**THE GREAT HISTORIES**

A series under the general editorship of H. R. Trevor-Roper, Regius Professor of Modern History, Oxford University

# SARPI

**HISTORY OF BENEFICES** and **Selections from HISTORY OF THE COUNCIL OF TRENT**

Newly Translated, Edited, and with an Introduction by Peter Burke ──────

**WSP** WASHINGTON SQUARE PRESS, INC. • NEW YORK

# SARPI

A *Washington Square Press* edition
1st printing ................................. October, 1967

**L**

Published by
Washington Square Press, Inc., 630 Fifth Avenue, New York, N.Y.

WASHINGTON SQUARE PRESS editions are distributed in the
U.S. by Simon & Schuster, Inc., 630 Fifth Avenue, New
York, N.Y. 10020 and in Canada by Simon & Schuster
of Canada, Ltd., Richmond Hill, Ontario, Canada.

*Acknowledgments*

I should like to thank the general editor, Professor H. R. Trevor-Roper, for encouraging an interest in Sarpi some years ago and for his illuminating criticisms of a draft of the introduction; my father, for making accessible various volumes of Sarpiana; and Mr. Tony Nuttall, of the University of Sussex, for advice on how to write English. I am also grateful to the University of Sussex for granting me a term's study leave, without which it would have been difficult to write the introduction.

# Contents

# Contents

# Introduction

Between Guicciardini and Gibbon, the Renaissance and the Enlightenment, one of the greatest of European historians was the Venetian friar, Paolo Sarpi. It is well known that in Renaissance Italy, an important contribution was made to the development of historical writing. Historians became more interested both in politics and in the analysis of motives. These trends are noticeable in Bruni's *History of the Florentine People*, Machiavelli's *History of Florence*, Guicciardini's *History of Italy*, and in the works of other lesser Florentines such as Varchi, Nardi, and Nerli. It is well known that another important contribution to the art of history was made in the eighteenth century. Historians became more interested in society, in long-term causes. This can be seen in the works of Giannone, Gibbon, Robertson, Voltaire, and many others. Between the Renaissance and Enlightenment, the seventeenth century tends to be thought of nowadays as a period of consolidation or of preparation rather than as a period of creative historical achievement in its own right; an age of scholars rather than of historians. This was the time of controversies about chronology, which engaged the attention, for example, of Isaac Newton. It was the time of Charles du Cange (1610–1688), who compiled famous glossaries of late and medieval Latin and Greek; of Jean Mabillon (1632–1707), who turned the dating of documents into the science of "diplomatic." However, the seventeenth century was not only the age of du Cange and Mabillon, important as these men were; it was also the age of Camden, Clarendon, de Thou, Hooft, Davila, and Sarpi. These men all wrote important works of synthesis and interpretation in the field of contemporary or sub-contemporary history. William Camden (1551–1623) wrote a history of Elizabeth's reign. Edward Hyde, Lord Clarendon (1609–1774) wrote about the civil war in England; Enrico Caterino Davila (1576–1631) wrote about the religious wars in France. Jacques-Auguste de Thou (1553–1617) wrote the history "of his own time." Pieter Corneliszoon Hooft (1581–1647) wrote about Henry IV of France, about the Medici, and about the war of the Netherlands with Spain. And Sarpi wrote about the Council of Trent.

These great seventeenth-century historians have not always been neglected. In the eighteenth and nineteenth centuries, as well as in their own time, they were much appreciated. To take Sarpi as an example: his *History of the Council of Trent* went into thirty-three editions at least in his own century, and eight more in the next. He was highly praised by Burnet, Gibbon, and Robertson. Dr. Johnson thought of translating him. In the nineteenth century, Ranke rated him above even Guicciardini, while Macaulay read the *Council of Trent* twice and called its author "my favourite modern historian." It is to be hoped that the later twentieth century will take Sarpi seriously once more.

Paolo Sarpi was born in Venice in 1552 and was baptized Pietro. His father was a merchant, though not a successful one; his mother was a Venetian noblewoman. A friend of her brother's was a Servite.[1] He educated the boy, and it was presumably through this man's influence that when he was thirteen, Pietro joined the Servites and took the name of Paolo. At the age of twenty-two, he was ordained a priest. His abilities gained him an invitation to Mantua as court theologian. After three years, disliking life at court, he moved to Milan, where he met Carlo Borromeo, the famous archbishop of Milan and saint of the Counter-Reformation. Then he taught philosophy at the Servite convent in Venice while studying at the University of Padua. He was still only twenty-seven when he became Provincial of the Venetian province of his order, and

---

[1] The Servites are an order of mendicant friars, founded in the thirteenth century.

thirty-two when he went to Rome to spend three years as Procurator-General of the whole order.

Then Sarpi's life changed, and he spent eighteen years (1588–1606) in studious retirement in Venice, apart from occasional visits to Rome. This was the life he really wanted. He even asked the Senate for a bishopric so that he would have the means and leisure to study permanently. He was a member of an "academy" which used to meet in the house of his friend Andrea Morosini, and he employed much of his time in scientific works. His interests included anatomy, astronomy, dynamics, magnetism, and optics. He supported the opinions of Copernicus and Vesalius, and became friendly with the young Galileo, who taught at Padua from 1592. Sarpi's papers were destroyed in a fire in the Servite convent in Venice in 1769, so we shall never know quite how good a scientist he was; but two statements can be made with some assurance. First, that he was the discoverer of the contraction of the iris. To support this statement, there is the testimony of Fabricius of Aquapendente—the physician under whom Sarpi, like Harvey, studied at Padua—in his book, *On the Eye*, published in 1600. Second, Sarpi was not the discoverer of the valves in the veins, which had been known since the 1540s, before he was born. Still less was he the discoverer—as some admirers have claimed —of the circulation of the blood. More of his philosophical work has survived than of his works on natural science, and this philosophical work includes a short treatise often referred to as the *Art of Thinking Well*. This treatise shows Sarpi to be a strong empiricist; owing something to the medieval philosopher William of Ockham, something to the neo-Aristotelean tradition of Renaissance Padua, and having affinities to Bacon and to Locke.

When he was fifty-four, Sarpi's life changed again. After those eighteen years of private study, events forced him out of retirement into the world of affairs, and he was never able to give himself up to science and philosophy again. The principal event which brought this change about was the Venetian interdict of 1606–7.

To anyone who knows medieval English history—or at least, something of the reigns of Henry II, John, and Edward I—the conflict between Venice and the papacy will seem familiar enough. The clash between Church and State was a clash over two issues. One was that of "criminous clerks"—that is, clergy who had broken the laws of the State. The other was that of ecclesiastical mortmain, or the accumulation of inalienable property in the hands of the Church. Two "clerks" had been imprisoned by the Venetian government; two laws prohibiting the donation or bequest of property to the Church had been passed by the Venetian Senate. Soon after this, in 1605, a new pope succeeded to the throne—Camillo Borghese, who took the name of Paul V. He ordered the clerks to be handed over and the laws repealed. The Senate would do neither. The Pope laid an interdict on Venice. The Senate forbade the clergy to observe it. The interdict lasted nearly two years.

Some months before the interdict began, Sarpi had been appointed theologian and canon lawyer to the Republic. During the interdict, he was excommunicated. Shortly after it was lifted, there was an attempt to assassinate him. As he described it in a letter a month later,

> I was attacked from behind by three cutthroats, and before my companion and I noticed what was happening, they gave me three wounds, two in the neck and one in the temple, all of them more than four fingers deep.

Rumor had it that the Pope's nephew, Cardinal Scipione Borghese, was responsible. Sarpi's own comment became one of his most famous witticisms; *agnosco stylum romanæ curiæ*—I recognize the methods (or "the dagger") of the court of Rome. Whether or not he ordered assassins to rid him of this turbulent priest, the Pope definitely regarded Sarpi as a dangerous enemy. And so in fact he was. He pleaded the cause of Venice before the educated men of Europe, as Coluccio Salutati, the famous humanist, had pleaded the cause of Florence during its interdict, some two hundred and thirty years before; and, like Salutati, he presented the conflict as a struggle for liberty against papal tyranny. In 1606, he wrote, with six other men, a *Treatise on the Interdict* to show that the interdict had not been legitimately published and that priests were not obliged to observe it —in fact, that they sinned if they did so. Although the interdict was lifted in 1607, the pamphlet war between Venice and the papacy continued, with Sarpi writing the pamphlets; on the prohibition of books, on the Inquisition, and so on. In Rome, there were plans to try Sarpi for heresy. In Venice, he became an institution. People frequently accosted him in the street to ask his advice. The government also consulted him frequently; they were still doing so when he was on his deathbed. Foreign tourists came to visit him as one of the sights of Venice. In the year of his death, 1623, it was ordered that a monument to him be erected.[2] It was in these years, when he was adviser and propagandist to the government of Venice, that Sarpi wrote all his historical works. There was his *History of Benefices;* the *History of the Interdict;* the *Addition* and the *Supplement* to the *History of the Uskoks;* and, most famous of all, the *History of the Council of Trent.*

What was it that made Sarpi seem so dangerous to the court of Rome and its allies? It was his ideas about religion and politics, and the skill with which he expressed them. Important to his thought is his conviction of the enormous difference between the modern Catholic Church (which he often calls *Chiesa romana*) and the primitive Church (*Chiesa di Dio*). He believed, for example, that the acquisition of temporal goods and temporal power had corrupted the Church spiritually, and that her salvation lay in being stripped of this wealth and power, if not all at once, then by stages. This conviction lies behind his book on benefices (see p. 3). Sarpi also thought that the Church had originally been a democracy, but that thanks to papal usurpa-

---

[2] This was eventually done—but only in 1892.

tion, it had gradually turned into a monarchy, with the Pope as the monarch. *La monarchia romana* is a phrase that recurs in his writings, with pejorative intent. His complaint against the Council of Trent (see pp. 116-7) was that it ended by strengthening the papal "monarchy" which it was originally summoned to reduce. He opens his *History of the Interdict* with the remark that it had been the lifelong aim of Paul V to acquire for the papacy "the spiritual and temporal monarchy of the whole world." This was usurpation because, according to Sarpi, the State (*il regno*) and the Church are two powers, each with its own sovereignty. They are composed of the same men, but one is concerned with earthly matters, the other with heavenly ones; and these two spheres must not be confused; they are distinct.

This sounds innocuous enough and not unlike the famous doctrine of the two swords; but it is important to emphasize that Sarpi operated with a relatively wide definition of earthly matters and a relatively narrow definition of heavenly ones; and that in clashes between Church and State, Sarpi's sympathies tended to be with the State. In this he belongs to a familiar European tradition. His position is much like that of a William of Ockham and Marsilio of Padua in the fourteenth century, an Anglican like Stephen Gardiner in the sixteenth, a Gallican like Edmond Richer (1560–1631) in the seventeenth century. Richer, a French contemporary of Sarpi's, illustrates the general significance of his ideas on Church and State very well. He was the syndic of the faculty of theology at Paris, and in 1611, he published a book, *On Ecclesiastical and Political Power*. It caused a great stir and led to his dismissal from his post of syndic. In this book he expressed views about the government of the Church which are very close to Sarpi's. He argued that Christ gave his authority to all the faithful, not to the clergy or the Pope. In the Church, the legislature was the general council, the judiciary was the bishops, and the executive power was delegated to the Pope. This book was answered in the following year by the Jesuit Cardinal Bellarmine, who argued that the power of the Pope was not delegated by the faithful but came direct from God—divine right of popes, one might say, for seventeenth-century controversies about the government of the Church are extremely similar to the controversies about the government of the "commonwealth" that took place at the same time. This controversy makes it easier to understand how contemporaries would have viewed Sarpi's historical works. The *History of Benefices* and the *History of the Council of Trent* were not simply academic works of history; they carried a political message in the same way that Sarpi's pamphlets did. And that message is explicit in Richer.

Sarpi may therefore be described as an anticlerical cleric, who equated the corruption of the Church with the dominance and wealth of the clergy, and he looked to the laity, to the State, for reform. These views of his entailed important consequences for foreign affairs, which he expounded in his letters addressed to the statesmen and scholars of Europe. Sarpi believed that the exorbitant power of the Counter-Reformation Church was a threat to political liberty in Europe. He considered that in his time, three absolute monarchs were in league: the Pope, the general of the Jesuits, and what he calls *Spagna*, which sometimes means the King of Spain, sometimes the Habsburg rulers in general. Sarpi called this alliance the *Diacatholicon*. It threatened Italy in particular, since the Pope was in Rome and the Spaniards were in possession of Naples, Sicily, and Milan. As Sarpi put it, "a man must be pretty blind not to see the yoke hanging over the neck of Italy."

He criticized those who preferred "bondage with ease" under the Spaniards to "strenuous liberty" without them (*che amano meglio servir in ozio che faticar in libertà*). His own city of Venice was in a particularly vulnerable position, having as her neighbors the Papal States, Spanish Milan, and Habsburg Austria. Venice consequently needed to ally not only with the King of France and the Duke of Savoy—Catholic princes opposed by interest to the Habsburgs—but also with certain Protestant powers such as England, the United Provinces, and the German Protestant princes. She needed, that is, to build up some kind of "third force" between the powers of Counter-Reformation Catholicism and the powers of militant Calvinism. She needed, too, to attack the Jesuits. For the Jesuits at this time were the great propagandists and missionaries of the Counter-Reformation, the essential ideological agents of both Spain and Rome. Or, as Sarpi expressed it, "The Spaniard without the Jesuit is no better than lettuce without oil" or again, "When the Jesuits are conquered, Rome is lost; and without Rome, religion will reform itself."

In this crusade against the hated *Diacatholicon*, Sarpi's religious and political hopes joined together; the salvation of Venice would also be the salvation of the Church.

Sarpi was not alone in these views. Similar criticisms of the *Catholicon* had been put forward in France towards the close of the religious wars, in the 1590s, when Philip II was hoping to acquire the kingdom for himself, and the French Jesuits were supporting him; we can see them, for example, in the famous *Satyre Ménippée* (1593), one of whose coauthors, Jacques Gillot, later corresponded with Sarpi and supplied him with material for his histories. In Venice, too, these opinions belonged not to an individual but to a party, that of the so-called "youngsters" (*giovani*), who in the late sixteenth century began to challenge the group in power. In 1606, one of these youngsters, Leonardo Donà (now seventy-two years old), became Doge of Venice; and a few days later, Paolo Sarpi became theologian and canonist to the Republic, which meant that he virtually joined the government. The importance of Sarpi's political ideas, then, does not lie in their originality but in the verve with which they were expressed in a period of political crisis. In the anxious years at the beginning of the seventeenth century, Sarpi was worth several hundred horsemen to the Republic of Venice.

With ideas like these, it is not surprising that Sarpi has often been seen as a crypto-Protestant. He seems to approve of the Lutheran doctrine of the priesthood of all believers, together with the Calvinist system of church government. He cultivated Protestant friends, supported Protestant movements, and published his works in Protestant countries. Bishop Bossuet called him a Protestant in friar's clothing—*Protestant habillé en moine*. Was he? What makes the question so difficult to answer is Sarpi's systematic effort to cover his tracks. He described himself once as being like a chameleon, all things to all men: "I am forced to wear a mask— *personam coactus fero*—it is impossible to be without one in Italy."

He had always been a reserved, introverted man—his anonymous contemporary biographer refers to his "withdrawal into himself" (*ritiratezza in sé medesimo*)—and the personal danger which he felt after the assassination attempt in 1607 made him all the more secretive. It was not unreasonable for him to feel in danger at a time when Bruno was arrested in Venice and burned in Rome (1600); Henry IV of France was assassinated (1610); and Galileo's opinions were condemned by the Inquisition (1616), not to mention the fate of lesser men, including two of Sarpi's assistants and some other seventeenth-century Italian historians. Sarpi himself was three times summoned before the Inquisition and twice narrowly escaped assassination. In 1609, he devised a cipher for his letters; t 13 stood for the Jesuits, t 33 for the Pope, m 28 for Spain, and so on. This, too, was no empty precaution, as his letters were in fact intercepted. Copies of some of them are still in the Vatican archives.

Given this secrecy, is it possible for us to unmask Sarpi? We know that he read Calvin's *Institutes;* that he corresponded regularly with Protestants (221 surviving letters have been printed in one volume); that he discussed with a German envoy, in 1608, the possibility of introducing Protestantism to Venice. His English friends, Sir Henry Wotton (ambassador to Venice) and William Bedell (Wotton's chaplain), were much concerned with this same plan. His assistant, Fulgenzio Micanzio, preached sermons telling the Venetians to pray in their own language, and he is said to have wanted to flee to Geneva. His acquaintance and translator, Sir Nathaniel

Brent, Vicar-General of the Archbishop of Canterbury, told his son that Sarpi and some of his friends "were Protestants in their hearts, though they durst not own it." This view of Sarpi is accepted by some modern historians; Gaetano Cozzi, for example, believes that Sarpi really accepted Calvinism, but lacked the courage to make an open break with the Church.

On the other side, it can be argued (as is done by Luigi Salvatorelli, for example) that Sarpi's criticisms of the Church and his desire to reform it belong to a Catholic tradition. Again, it was possible to believe in making alliances with Protestants without being a Protestant; the policy advocated by Sarpi is much like the policy pursued by Cardinal Richelieu at the time of the Thirty Years' War. He could have been trying to use the Protestants to force reform on the Church from within, just as they tried to use him to attack it from without. If he made friends with the English ambassadors to Venice, he made friends with the French ambassadors as well. As for Brent, he could have been making the same mistake that an English liberal travelling in Eastern Europe might make today when he takes criticisms of the regime for an affirmation of faith in Western-style democracy. It seems helpful to see Sarpi as a Venetian "Gallican," with attitudes similar to those of his French friends the pamphleteer Gillot and the historian de Thou, and to describe his more spiritual criticisms of the Church of his day by calling him a Jansenist before Jansen—for his moral rigorism, his admiration for the primitive Church, and his dislike of the Jesuits all fit the Jansenist pattern. At much the same time as Sarpi, Jansen himself was corresponding in code with his friends about the evils of the Jesuits and taking a sympathetic interest in the activities of the Calvinist synod of Dort. And so, however radical Sarpi's criticisms of the Church of his day may seem at first glance, the verdict on his Protestantism must be "not proven."

It was the interdict which turned Sarpi into a historian. Not that he had been uninterested in politics before; he had been accustomed to frequent the *Golden Ship*, a shop in Venice where one could meet merchants and foreigners and learn news, and he had been particularly interested to learn about the religious wars in France. But, as he told a German visitor: "If it had not been for the interdict, I should have written nothing." From 1606, he had assistants, such as Fulgenzio Micanzio and Marco Franzano (Servite friars like himself), which made it easier for him to write. Although he never became official historian to the Republic, a post which was held in his time by Paolo Paruta and Niccolò Contarini, he was, like them, given access (from 1607) to the secret archives of the State. His historical works were not official either (unless the books on the Uskoks are an exception), but they sprang, as will be seen in a moment, from the same researches as did Sarpi's written advice to the Republic and his polemical writings on its behalf.

It is thus appropriate that Sarpi's first historical work should have been a history of the interdict. It was a piece of straight narrative—*une semplice narratione*, he called it. Divided into seven books, it tells the story of events from August 1605 to May 1607 in chronological order and in considerable detail. It is beautifully written, yet it was not intended for publication in its original form. The conflict between Venice and the papacy had been followed with considerable interest in Gallican and Huguenot circles in Paris. Jérôme Groslot de l'Isle, a Huguenot gentleman, visited Sarpi in 1607 and suggested to him that he furnish the French historian Jacques-Auguste de Thou with an account of the controversy, so that de Thou could describe it in the next volume of his *History of His Own Time*. Sarpi wrote to de Thou saying that he would send him a narrative which de Thou could summarize, just as Pliny gave Tacitus two hundred verses which Tacitus reduced to twenty-five words. That was in June; by December the narrative was written. Sarpi's only problem was that of getting the manuscript to de Thou without any risk to it or to himself. This problem was all the greater because the Venetian government, having now made peace with the Pope, did not want to do anything that might offend him. Sarpi thought of sending the manuscript to Paris first with one Venetian envoy, then with another, but something always went wrong. The opportunity was lost, the papal party grew more powerful, Henry IV was assassinated, Sarpi's letters were intercepted, and he did not dare send the manuscript. His next plan was still more complicated. He had allowed Bedell, Wotton's chaplain, to make a copy of the memoir, provided that the copy was in English. Bedell had returned to England in 1610; so Sarpi thought of letting de Thou have the manuscript by way of England, and he sent Groslot a letter to send to Bedell, asking him to send his copy to de Thou. But Bedell did not do this. Meanwhile, de Thou was also making efforts to obtain the manuscript, again unsuccessfully. Finally, in 1617, Sarpi did in fact send the manuscript to Paris: When it arrived, de Thou was dead. The work was published in Geneva (in Italian) in 1624, the year after Sarpi had died, too.

These details are still of interest in that they help recapture the atmosphere in which Sarpi lived and worked. The modern reader may find it helpful to think of those East European writers who have published books in the West, in order to appreciate Sarpi's problems. He should not find it difficult to understand why Sarpi's second historical work, his *History of Benefices* (written c.1609), was not published in his lifetime either. It, too, was inspired by contemporary events. In 1608, there was another, lesser conflict between the Republic of Venice and Paul V. Its occasion was Paul's bestowal of the abbey of S. Maria della Vangadizza, in the Polesine, on his nephew, Paolo Scipione Borghese. The Venetians claimed that since Vangadizza was in Venetian territory, the benefice could only be conferred on a Venetian citizen. In an age accustomed to arguments from precedent, a history of the Pope's power over benefices was obviously of great contemporary relevance. At about this time, Sarpi wrote a memorandum for the Venetian government on the foundation, progress, and abuse of the "commendam," that is, the appointment to benefices by papal (or other) recommendation, instead of by election. This, too, is a theme which he takes up in his *History of Benefices*.

Again, the interdict controversy had arisen partly because of the law passed by the Venetian Senate to the effect that goods could not be alienated to the Church without their permission. Sarpi had already written a defense of this law; and this theme of the importance and danger of ecclesiastical mortmain finds its place here again. Some parts of the *History of Benefices* betray their legal origin; for example, the digression (p. 34ff.) which discusses whether tithes are levied by the law of God or man. This may well remind the English reader of John Selden's *History of Tithes* (1618), a book which caused a brisk controversy with the Anglican Church. The parallel extends to more than that particular section. In the work of Selden—and Coke—as in that of Sarpi, politics, law, and history are all connected. Selden did research in the Tower archives to prove that Charles I's absolute power was illegal. Sarpi did research in the Venetian archives to prove that Paul V's absolute power was illegal. Like them, he provides a constitutional movement—the movement towards democracy in the government of the Catholic Church, a movement which it is convenient to call "Gallicanism" or "Richerism"—with a historical myth. It is not surprising to find that some Frenchmen had recently been working on the same lines. Jacques Gillot sent Sarpi his *Discourse on Benefices*, which pleased him very much. Jérôme Groslot put him in touch with a friend of his, Jacques Leschassier, who had, in 1606, written a brief memoir on the acquisition of property by the clergy, which was not published till 1649. Leschassier also helped Sarpi a great deal by his knowledge of the history of canon law.

Sarpi's *History of Benefices* also has its place in a still more important controversy. One of the great debates of the Reformation concerned the question, was the Church of Rome the true or direct descendant of the primitive Church or not? If not, then when did the break come? This is obviously a historical question, and in fact the attempts of Catholics and Protestants to answer it led to a great deal of historical research. On the Protestant side, the great work was the *Ecclesiastical History*, produced by a research team at Magdeburg who became known as the "Centuriators" because they produced their history century by century. This work was published in Basel between 1559 and 1574. The chief Catholic reply was the *Ecclesiastical Annals* of Cardinal Cesare Baronio, better known as Baronius (1538–1607). Sarpi has some very harsh things to say about Baronius. In a letter of 1612 to the Huguenot scholar Isaac Casaubon (1559–1614), he refers to Baronius's "forged and distorted evidence, his extremely irritating long-windedness, and his perverse and silly judgments," and encourages Casaubon to refute him, which Casaubon most effectively did. Similarly, the *History of Benefices* mentions Baronius several times—to criticize him. Sarpi, however, does not take up the same position as the Centuriators. He does not try to prove that the Pope is Anti-Christ; he simply addresses himself to the question, how far the Catholic Church has departed from the practice of the primitive Church in economic matters; when; and why. From the religious point of view, this position illustrates Sarpi's moderation; like Venice in international politics, Sarpi's book occupies the position of a third force between Catholic and Protestant. From the point of view of historical method, its significance is greater still. In this particular controversy, it is Sarpi who takes the decisive step from medieval explanations of Church history in terms of the conflict between good and evil, God and the devil, to modern ones in terms of secondary causes—circumstances and men. Gibbon was to apply this approach to explain the rise of Christianity itself in terms of secondary causes in the famous fifteenth and sixteenth chapters of his *Decline and Fall*.

Sarpi's most famous work, the *History of the Council of Trent,* also took shape in those crucial years around the interdict. His letters of 1608 show him reading all the printed material he could find; and in August of that year he announced to a visitor: "I have the affairs of the Council; I need three months to organize them."

In fact, it was to take much longer. In 1614, the English ambassador to Venice, Dudley Carleton, wrote to his cousin George Carleton (later Bishop of Chichester), who had published an attack on the Council of Trent, saying that Sarpi was "about a work not altogether differing from your subject." In 1616, Sarpi's friend Sir Henry Wotton read the completed manuscript. Now all that remained was to publish it. This, however, was an enterprise even more complicated and dangerous than sending the memoir of the interdict to de Thou. And so the publication was surrounded by deliberate mystification, which makes it difficult to reconstruct the story today and to decide on Sarpi's intentions.

The *Council of Trent* was first published in London, in 1619—in Italian. Its author, according to the title page, was one Pietro Soave Polano, a name which turns out to be an anagram for Paolo Sarpi Veneto; but Sarpi would never admit to having written it. When, in 1620, the Prince de Condé asked him point-blank who was the author of the book, Sarpi would not commit himself beyond saying that "at Rome they knew very well who had written it." This comedy was kept up for a long time. When the Jesuit Sforza Pallavicino published his anti-Sarpian *History of the Council of Trent* (1656), the Venetians would not let it into their territories, and they gave as their reason the fact that Pallavicino referred to Sarpi as the author of the previous *History*.

There are also two rival stories as to how the book came to be published. The first story is that, in 1618, the Archbishop of Canterbury, George Abbott, sent Sir Nathaniel Brent, his Vicar-General, to Venice to see Sarpi; and that Brent and Wotton (now ambassador again), sent the manuscript over piece by piece through a network of contact men, referring to the pieces by the code name of "songs" (*canzoni*). This version comes from Wotton's friend Izaak Walton, from Brent's son, and from Abbott's letters, acknowledging the receipt of some of the *canzoni*. The second story is that Sarpi lent the manuscript to Marcantonio de Dominis (1566–1624), a Dalmatian who, after having been Bishop of Senj and Archbishop of Split, went to England in 1616, turned

Protestant and became Dean of Windsor. It is claimed that de Dominis, who had made a copy of the manuscript, and who wrote the preface to the first edition, published the book without Sarpi's knowledge, let alone consent. This story comes from a letter written by Sarpi's assistant Micanzio to de Dominis in 1619, saying that Sarpi was displeased with the publication, and this is supported by de Dominis's preface, in which he declares this; it should be emphasized that he received a great decision to publish. Could the smuggling of the manuscript have taken place without Sarpi knowing? It is more likely that the letter and preface are simply a disclaimer of responsibility for the publication, a second line of defense for Sarpi in case the secret of his authorship was divulged. It is, anyhow, appropriate that a book which sets out to tell the "inside story" of the Council of Trent should have an inside story of its own.

The caution is understandable, for the book was seen by both sides as a weapon in the religious wars. Its publication was intended by the English government to coincide with the opening of the synod of Dordrecht (or "Dort") in 1618, a synod which has been described as a "Calvinist Council of Trent" (and at which, incidentally, George Carleton represented the Church of England). De Dominis provided the book with a title page, dedication (to James I), and even index entries stressing the antipapal nature of the contents. Its seventeenth-century circulation was largely Protestant; twenty-four editions were published in Protestant countries, compared with five in Catholic ones, and four in places unknown. A French translation was made by a well-known Calvinist, Giovanni Diodati, and a French abridgement was made by the famous Huguenot pastor, Pierre Jurieu. It is unlikely that Sarpi would have approved of all this; it should be emphasized that he received a great deal of help when writing the work (as when writing *On Benefices*) from French Gallicans like Gillot, who sent him documents, and that his book was published in France as well as in Protestant countries.

However, the book was dangerous enough without all this Protestant varnish, for the message of the *History* is that the Council of Trent was an unmitigated disaster. The Council should have passed reforms which would have begun to lead the corrupt Church back to her primitive state, poorer and more democratic. It was time to attract the Protestants back to the Church—men who had left it largely because of this very corruption. They should, therefore, have played an important part at the Council, which would then have become truly "general." These opportunities were all missed. Matters became worse, not better. To quote from Sarpi's bitter opening paragraphs:

> This Council, which pious men desired and procured to reunite the Church (which was beginning to split apart), has, on the contrary, made the split a permanent one and the parties to it irreconcilable. It was planned by the princes to reform the Church; but it has brought about the greatest corruption of the Church since the name of "Christian" was first heard. . . .[3]

To explain this disaster, Sarpi has recourse to what might be called his "conspiracy theory of history"—he suggests that the aims of the princes were defeated by the intrigues of the popes and the Curia. It is not surprising that he dared not put his name on the title page, and that the book could not be published in Italy—even in Venice.

The same conspiracy theory runs through Sarpi's works on the Uskoks, his only venture into purely secular history. The Uskoks were Christian refugees from the Turkish Balkans, turned pirates on the Adriatic. They operated from Senj, in Dalmatia, and preyed on the Venetians as well as on the Turks. They were a cause of conflict between Austria (that is, the territories of the Archduke of Styria) and Venice, because the Venetians regarded the Austrians as responsible for the Uskoks' activities. Added to this was a conflict between the Empire and Venice over the dominion of the Adri-

---

[3] See p. 117.

atic. These conflicts turned into an open war in 1615. The war can be seen as a kind of trial run for the Thirty Years' War, because the Archduke of Styria was soon to become Emperor Ferdinand II, and because England and the United Provinces supported Venice, whose alliance with Protestant powers against the Habsburgs thus anticipated the policy of Cardinal Richelieu in the Thirty Years' War. In 1618, when this war was coming to an end, the revolt in Prague against Ferdinand occurred which was to begin the Thirty Years' War; and the Venetians discovered the famous Bedmar conspiracy, planned by the Spanish Duke of Osuna, Viceroy of Naples, and aimed at making Venice part of the Spanish Empire.

Minuccio Minucci, Archbishop of Zadar, in Dalmatia, had written a history of the Uskoks (his neighbors) in about 1602. Sarpi brought his story up to date in an *Addition* and a *Supplement,* published together about 1617. He also wrote a history of the peace negotiations, which ends in the year 1619; but this work remained unpublished until as recently as 1965. These books on the Uskoks give the modern reader a chance to assess Sarpi as a historian without possible Catholic or Protestant prejudices coming into play; but the ideas expressed in them have much in common with the ideas expressed by Sarpi elsewhere. It is ironic that the *Addition* and the *Supplement* should have appeared bound together with the *History* of Minucci, because Minucci argues that the Habsburgs were not responsible for what the Uskoks did, whereas Sarpi argues that they were. Sarpi sees their depredations as part of the great conspiracy of the *Diacatholicon* against the Republic of Venice. The Pope is involved; he supported the Uskoks on the grounds that they were crusaders who attacked the Turks. For Sarpi, these grounds are a mere pretext. Spain is involved because the Habsburgs are all one family; for Sarpi, the Uskok war and the Bedmar conspiracy are all part of the same plot. Thus all Sarpi's historical works, religious and secular—and even his private letters—are united by their dominant ideas, and by their author's identification with the official point of view of Venice.

In what does Sarpi's greatness as a historian consist? He and his works occupy an important place in the rise of problematic history, the rise of pragmatic history, and the development of historical explanation. These are three great trends of the historiography of his time. Let us consider them in order.

Sarpi's historical works are early examples of the monograph. They belong to the rise of "problematic history," a term recently coined to describe history which is organized around problems, not periods. The revival of problematic history (which was practiced in the ancient world, as Sallust's books on the conspiracy of Catiline and the Jugurthan war may remind us) means the emancipation of history from the chronicle. This emancipation is one of the dominant themes in the development of modern history writing in the West. The great Renaissance historians still tended to write the histories of nations or of city-states; Guicciardini's history of Italy and Machiavelli's history of Florence are obvious and distinguished examples. All Sarpi's works, on the other hand, deal with special topics; the interdict, benefices, the Council of Trent, the Uskoks. Simply to think of writing a monograph was still an achievement at the beginning of the seventeenth century; but the historian's problems did not end with this decision. On the contrary, that is where they began. How was one to plan such a book? Sarpi realized, for example, that his problem in composing the *Council of Trent* was an unusual one; he remarks, "I believe that every subject needs its own appropriate form, and that mine cannot follow the usual rules."

He describes his method as annalistic, but it is not so simple as that. For one thing, as he points out himself, he writes a day-by-day account when the Council is sitting, but a year-by-year account when it is not. More important still, he tries to integrate the general political history of the period into the history of the Council, and yet to do this in such a way as not to distract the reader's attention from his main themes. The sack of Rome, for example, or the battle of Dreux is briefly but vividly described. Such passages make it clear that the Council did not operate in a vacuum, locked away from the world like the cardinals in conclave, but that news of what the Council was doing influenced events outside Trent, and news of events outside, in turn, influenced what the Council was doing. These "digressions," which are in fact necessary to understand how the Council turned out as it did, serve an important literary function as well; they form a sort of subplot and relieve the reader from the strain of attending to the debates of ecclesiastics for so many hundred pages.

Equally important is another kind of digression: the excursus into earlier Church history in order to clarify the issues raised at the Council. It may be the history of the manner of declaring opinions in past councils; it may be the history of censorship. These digressions show Sarpi's supreme gift for putting complicated issues in the clearest possible way and for discussing trends over a long period of time.

These gifts are shown even more spectacularly in the *History of Benefices,* where Sarpi needs to adopt a chronological framework because of his main theme, the gradual corruption, the simultaneous economic rise and moral decline of the Church. On the other hand, he needs to adopt an analytic framework because there are so many kinds of benefices to be distinguished, so many technical terms (commendams, expectatives, regresses, and so on) to be explained. He has also to give something like a short history of the decline of the Roman Empire and the rise of feudal Europe. Somehow he succeeds in all these tasks—and in some thirty thousand words.

Sarpi's historical works are also important in the rise of what I should like to call "pragmatic history," borrowing the term from Reineccius (a late sixteenth-century German writer on historical method) and using it to refer to history written in reaction against the rhetorical "humanist history" of the fifteenth and sixteenth centuries.

During the Renaissance, in Italy first of all and then all over Europe, the writing of history changed in two ways. First, it became more political and more causal. Men no longer considered it sufficient to chronicle events; they felt the need to explain them. Secondly, historians became more interested in rhetoric. They concentrated on the production of set pieces, such as the description of a battle, the moralizing character sketch, and the speech (usually invented by the historian), which was used to reveal character and explain motives. Battles, characters, and speeches were all somewhat self-consciously literary; phrases were sometimes taken over from the great classical historians for stylistic reasons, regardless of the fact that the classical writers were describing different situations and different men. Humanist historians had also a great respect for what they called the "dignity" of history. Descartes' criticisms of historians in general are quite just when applied to them. To make their books worthy to be read, they left out whatever was beneath this dignity of history (*les plus basses et moins illustres circonstances*, as he puts it), with the result that their books were as much fiction as the still-popular romances of chivalry.

Pragmatic history carried on the tradition of humanist history in the first respect; that is, it continued to be political and causal. In that respect, Sarpi is the heir or the disciple of Guicciardini, whom he much admired. But the pragmatists broke with the rhetorical tradition, because they wanted to write something useful. They did not imitate Livy, but Polybius, who scoffed at other historians for inventing speeches, who wanted history to be useful (*pragmatikos*), and who did not see the point of narration without explanation. An early example of a historian of this pragmatic school is Johann Sleidan (1506–1556), who wrote *Commentaries* on the reign of Charles V, and who anticipated Ranke in declaring that one should write history "as it actually happened" (*prout res acta fuit*). In Sarpi's time, Camden and de Thou belonged to this school of historians; and there are many lesser seventeenth-century figures as well, especially in Italy. They all try to write history in a manner at once simpler and truer.

And so, when Sarpi declares, at the beginning of his *Supplement to the History of the Uskoks,* that "apart from the truth and sincerity of the narration and from my suspension of judgment, . . . I have not obeyed the laws of history," and that he is not writing for posterity (just as when he declares, at the beginning of Book Three of the *Council of Trent,* that he thinks few people will ever read his work), his words should be seen not as modesty but as irony; so much the worse for the laws of history, for posterity. This is Sarpi's way of writing a manifesto for a school of historians who consider the deeds of "low" people, like the Uskoks, worthy of their attention and are not afraid of detail, because they believe that the study of past events is of practical value—that history teaches wisdom. His words should be interpreted in the light of his letter to Isaac Casaubon, thanking him for the gift of his new edition of Polybius and praising Polybius as a writer particularly useful to the world at the present time.

Even when writing the history of "the Iliad of our age" (as he called the controversy over the Council of Trent), Sarpi tried not to write in an epic style. For example, he tends to shorten the humanist "character" to a thumbnail sketch of no more than a line or two. This is how he characterizes the three legates to the Council, Cardinals Pole, Marcello Cervino, and del Monte:

> In choosing the first, the Pope chose his noble blood and his common reputation for piety . . . in the case of Marcello, his constancy and perseverance . . . in the case of Monte, his realism and open-mindedness, together with his loyalty.

In his *History of the Interdict,* even his characterizations of the principal figures, such as Pope Paul V and Doge Leonardo Donà, are extremely brief.

Again, Sarpi does not invent speeches; he prefers to summarize them in the third person, so that space is saved, and the reader is not under the illusion of hearing the actual words. A third, more positive difference from the practice of the humanist historians is that Sarpi keeps closer to documents, often quoting them or paraphrasing them. Giucciardini, too, did research in archives, but he kept the documents more in the background of his book. For Sarpi, as for other pragmatic historians, documents tend to replace the great literary set pieces of the humanists.

The total effect of this approach to history is to produce a story which is less highly colored and less dramatic than that of the humanist historians. It runs the danger of dullness—as Sarpi admits. "I know that a plain narration of events of the same sort is dull for both the writer and the reader." What saves him from dullness is his brevity, his irony and wit, and the impression which he communicates throughout of things being different from what they seem. This last impression fits in with Sarpi's attitude toward historical explanation.

Sarpi's theory and practice of historical explanation is the third of his great qualities as a historian. In the *Council of Trent*, this interest in causation is apparent from the very beginning, where he states his purpose: "to describe all the causes of the Council of Trent." Similarly, at the beginning of the *Supplement*, he declares that he will explain "the causes and the motives" of the war with the Uskoks.

Sarpi's concept of causation is worth exploring in some detail. He is sceptical of explanations in terms of the hand of God. He does not deny them outright, but he treats them in an ironic, almost Gibbonian way, as in his comment on Pope Clement VII's recovery of power in 1529: "In Italy . . . everyone attributed it to a miracle, and those who loved the Curia called it a sign of God's favor towards His Church."

Again, when he relates the circumstances supposed to have surrounded the death of Luther, he adds dryly that nothing happened that might not be expected at the death of a man sixty-three years old. As the *Council* progresses, incidental comments like this one seem to cohere into a definite view of the role of God in history, which Sarpi states explicitly, too.

> Certainly it is pious and religious to attribute the disposition of every event to Divine Providence. But to decide to what end that Supreme Wisdom has determined events is not far from presumption. Men are so much in love with their own opinions, that they persuade themselves that God favors them as much as they do themselves.

This view that, although Providence disposes, we are never in a position to say that it has done so, is important as a stage in the steady secularization of historical thought between Renaissance and Enlightenment. It prevents the historian using God as an excuse not to think out all the causes. Sarpi does not deny God any role in history at all, any more than Descartes denied Him any role in nature. Descartes's God sets the world in motion, and Sarpi's God provides the *occasione* —one of the key concepts in his historical thinking.

With his concept of *occasione,* or *opportunità,* Sarpi strikes a balance between two rival theories of history. A common Renaissance theory of history stressed the individual; a common Reformation theory (Lutheran or Calvinist) minimized him. At the same time, Sarpi seems balanced between the traditional view that the explanatory alternatives are "man" and "God," and the Enlightenment view that they are man and "circumstances" or "environment." Early on in the *Council,* the need to explain an event as complex as the Reformation forces him to be explicit on this point and say whether he thinks that it is fundamentally the work of one man, Luther, or the result of a situation, the corruption of the Church. Sarpi suggests that both man and situation are necessary conditions of the Reformation, and that neither is a sufficient one.

> *Occasions* often occur which are sufficient to produce notable effects, and they vanish because the men are lacking who would have known how to

take advantage of them. And what is more important, it is necessary that to effect anything, the time should be ripe, in which God is pleased to correct the deficiencies of man. All these things *coincided* (*s'incontrarono*) at the time of Pope Leo. . . . [my italics]

Similarly, the failure of a plan of Charles V for a general council prompts the reflection: "Just as the most fertile seeds, when sown out of season, do not grow, so great plans which lack opportunity come to nothing."

As Sarpi once said to a German visitor: "A man can do nothing without the occasion. . . . Often, men do not become great because the occasions are lacking. Often, if men do not use their brains, the occasions vanish." Man and occasion must coincide, must conjoin; in his *Addition*, Sarpi writes at one point of "the conjuncture of those times" (*le congionture di quei tempi*).

In these passages, Sarpi appears as a dualist, believing that man and occasion are of equal importance. Elsewhere, however, he seems to suggest that occasion gives the more fundamental explanation. The irony of the opening pages of the *Council* comes from the fact that Sarpi believes that "What emerged was quite contrary to the plans of those who had fought for it and the fears of those who had done their best to hinder it."

He sometimes suggests that there is a hierarchy of causes. After the death of Zwingli, the Swiss cantons continued to make progress in the new religion: "a manifest argument, that this came from a higher cause than the work of Zwingli."

His comment on the death of Luther is similar:

The fathers in Trent and the Curia in Rome became extremely hopeful when they saw dead . . . the principal and almost sole cause of the divisions . . . but the events that followed, up to our own time, have made it clear that Martin was only one of the instruments, and that the causes were different, more powerful and more hidden.

Of what sort are these more powerful, hidden causes? No doubt many contemporaries thought that Sarpi meant that God was on the side of the Reformation—but this is just the "presumption" that he denounced in the passage quoted above. It is more likely that he was thinking of the deeper causes of the Reformation as connected with the corruption of the Church, as he analyzed it in his book on benefices. But what are the hidden causes which made a farce of the Council of Trent? In this case, Sarpi believes that the explanation is political. In the *Council* he is a reductionist, who explains religious history in political terms. Like Marx, Sarpi sees religious arguments as a mere "ideology," though unlike Marx, Sarpi's ultimate reality is not economic but political, and his reductionism is concerned with levels of motive, not with structural factors. His fundamental explanation for what went wrong at the Council is that the popes desired absolute power over the Church, and that they acted as temporal rulers first, spiritual leaders second. For example, Sarpi quotes a criticism of the papal maxim that it is better to persecute heretics than infidels, on the grounds that this maxim "was better suited to the maintenance of the Pope's power than to the benefit of Christianity."

Again, Sarpi emphasizes how the religious policy of Charles V was affected more by political than by religious considerations—he wanted more absolute power in Germany than his predecessors had had. He made war on the German princes "not for religious but for political reasons" (*non per causa di religione, anzi per rispetti di stato*). But—as Sarpi once phrased it in a private letter—"everything is covered by the mask of religion" (*tutto si cuopre con la maschera della religione*).

The instances just quoted are not isolated; this fundamental idea of the enormous difference between appearance and reality in human affairs echoes through the whole work. On one hand, there is what is *apparenza*, or *palese*, or *manifesto*, or *pretesto*; on the other, what is *sostanza*, or *coperto*, or *latente*, or *secreto*, or *arcano*. The same terms recur when Sarpi writes secular history. The Austrians, he writes, claimed that they could do nothing about the depredations of the Uskoks, calling them indomitable, incorrigible; "but this was nothing but a cloak to cover their decision not to do anything about them."

Sarpi believes that the task of the historian is *scoprire*, to discover (or rather, to "uncover"), unveil, unmask the truth; to make the latent causes manifest. It is his passionate attempt to penetrate the surface of historical reality, to discover the hidden causes, which makes Sarpi a great historian. This quality did not go unnoticed in his own century. Milton wrote in *Areopagitica* of "Padre Paolo the great unmasker of the Trentine Council." The portrait of Sarpi in the Bodleian Library, Oxford, bears an inscription (composed by Sir Henry Wotton) calling him *Concilii Tridentini eviscerator*—the man who "disembowelled" the Council. Of course, Sarpi was not the first historian to notice that one cannot trust appearances in history; Tacitus, Machiavelli, and Guicciardini are celebrated examples to the contrary. But they did not do what Sarpi has done, and make this awareness the organizing principle of their historical works.

Sarpi is a great historian; he is not a faultless one. The principal fault charged against him is that of bias. At first sight this seems odd. Sarpi gives the first impression of calm objectivity and claims on occasion to write with "suspended judgment" (*la suspensione nel giudicare*). Yet he has been frequently and violently criticized for his bias. Hubert Jedin, for example, a distinguished modern historian of the Council, suggests that "he gives a seemingly temperate description . . . of the first period of the council, while it actually quivers with fierce hatred for the curia."

There is some truth in this criticism. The prose is deceptively flat; the dry, calm manner of narration is partly artifice. There is no doubt that the Pope and the Curia are the villains of his story. Sarpi is convinced, for example, that popes do not want councils. If they seem to do so (as in the case of Paul III), it must be a trick.

The modern reader may well feel that, although the popes may have been as Sarpi paints them, there is nothing that they could have been shown to have done that would have made Sarpi change his mind about them. His opinion, then, was not the result of historical research alone, but of prejudice. "Suspended judgment" sometimes means no more than the practice of projecting his opinions onto the characters in his story, or at least emphasizing those contemporary opinions with which he happened to agree.[4] This method suits Sarpi's cautious nature very well, his love of seeming transparent, like the chameleon (his own image), of seeming less interesting and less involved than he really is. Yet a colorless liquid may turn out to be an acid. It should not be forgotten that Sarpi was a professional propagandist as well as a historian. This fact is an important clue to the nature of his bias. It is not simply personal, the result of malice, as modern Catholic writers sometimes suggest. It probably owes something to the nature of the sources accessible to him; French documents were made available to Sarpi, while Roman documents were not, and his treatment of the conflict between France and Rome is surely influenced by that fact. But more important still, Sarpi's bias is the expression of the official Venetian point of view, with which Sarpi seems to have identified himself completely; his pro-French attitude in Books Seven and Eight of the *Council* reflects the Venetian desire to cooperate with France against Rome in the seventeenth century. His bias is much like the national bias of such writers of official national histories as Camden and Pufendorf, to take only seventeenth-century examples.

On the other hand, by the standards of his age, when the religious wars were still raging and when historians

---

[4] For example, the famous remark about the Holy Spirit coming to the Council in the papal bags (*nelle valise*) (see p. 217) is introduced as a "blasphemous proverb," but it is clearly one with which Sarpi agrees. In fact, Sarpi does not seem to have been the inventor of this mot, but it was not a proverb either. According to his table talk, when de Thou was at the Estates of Blois, in 1588, he saw a letter by Lansac, French ambassador to the Council, *"du Saint Esprit venu au concile dans une valise."*

tended either to blacken or whiten their characters, Sarpi
is extremely moderate in his opinions, stated and implied.
His discussion of the Reformation is one of the most
impartial that can be found in his century. He thinks
that there were faults on Luther's side and on the side
of the Pope's defenders, too.

> The dispute became more and more heated, and
> the higher the others raised the authority of the
> Pope the more he lowered it . . . neither side was
> able to keep silent. They provoked one another, and
> the controversy grew more bitter still.

Another serious criticism of Sarpi concerns his ac-
curacy. The Jesuit Sforza Pallavicino launched a famous
attack on Sarpi's errors. More valuable is Ranke's discussion of how Sarpi handles his sources. He gives two
instances in which Sarpi's story is significantly different
from that told by his source. The first: Sleidan says that
the German cities heard rumors that if they did not submit to the Council, something unpleasant would happen
to them (*futurum ut acrius multo quam nuper plectan-
tur*). Sarpi makes a definite individual, Granvelle, deliver
a more precise threat—that they would have to pay
more money. The second instance concerns the Pope's
instructions to Cardinal Contarini. Sarpi makes the
Pope's words more precise than the manuscript of
the instructions does, with the result that the Pope seems
less willing to compromise than he actually was. In each
case, it is possible that Sarpi had other evidence in mind
when departing from his main source; it is equally possible that he was, consciously or unconsciously, distorting
the truth. It should be emphasized that at this period,
the "laws," or rather the conventions of history, allowed
for much more invention than we find tolerable now.
History's neighbor-subject was not sociology but poetry.
Sarpi, as a pragmatic historian, was more concerned
with detailed facts than his predecessors; but even revo-
lutionaries cannot emancipate themselves completely
from tradition.

Not that tradition was simply an obstacle for Sarpi to overcome; it was also an impulse behind him. If we seek to explain his achievement—and it is a fact in European cultural history which the historian must try to explain—then one of the most obvious factors to suggest is quite simply the great tradition of Italian historiography. Sarpi wrote his books some two hundred years after Leonardo Bruni Aretino wrote his *History of the Florentine People*, a work which is often taken to mark the beginning of "modern" historical writing in Italy. In every generation between Bruni and Sarpi, some historical work of importance had been produced in Italy— above all, in Venice and in Florence. The very existence of these works made it easier for a man of ability to think of writing history rather than something else, and easier for him to solve his problems when writing had begun. Had Valla and Guicciardini and other predecessors not existed, had they not been Italians even, Sarpi might not have been able to write as he did. He did not follow them blindly or even closely; but both to possess a tradition and not to feel bound by it seem important conditions for achievement.

To explain the achievement of Sarpi the historian, it is tempting to refer to Sarpi the scientist. His early training may well have been important in making him write history in one way rather than in another. It may have given him his taste for a plain, objective-seeming, prose style. It may have given him his taste for a history which is detailed, useful, concerned with explanation, and without rhetorical pretensions—in a word, for "pragmatic" history. More interesting still, Sarpi's view of hidden and apparent causes in the historical world is parallel to his friend Galileo's view of primary and secondary qualities in the world of nature; and just as his acquaintance Giordano Bruno believed that he had torn the veil from nature (*nudata la ricoperta e velata natura*), so Sarpi believed that he had exposed papal motives in their nakedness. Similarly, Sarpi had once defined philosophy as the study which leads to the uncovering of linguistic and conceptual confusions (*tende a scoprir gli inganni delle parole e ancor de' concetti*); he might have defined his historical studies as leading to the uncovering of the *inganni,* or deceits, of the court of Rome.

Sarpi's political experiences seem even more relevant to his history. Without them, he would not have become a historian at all. A number of great historians (Thucydides, Machiavelli, Guicciardini, Bacon, Clarendon) wrote history in their enforced retirement after an active life in politics. With Sarpi, it was the other way around. His political career and his career as a historian began at the same time, around 1606. But he had held the post of Provincial of his order years before; he had not spent all his life in his cell reading, but had years of administration behind him when he came to write history. Add to this the fact that the Servite order was split by factions in his day, and that he had had to visit Rome five times on business. If Gibbon found that the lieutenant of the Hampshire militia was not altogether useless to the historian of the Roman Empire, Sarpi might well have commented that the Provincial of the Servites had been of some use to the historian of the Council of Trent.

Sarpi's political experiences not only turned him into a historian, they also encouraged him to see history in a certain way. His greatest predecessors had also had experience of crises which made them come of age as historians. Leonardo Bruni experienced the Florentine crisis of about 1400, the struggle for liberty with Milan; Machiavelli and Guicciardini lived through the Italian crisis of 1494, the French invasion. The year 1606 was Sarpi's 1494. For him it was a double crisis, political and religious; a threat to his native city, Venice; and a revelation of the state of the papacy, of the Church. To explain this crisis he was forced back into history. And so Sarpi joins the group of famous historians who were attracted to the subject of their masterpieces because they had a disaster to explain. They studied the past and wrote about it precisely because they felt that the past should not have happened. Thucydides was unable to accept the decline of Athens, the loss of her empire. Guicciardini was unable to accept the decline of Italy, the French invasion. Clarendon was unable to accept the Great Rebellion and "the prosperous wickedness of these times." Sarpi could not accept the Council of Trent and the rise of papal absolutism. In each case, this refusal to accept what had happened makes a sense of tragedy pervade the work; and this sense of tragedy is part of its greatness. In each case, the historian is driven to reject conventional explanations of the disaster and to strain his eyes, peering back into the past to discern the true, underlying causes.

Sarpi's particular achievement can also be linked to the fact that he lived when and where he did, in Europe in the late sixteenth and early seventeenth century. He grew up in the years when Spain was trying to incorporate Italy into her empire and at the time of the revolt of The Netherlands and the religious wars in France. In later life, he witnessed the first years of the Thirty Years' War, as well as the events leading up to it. The years in which he wrote were years of an uneasy lull between religious wars, years, as we might say now, of "cold war"—years, as was said then, of "hidden war" (*guerra occulta*). It is likely that all this left traces on Sarpi's history. To live at a time when religious wars were turning into political wars is to be made forcibly aware of how religion can be made what we call an "ideology," what they called a "cloak" or "veil." For example, the *politique* party in France argued that the religious wars there were not religious at all, but were inspired by ambitious nobles. The historian de Thou, a *politique* himself, wrote of "those who use religion to make a Spanish cloak to cover their ambition." It is not surprising to find the same theme turning up in the *Council of Trent*.

Again, the combination of Spanish rule in Italy and an intensification of persecutions for heresy after 1550 made it dangerous for Italian intellectuals to express their opinions if they did not wish to come to grief. Hence Sarpi's complaint that he was forced to wear a mask. The literature of the time, perhaps for these reasons, is full of allusions to the world as a stage in which the actors wear masks. A man who is conscious of wearing a mask himself is likely to be that much more aware of the disguises of others. The age was therefore propitious to the development of what Karl Mannheim has called the "unmasking turn of mind." In Europe in general, and in Italy in particular, there grew up a literature of "reason of state," which shows awareness of the techniques of political manipulation. Tacitus became more popular, of all ancient historians the most conscious of men's deceits. At such a time it is least surprising to find an unmasker of the techniques of reason of state, a Tacitus who wrote the annals of the papal court, a Paolo Sarpi.

It is clear that Sarpi's achievement cannot be explained without reference to a "conjuncture" of different factors. His books are the expression of his personality—austere, elusive, and ironic. His work also has its place in the development of European history writing from Renaissance to Enlightenment, a development which would have taken place had he never been born or written. His work is also related to his environment—to his life as a Venetian, as a Servite, as a European of the age of the late religious wars and the early baroque. What the historian cannot explain in this way is the quality of his achievement; the fact that between Gibbon and Guicciardini, one of the greatest European historians was Paolo Sarpi.

The translation follows the text as presented in the standard edition of Sarpi's works (Bari, Laterza, 1935–65), which differs considerably from some seventeenth- and eighteenth-century editions.

The *History of Benefices* is presented unabridged.

The passages translated from the *Council of Trent* form only a small portion of that work. It seemed necessary to translate long passages in the main, to give the reader some sense of Sarpi's art as a historian, his capacity for organizing masses of detail. But it also seemed unfair to the reader not to give him a coherent impression of what happened at the Council, so the reproduction of two books entire (say) and the omission of the rest was ruled out. I decided to draw upon books One and Two, which explain why the Council met and describe the first sessions, which set the pattern for those to follow; to omit books Three, Four, and Five (summarized on pp. 201-203); and again to draw upon books Six, Seven, and Eight, which deal with the period 1562–5, in which the important decrees were passed, and about which Sarpi was best informed.

The division into books is Sarpi's own. The division into chapters is the work of an eighteenth-century French translator, Le Courayer, whose arrangement is followed by modern editors.

Names of places and people have posed something of a problem; Sarpi tends to Italianize them. Where no well-known English form exists, I have tended to give place-names in their current modern form. Thus *Senj* not *Segna*, *Pecs* not *Cinquechiese* or *Fünfkirchen*. I have tried to give personal names in the form of their bearer's native language.

The *History of Benefices* was first published in 1675, some fifty years after Sarpi's death. The standard modern edition is contained in Sarpi's *Scritti Giurisdizionalistici* (ed. G. Gambarin, Bari, Laterza, 1958). The book has been translated into English by W. Denton (1680); C. Hayes (1727); and T. Jenkins (1736). I have made a new translation for this edition.

The *History of the Council of Trent* was first published in 1619. The standard modern edition is that in three volumes (ed. G. Gambarin, Bari, Laterza, 1935). An English version appeared in 1620, the work of Sir Nathaniel Brent, who had helped in the smuggling to England of the original manuscript. The book has not been translated into English since. Dr. Johnson commented on Brent's version that "you cannot read three pages . . . without discovering that the Stile is capable of great Improvements." He meant to do the job himself, but gave up after a dispute with a rival translator. A copy of Johnson's specimen version of the opening paragraphs was discovered recently in the John Rylands Library, Manchester.

Sarpi's *History of the Interdict* and his various works on the Uskoks are all accessible in Italian in the Laterza edition, but translations of them do not exist.

A thorough bibliographical study of Sarpi's publications has never been made; given the amount of anonymous and pseudonymous work he published, such a study would be both difficult and valuable. But it should be mentioned that Lord Acton based many of his moral criticisms of Sarpi on a pamphlet of advice to the Venetian Senate, which it is now generally believed was not written by Sarpi at all.

An anonymous life of Sarpi, often believed to have been written by his assistant Fulgenzio Micanzio, was published at Leiden, in Italian, in 1646. It was translated into English by "a person of quality" in 1651. Together with his letters, it is the fundamental source for our knowledge of Sarpi's personality.

Modern writings in English on Sarpi include: H. F. Brown, *Paolo Sarpi the Man,* in his *Studies in the History of Venice* (London, 1907); F. A. Yates, *Paolo Sarpi's "History of the Council of Trent"* in the *Journal of the Warburg and Courtauld Institutes,* 1944 (which deals especially with Sarpi's relations with England); and W. J. Bouwsma, *Three Types of Historiography in Post-Renaissance Italy,* in *History and Theory,* 1965 (which compares Sarpi with his contemporaries Ammirato and Baronius). Professor Bouwsma is preparing a book on Sarpi and his times.

In Italian, the numerous studies of Sarpi include the biography by A. Bianchi-Giovini (Brussels, 1836, not yet superseded; there is a French translation); F. Chabod, *La politica di Paolo Sarpi* (Venice and Rome, 1962); and two articles by G. Cozzi, one in the *Rivista Storica Italiana,* 1956 (on Sarpi, Anglicanism, and his *History of the Council of Trent*) and the other in the *Bollettino dell'istituto di storia della società e dello stato Veneziano,* 1959 (on Sarpi's relations with Canaye du Fresne and Isaac Casaubon).

On the Council of Trent itself there is a huge literature; the standard modern work, still unfinished, is by Hubert Jedin, translated into English as *A History of the Council of Trent* (London, Nelson, 1957, 1961).

| | |
|---|---|
| 1552 | Sarpi born in Venice. |
| 1559 | Treaty of Cateau-Cambrésis—Spain received Milan, Naples, Sicily. |
| 1562 | Council of Trent reassembled; religious wars in France began. |
| 1566 | Sarpi joined the Servites. |
| 1570 | Sarpi became court theologian at Mantua. |
| 1574 | Sarpi in Milan. |
| 1579 | Sarpi became Provincial of Venetian province of the Servites. |
| c.1580–90 | Sarpi wrote *Art of Thinking Well*. |
| 1585–8 | Sarpi in Rome as Procurator. |
| 1586 | Gentillet's *Le bureau du Concile de Trente* published. |
| 1588–1606 | Sarpi in retirement in Venice. |
| c.1602 | Minucci's *History of the Uskoks* published. |
| 1605 | Venetian Senate forbade alienation of goods to the Church. |
| 1605 | Paul V elected Pope. |
| 1606 | Leonardo Donà became Doge of Venice (January 10). |
| 1606 | Sarpi became theologian and canonist to the Republic (January 28). |
| 1606 | Paul V laid Venice under interdict (April). |
| 1606 | Sarpi's *Treatise on the Interdict* published (September). |
| 1607 | Sarpi excommunicated (January). |
| 1607 | Attempt to assassinate Sarpi (October). |
| 1607 | Gillot's *Actes du Concile de Trente* published. |
| 1607 | *History of the Interdict* written. |
| 1608 | Vangadizza affair. |
| c.1609 | *On Benefices* written. |
| 1610 | *On the Prohibition of Books* written. |
| 1612 | Doge Donà died. |
| 1613 | *On the Inquisition* written. |

| 1615 | War began between Venice and the Archduke Ferdinand. |
| c.1617 | *Addition* and *Supplement* published. |
| 1618 | Bedmar conspiracy; Thirty Years' War began; synod of Dort met. |
| 1619 | Alliance between Venice and the United Provinces. |
| 1619 | *Council of Trent* published. |
| c.1620 | *Treaty of Peace* written. |
| 1623 | Sarpi died in Venice. |
| 1624 | *History of the Interdict* published. |
| 1656 | Pallavicino's *History of the Council of Trent* published. |
| 1675 | *On Benefices* published. |

# History of Benefices

## (Delle Materie Beneficiarie)

retaining what the rules supplied. And so it has to work
necessary to pass laws forbidding excessive acquisition,
and plous men feel a strong desire to devote past wealth
of explaination to ward off the anger of men...

...
they themselves...
beyond all remedy...
as much grace to...
ancestors, we would not be guilty of jesting the cause,
marvels in our age as in history. It was the stage that the
situation became so urgent and as a result that...
necessary for it to be narrowed into that of reform. In the
primitive patricians it is only clear that this course is not
open unless it is clearer how important goods were to be
administered in the household, and how this adaptation
came to degenerate. And here it is necessary to say
anything else to explain how the church has come into
the age to acquire worldly goods, and how in bad times
to deprive members of the clergy so illiterate to present
them. This will make clear that the obstacles are less
thorough reformation of the present kind, and it will
also show how they take to be symmetry. This is to show
in the present work on the first chapters of reformer.

The ancient fervor of Christian charity not only moved princes and private individuals to give many worldly goods to churches, but also moved the clergy to devote those goods to pious uses. Now that this fervor has grown cold, it is no wonder that the clergy are no longer generous, but are diligent only in acquiring goods and in retaining what they have acquired. And so it has become necessary to pass laws controlling excessive acquisitions, and pious men feel a strong desire to see the use made of ecclesiastical property return to the ancient model, or at least to a tolerable compromise with it.

The defects that can be seen today did not affect all the clergy together nor all at once. From a state of absolute or divine perfection, the clergy descended step by step to that imperfection now obvious to all, which they themselves admit and which some of them consider beyond all remedy. Yet if it pleases Our Lord God to give as much grace to the faithful now as He gave to our ancestors, we ought not to despair of seeing the same marvels in our age as in theirs. It was by steps that the situation became so serious, and it is by steps that it is necessary for it to improve, in order to return to the primitive perfection of the holy Church. This cannot happen unless it is known how temporal goods were administered in the beginning, and how this administration came to degenerate. And so it is necessary before anything else to explain how the Church has come over the ages to acquire worldly goods, and how it has come to depute members of the clergy to distribute or possess them. This will make clear what the obstacles are to a thorough reformation at the present time, and it will also show how they are to be overcome. This is my aim in the present work on the huge subject of benefices.

The history of ecclesiastical property begins at the time when Our Lord Jesus Christ still lived on earth, and it originated in the gifts of the pious, gifts which were handed to someone to look after and used for two purposes only: for the needs of Our Lord and the apostles, preachers of the Gospel, and for giving alms to the poor. All this can be seen clearly in the Gospel of St. John, where he says that Judas was the one who had the box or purse in which was the money given to the Lord, and that he bought necessities or gave to the poor, according to what the Lord told him each day. St. Augustine thought that since Christ was served by angels, He had no need of money but that all the same He wished to have a purse to give example to the Church of what it should do. So the Church has always understood that His Divine Majesty has shown it by His own example how to get money and how to spend it. If we do not see such a good custom observed in our own time, we ought to consider what the Bible relates for our instruction and consolation: that Judas, too, was a thief and embezzled the goods of the apostles, and reached such a peak of avarice that what he took did not seem enough to him, and to make more money he sold Christ Our Lord Himself to the Jews. Whether we read history or observe the events of our own time, we see that ecclesiastical goods are largely devoted to uses other than pious, and that some of those who have charge of them, not satisfied with taking for their private use what ought to be devoted to the needs of the Church and of the poor, go further and make money by selling sacred things. We should not ascribe this to the special vices of our own or any other time, but rather to the will of God in order to test good men, seeing that even in its first years the Church was subject to the same imperfections. We should all try to remedy this according to our rank and calling. He who can do nothing else should pray. He who can should fight this evil by opposing abuses, remembering that although Judas received no human punishment (because those who should have punished him were his accomplices), nevertheless Divine Providence showed what punishment he deserved, and made him his own executioner, in order to make their duty clear to those whom His Divine Majesty would later make defenders of the Church.

After Christ Our Lord had ascended into heaven, the blessed apostles followed the same system in the church of Jerusalem; that is, they spent their money on the needs of the ministers of the Gospel and on the relief of the poor. The source of this money was, as before, the offerings of the faithful, who lived in common and sold their individual possessions to raise money for this purpose. So the property of the Church was not distinct from that of each of the faithful, as is still the case in some religious orders, faithful to their original constitutions. In those early days, Christians were extremely ready to give away their possessions for alms, because they expected the end of the world to come soon, since Christ Our Lord had not made the matter clear. Although it was to last as long as He willed it, they thought of it as if its end were imminent, being certain that the world, in the sense of their lives, would pass away; and so gifts to the Church grew larger and larger. The custom of having all goods in common and no individual possessions, so that no one was poor or rich, but all lived as equals, did not spread beyond Jerusalem. It was not followed in the other churches which the blessed apostles built, and it did not last long even in Jerusalem. Twenty-six years after the death of Christ we read that public property was distinct from private, each man knowing what was his. In that church as in others, there was a common stock of money derived from offerings, which was put to common use, for the ministers and for the poor, but no one who had property of his own was allowed to live at the expense of the Church. St. Paul laid it down that widows who had relations should be maintained by them, so that the goods of the Church could be applied to those who were genuinely helpless and poor. On the first day of the week (which was therefore called the Lord's Day) the faithful would meet, and each would contribute whatever he had put aside the week before for the needs of the community.

The stewardship of the common goods which Our

Lord had given to Judas while He lived on earth was exercised after His ascension by the apostles for a short time. But they saw that murmurings and sedition arose among the faithful about the distribution of the common goods since some thought that they were not receiving their fair share, or that others should have made larger contributions—an evil which has always arisen when the goods of the Church have been divided. They realized that they could not attend to this efficiently at the same time as preaching the word of God: and so they decided to preach and teach themselves, but to confide the administration of worldly goods to another class of men. This is the opposite of what we see in our own time, when the leading prelates of the Church administer its goods, but the office of preaching and teaching the word of God and the doctrine of the Gospels is left to the friars or to some poor priests low in the ranks of the Church. This new class of men, founded by the apostles to administer temporal affairs, was called the class of deacons. Seven of them were chosen from the whole body of the faithful for the purpose, and the apostles ordained them to this ministry. Wherever they founded churches, they ordained deacons in the same way as they ordained bishops and priests and other ministers of the Church, that is to say, they began with fasting and praying and proceeded to the common choice of the faithful, always following the rule of appointing to ecclesiastical posts those men only who had previously been elected by the whole Church, that is, by all the faithful together. This custom continued to be observed in the Church for about two hundred years, the common goods being spent on the support of the clergy and the poor, and the only source of revenue being the gifts of the faithful. Revenues were most abundant all the same, because everyone was so generous that he offered all that his means allowed. When the faithful in any particular city were able to do more than supply the needs of their own church, collections were made for other, poorer churches. In this way, St. James, St. Peter, and St. John, when they recognized St. Paul and St. Barnabas as colleagues in mission work, recommended them to collect alms for the poor church of Jerusalem, and St. Paul says that they did so in Macedonia, Achæa, Galatia, and Corinth. This custom was observed not only while the blessed apostles were alive, but after their death as well. In the city of Rome, which was extremely rich, offerings were most abundant and, about the year 150, they were sufficient not only to sustain the clergy and poor Christians of that city, but also to make large sums available to other churches, not only those near at hand, but also distant ones; and they supplied the necessities of life to Christians in various provinces who had been condemned to the mines, to prison, or who were in other ways unfortunate. To show the size of the offerings I will give just one example. Marcion, on one occasion, about 170, offered five thousand gold drachmas in the church at Rome. But because he held certain opinions on matters of faith which were not as they should have been, he was expelled from the Church and all his money restored to him, since it seemed to the Holy Church that it would be contaminated by retaining the possessions of a heretic. The church of Rome became so rich that, after the year 250, the Roman emperors themselves became interested, and Decius imprisoned St. Lawrence, Deacon of Rome, to obtain from him the treasure of the church, so great was it. However, he was mistaken in thinking that these treasures were laid up and preserved, because that saintly deacon, suspecting the rapacity of the tyrant and foreseeing imminent persecution, had given it all away, as was the custom in time of such dangers. This was the cause of most of the persecutions of the Church after the death of Commodus; that is, the princes or prefects, finding themselves in need of money, adopted this method of acquiring that of the Christian Church.

After the churches had become rich, the clergy began to live more comfortably, and some of them, not content with the communal life of the churches, wanted to live apart in their own houses and have their share of the church's goods in money every day or monthly or for longer periods still. This was a falling off from the original perfect state, but it was tolerated by the Fathers all the same. Decline did not stop there. The

7

bishops began to neglect the customary alms to the poor and to keep for themselves what should have been given away. Having become rich on the common property of the church, they practiced usury to increase their wealth and abandoned their charge of teaching the doctrines of Christ, giving themselves up entirely to avarice. St. Cyprian complained of this in his time, and he came to the conclusion that God permitted the great persecution of Decius's reign in order to purge His Church of these errors, and that He has always reformed His Church either gently through its own rulers, or, when corruption has gone too far, through persecutions.

Although the Church was so rich, at this time it did not possess landed property. This was because it was not interested in such possessions, believing that the end was at hand and all worldly things transitory, and that they weighed a man down on his way to heaven. Secondly, Roman law did not allow any college or community or corporation to be given or bequeathed landed property, nor could they for any reason possess such property unless the Senate or the emperor approved. This cannot be doubted, although there are going about some letters in the name of ancient popes which explain why the apostles sold their property in Judæa and why the Christians who came after kept to this by saying that this was because the apostles foresaw that the Christian Church must not remain in Judæa but spread among the Gentiles—as if the cause of the sale was not explicitly stated in the Gospel, where Christ said to His Church, "Fear not, but sell all you have and give to the poor." Although Jerusalem was destroyed, Christians did not give much help in rebuilding it, and the cities where the Gentile churches had property were not destroyed. But it is unnecessary to make efforts to show how this argument is false, since it is certain that these epistles are forgeries dating from about 800, the work of those who preferred pomp and riches (as men still do) to the moderation of apostolic times, as ordained and commanded by Christ. In the long confusion that followed the imprisonment of Valerian, the laws of the empire were not much observed, especially in

Africa, France, and Italy. So some people left or gave landed property to churches, which was all confiscated by Diocletian and Maximian in 302, although in France, thanks to Constantius Chlorus (the Cæsar who governed there), the decree of the emperors was not executed. After these princes had given up the empire, Maxentius (eight years later) restored all its possessions to the Roman church. Shortly afterwards, Constantine and Licinius gave Christians freedom of worship and approved the ecclesiastical colleges, which they called by the Greek word *ekklesia* [churches]. They made a general concession throughout the empire to the effect that these "churches" could acquire landed property, whether given or bequeathed to them, and they also exempted the clergy from military duties in order to enable them to attend more easily to the service of religion.

They did not at this time observe our custom of giving or leaving property to the Church on condition that it was used for some specified purpose, such as building, dowries, food for orphans, and so on—still less on condition that Masses were said or other services performed. This custom did not grow up until long afterwards. Property was given or bequeathed unconditionally. What was given was added to the common stock, to be used for all pious works. It is therefore true to say that the goods of the Church in its early days were not allocated to any special purpose. Nor could they be spent on anything at all; they were used for pious works in general, and these only. The property of the Church was increasingly exempted from taxation by princes, and these exemptions were thoroughly observed, to the satisfaction of both princes and people. This was not to the disadvantage of society, and the common people did not complain about it for two reasons. The first was that in the last resort the goods of the Church were the goods of the poor, of the people, and so to exempt them was simply to exempt the have-nots and tax the haves, something which has always been considered just. The second reason was that to exempt someone when he possesses little or less than is sufficient does not make others feel aggrieved. However, no one should draw the conclusion

9

that this liberality of rulers towards the Church is just and fitting in modern times as well. Now that it has become so rich that it possesses a quarter or more of all property and spends its riches on the poor no longer, to exempt the Church would be to do the contrary of what good rulers have done, by exempting the rich and making the poor bear the burden of taxation. The rulers of today are no less pious than rulers used to be, but the situation is different. Those of today would still exempt the Church if it were still poor. The rulers then would not have exempted it if it had been rich.

The great devotion of princes and peoples thus vastly increased the riches of the Church; and this increase aroused in the clergy the desire to become more rich still. This desire affected even those with the highest motives. Seeing that the distribution of the goods of the Church was to the glory of God and the good of society, they concluded that the more the Church had to give away, the better. And so they used every means and every art to acquire riches, without caring whether the means they used were legitimate or just. Provided that the Church grew richer, it seemed to them that they had made a sacrifice to God. It is certain that this sort of zealous people, who have no discretion, is responsible for innumerable and immense evils. It seems to them that everything that serves the cause of religion is good, whatever the means; so they often do what is inhuman and throw the world into confusion. And so it was in the early Church. After the Church was permitted to acquire landed property, some religious people believed that they were serving God by depriving their own sons and other relations to give to churches. The churches, too, omitted nothing in order to induce widows, girls, and others easily persuaded to deprive their own families in order to leave property to the Church. The practice went so far and so nearly became irremediable that the secular authority had to intervene; and in 370, a law was passed, which although it did not absolutely forbid churches to acquire property, forbade the clergy to enter the houses of widows and wards, or to receive anything from women by gift or will not only directly,

but even through the medium of a third person. St.
Jerome declared that this law was a remedy for the
corruption of the Church, which had gone too far in
desiring to acquire worldly goods. This law was not
enough, for a few years after, in 390, another law was
passed, which forbade any widow who dedicated her-
self to the service of the Church to give or bequeath it
landed property or valuable movable goods. This law
is discussed at length elsewhere.

St. Augustine, who lived at this time, did not much
like excessive acquisitions either. He said openly that
it would please him more if the inheritance were to go
to the family than if it were to go to the Church. In
fact, he refused inheritances which were left to his
church, declaring that the function of the Church was
not to give much, but to give well. He criticized a new
means of acquiring property which the churches had
discovered at this time, which was the purchase of
landed property out of surplus income. The Saint always
hated this and never wanted to permit it in his church,
but said in public sermons that he would rather live
on offerings and collections, as was done in the early
days of the Church, than have to think about property.
This was difficult for him and hindered him from attending fully to a bishop's main duty, which was concerned
with spiritual matters. He added that he was prepared
to give up property altogether, provided that the servants of God were provided for, as in the Old Testament,
by means of tithes and other offerings, so that they
were not subject to the distractions which earthly things
brought with them.

However, in spite of the limitations imposed by the
holy Fathers, by means of exhortations, and by the
princes, by means of laws, it was not possible to prevent
the goods of the Church increasing more than they should
have done. Yet the administration and distribution of
them was not changed, and this state of affairs continued till 420 without notable alteration. All the offerings and other income of the Church, derived from property, were still held in common and administered by
the deacons, helped by the subdeacons and others, and

11

they were spent on the maintenance of the clergy and the poor. The whole body of priests and the bishop in particular supervised this. In brief, there was a common income and a common expenditure, with the bishop making all the decisions, the deacons carrying them out, and all the clergy living on the property of the Church, although they did not all take part in its administration. St. John Chrysostom mentions the fact that at this time the church of Antioch maintained more than three thousand people at public expense. It is also certain that the church of Jerusalem paid the expenses of an infinite number of people who arrived there from all parts of the world. It is recorded in the histories that Atticus, Bishop of Constantinople, helped the church of Nicæa in Bithynia because so many poor people had flocked there—ten thousand were counted in one day.

After France, Spain, and Africa had been separated from the empire and had become independent kingdoms, after the heirs of Theodosius had become extinct, and after various barbarian invasions, Italy fell into the hands of the Goths. The East became separated from the West, and the Church began to be administered in a different manner. In the East, goods continued to be held in common, but in the West, the bishops and administrators began to take the goods of the Church for themselves or divide them in the way that best pleased them. Hence, there was great confusion in the distribution of these goods, and great harm done both to church buildings, which decayed, and to the poor, who were abandoned. And so, in about 470, it was laid down in the West that the income of churches should be divided into four parts. The first part was for the bishop, the second for the rest of the clergy, the third for the fabric of the church, which included not only the church itself but the houses of the bishop and other clergy and the sick and widows; and the fourth part was for the poor. But in most places, as St. Gregory explains, the "poor" meant only the poor of the district, because the duty of hospitality was the bishop's. It was he who was obliged to put up visiting clergy and to feed the poor who came from outside. It must not be thought that this division was into four arithmetically equal parts; it was proportional. In some churches, the clergy were so numerous that more had to be spent on them than on the poor; in others it was just the opposite. In large cities, building expenses were considerable, but in ordinary towns this was not the case. So each church divided its income into four parts according to the decree, but made the parts of different size, according to its own needs. I know that some people date this division to Pope Sylvester's time, a hundred and fifty years before, basing themselves on certain manuscripts forged later—a dating which is not to the honor of those ancient times, which were not yet so smirched. In the Theodosian Code can be found a law of Constantius and Julian, in 359, which exempts clerics who were merchants from paying tax because what profit they made went to the poor; so far are we from the division of the goods of the Church, for here their profits were still in common. But in the years around 500, although the revenues were divided into four parts, their sources were not, whether property or gifts and offerings, but all were administered together by the deacons and sub-deacons, and the proceeds were divided into four parts. It is necessary to recapitulate this here, because in the following period I shall describe a change so great as to be completely contrary to ancient practice. The method of choosing the clergy was, as I said above, founded by the blessed apostles. Bishops, priests, and other ministers of the word of God, and the deacons who were in charge of temporal affairs were chosen by the whole body of the faithful and were ordained by the bishop laying his hands on their head. And this custom did not change. The bishop was chosen by the people and ordained by the metropolitan in the presence of all the bishops of the province, or with the written consent of those who were not able to attend; and if the metropolitan himself was unable to attend, the ordination would be made by three neighboring bishops with the agreement of the metropolitan and the other absent bishops. After many provinces had been given a primate as a better form of government, his consent was necessary, too. Priests and deacons and other clerics were presented by the people and ordained by the bishop, or nominated by the bishop, and with the consent of the people ordained by him. No strangers were ever appointed. The bishop never ordained anyone who was not approved, praised, or nominated by the people. Their consent and participation was considered so necessary that St. Leo [Pope Leo I] claimed that the ordination of a bishop could not be valid unless he was requested and approved by the people. All the saints of those times said the same. St. Gregory thought that Constantius, who had been elected by the clergy, could not be consecrated bishop of Milan unless the citizens agreed, and they had fled to Genoa from the barbarian invasions; so he sent to ask their opinion first. This is something worthy of note in our times, when elections in which the people claims its share are declared to be illegitimate and void. How things have changed! They have become the opposite of what they were. What used to be called wicked is now called legitimate. What used to be considered holy is now thought of as unholy! Sometimes a bishop, when he was old, would choose his own successor: St. Augustine nominated Eradius, for example. But this nomination was of no value unless it was approved by the people. It is necessary to keep all these things in mind to contrast them with the customs that came into use at a later date.

Now it is necessary to make a small digression for a new reason, on account of something which has greatly increased the goods of the Church, and which began at this same time, about 500. This was another sort of religious corporation, called monasteries. Monasticism began in Egypt about the year 300, among refugees from persecution. From there it passed to Greece, where, around 370, Basil organized it into its present form in those parts. But in Italy, around 350, it was brought to Rome by Athanasius, and there and in the country around it had little success or support until this time, 500, when St. Equitius and St. Benedict gave it a permanent form and caused it to spread. In fact, St. Equitius's organization did not spread far and soon died out, but that of St. Benedict extended itself throughout Italy and even passed beyond the Alps.

Monks at this time, and long after, were not clerics, but laymen, and in their monasteries in the countryside they lived by doing agricultural and other work and also received various offerings from the faithful, which were looked after by the abbot. In cities they lived on the proceeds of their work and on what the Church gave them. These latter maintained their ancient discipline much longer. After the goods of the Church had been divided, the clergy lost the devotion of the people, and so few people gave them or bequeathed them anything any more. This might have been the end of the acquisitions of the Church. But the monks, who continued to live in common and do pious works, were the reason why the generosity of the people did not become extinct: gifts went no longer to the clergy but to the monks, who were an important means of increasing the wealth of the Church. In the course of time they increased greatly in property and income given and bequeathed them, which they continued to make good use of in maintaining a large number of monks, in hospitality, in education, and in other pious works. The abbot Trithemius declares that there were as many as fifteen thousand Benedictine monasteries, besides priories and small convents. The monks themselves elected their abbot, who was their spiritual ruler and who administered their property, too, both the charitable offerings of the faithful and what the monks had earned themselves by their enterprises—and later, their income from property as well.

But the bishops, in the period after 500, having gained absolute control over a quarter of the goods of the Church, began to think a little more about worldly matters and to gain a following for themselves in the cities. Elections had less to do with the service of God and more with intrigues, and often they passed from intrigues to public violence. And so secular rulers, who up to that time had not much considered who should be chosen to fill which office in the Church, began to take thought about it. They were told by holy men of that time that God had committed the Church to their protection, so that it was their duty, by command of His Divine Majesty, to ensure that Church affairs were carried on in a proper way. Besides, princes could see the danger to the tranquillity and good government of the state in the private interests of ambitious clerics and in their seditious intrigues to acquire offices in the Church. And so, both for unworldly and worldly reasons, they came to forbid the clergy and people to choose their bishop in their own way. This was partly because things had changed, and a bishopric was no longer something men avoided, but something they were ambitious to obtain; so that men intrigued for it, and there were plots and murders as a result of the competition. It was also because the men who were chosen bishops were sometimes factious people and had secret understandings with the ruler's enemies, of whom there was no lack at this time of confusion in the West. At other times men were elected who had a following among the people and who attempted to take over the power of the magistrates, inciting the people to help them in this enterprise. So the rulers laid down that no bishop-elect could be consecrated without their permission or that of the magistrate, reserving for themselves the confirmation of the greater bishoprics, like Rome, Ravenna, and Milan in Italy, and leaving their subordinates to look after the lesser bishoprics. But they cared more about the reality than about the appearances, and when there was in a city a universally popular candidate, and the people knew that he was satisfactory to the prince, and the prince knew that he pleased the people, then he was consecrated without delay. Sometimes it happened that by the accident of war or plague someone was ordained before he had the permission of the prince, as was the case with Pelagius II, the predecessor of St. Gregory, during the siege of Rome by the Lombards. But when the siege was raised, he sent St. Gregory, who was then a deacon, to make his excuses to the emperor and to beg him to ratify what had been done out of necessity.

The popes and bishops in Italy were elected in this way with the confirmation of the emperor till 750. But in France and in other places on the far side of the Alps, the authority of the king or the mayor of the palace was more absolute, so that the people had nothing to do with the election when the prince took an interest in it. Good men did not intervene because they believed that the kings' beneficence made intervention unnecessary; bad men did not intervene because they believed it impossible. So during this period, kings appointed bishops by themselves. In the history written by Gregory of Tours, from Clovis, the first Christian king of France, to 590, one finds no bishops appointed except at the command or with the permission of the king. And St. Gregory, who was made pope in that year, writing to the kings of France on various occasions complains that they do not give bishoprics to the right men, and he begs them to choose people who are good and intelligent. But he never complains of royal appointments when the men appointed are worthy. It was easy for the bishops, who did not owe their own appointments to the people, to exclude them from the choice of priests, deacons, and other ministers of the Church as well and to give the power of nominating them to the prince alone. Besides, some of the people had withdrawn from church meetings to attend to their own affairs; others had withdrawn because they disliked the results of faction, others because they saw that they were not respected by the bishop, who had become powerful, both because of his riches and his close relations with the prince who had appointed him or confirmed his appointment. The prince sometimes appointed priests and at other times left this entirely to the bishop, especially when he had full confidence in him. This confidence was also the reason for the prince's often making use of the bishop to compose the difficulties among his subjects, or to end difficult lawsuits, because the general respect for religion meant that bishops were trusted more than magistrates. So the bishops devoted themselves to these tasks more than to teaching Christian doctrine, their original duty. And so it came about that when it was a question

17

of appointing a bishop, it was considered more appropriate to look for a worldly-wise man than for one who had understanding of matters of faith. This view is still held, and people say that (apart from places on the borders of Christendom) it is better to make a good lawyer a bishop than to choose a good theologian. And this would certainly be reasonable, if the main duty of a bishop were to be a judge. Christ Our Lord, ordaining the apostles, said: "I came upon an errand from my Father, and now I am sending you out in my turn," which is to be understood as, sending to teach. If nowadays everyone has been sufficiently taught and there is no more need of this, they can attend to something else!

Formerly, the principal duty of the bishop was to teach, his second, to look after the poor. In the second, as in the first, there was a certain falling away. In the case of the division into four parts mentioned above, the administration of the goods was in the hands of the clergy, and it was they who made the division in their own way. Where the bishop and priests were conscientious, the division was a just one; where they were too attentive to their own interests, there was no one to protect the poor, still less the buildings, and these received very small shares. In some places they received nothing at all, and everything was divided between the bishop and the clergy. Even where the division was made in just proportions, the administration of the buildings and of the share of the poor always remained in the hands of the clergy, and so, little by little, these two parts diminished, and the other two parts increased. This can be seen from the fact that in only very few places is there a separate building fund; and for the poor, there remain only poorhouses, none of which are of ancient date.

The share of the clergy was originally not distributed among them, but it was the bishop's duty to give to each according to his deserts. Then the clergy took over the task of distributing it and excluded the bishop. When they had their own share, with which neither the bishop nor anyone else had anything to do, this was divided yet again among them, so that each individual began to think of his share as his own and gave up living in common. Although the proceeds were divided in this way, the sources of income continued to be administered by the deacons and subdeacons, and what they collected was then passed on to the bishop and each of the clergy according to their share. At this time, in Italy, the property of the churches was called "patrimony." I wanted to mention this here so that no one should think that this name means some supreme power or some jurisdiction belonging to the Church of Rome or to the Pope. The property of some family which came to them from their ancestors was, at the time of which we are speaking, called their "patrimony," and the property of the prince was also called his "patrimony." To distinguish it from the patrimony of private individuals it was called *sacrum patrimonium,* as may be read in many laws in Book XII of the Codex. For the same reason, the property of each church was called its patrimony. In the letters of St. Gregory there are references not only to the patrimonies of the Roman church, but also to those of the church of Rimini, the church of Milan, the church of Ravenna. Those churches which were built in cities where the inhabitants had only moderate fortunes were not bequeathed property outside their own district; but churches in imperial cities, like Rome, Ravenna, or Milan, where senators and other famous people lived, were left property in various parts of the world. St. Gregory mentions the patrimony of the church of Ravenna in Sicily and another patrimony in Sicily belonging to the church of Milan. The Roman church had patrimonies in most parts of the world. Mention is made of the patrimony of France, of Africa, of Sicily, of the Cottian Alps, and of many other places. In the time of St. Gregory himself there were lawsuits between him and the bishop of Ravenna for the patrimonies of both churches, which were settled by compromise. In order that church property might be more respected, it was customary to give it the name of that saint which that particular church venerated particularly. So the church of Ravenna called its property that of St. Apollinaris; the church of Milan, that of St. Ambrose; the church of Rome, the patrimony of St. Peter in the Abruzzi, the patrimony of St. Peter in Sicily, and so on, in the same way that in Venice the income of the State is called that of St. Mark. In the patrimonies of the prince (when they were not under military rule), a governor was appointed with jurisdiction in appropriate cases. Some ecclesiastics of the Roman church attempted to usurp similar powers over the patrimonies of that church, wishing to try their own cases and not to have recourse to a public tribunal; but St. Gregory condemned this attempt and forbade it on pain of excommunication. Church property used to pay contributions to the prince, as clearly appears from the canon *si tributum* of St. Ambrose. It is clear that Constantine Pogonatus, in 681, granted exemptions from the contributions which the Roman church paid for the patrimonies of Sicily and Calabria, and that Justinian Rhinotmetus, in 687, remitted the contributions levied on the patrimonies of the Abruzzi and Basilicata. The Roman church did not receive such a large income from its patrimonies as some think. Where the histories describe how Leo the Isaurian, in 732, confiscated the patrimonies of Calabria and Sicily, they mention the fact that the income from this property together was three silver talents and half a gold one, which makes in our money (not to describe in detail the variety of opinions about the precise modern equivalent of a talent) not more than 5500 scudi. The patrimony of Sicily, which was a very large one, did not bring in more than 2100 scudi.

It is not irrelevant to mention these events which occurred while the property of the Church remained united and under the same administration, although the proceeds were divided. This state of affairs could not last long, however, because of the disputes that arose between the administrators and the others who were in their power. As a more satisfactory solution, each minister began to keep what was offered in his church—offerings which he had previously taken to the bishop to be divided. In recognition of the superiority of the bishop, each minister gave him a third or a little more, which was called the *cattedratico* because it was given out of reverence for the bishop's throne [*cattedra*]. The sources of revenue were also divided, and each individual had his share. These changes did not take place everywhere at the same time, nor by means of a public decree, but as is the case with customs, they began in one place and spread gradually to others. This is especially true of bad customs, which move faster and meet fewer obstacles than others.

At this time, the princes distributed the lands of the State to soldiers, telling one to guard the frontiers, another to serve his prince in the civil administration, another to follow him to the wars, yet another to guard the cities and fortresses. These lands were called *fiefs* in the Frankish and Lombard languages, and in Latin, which was not yet totally extinct, they were called *beneficia*, because the prince gave them out of beneficence. Shares of Church property, or rather the right to such shares, were also called "benefices," because they were given by the prince, like bishoprics, or by the bishop with the prince's consent, like the other benefices, and because the clergy were soldiers of the faith and carried on spiritual warfare. The abbeys on the far side of the Alps had become large and rich, and so the mayors of the palace took over the power of appointing abbots. This they had an obvious right to do, because in those days monks were laymen, as I said before. They did not always appoint abbots; sometimes, as a favor, they allowed the monks to choose their own. But in Italy, monasteries were not particularly rich until about 750, as I said, so the kings of the Goths and the emperors and the kings of the Lombards did not pay much attention to them, and elections were held by the monks with only the bishop to supervise them. Sometimes the bishops, eager to increase their powers, did the monasteries harm, and so the monks and abbots, to free themselves from this subjection, went to the Pope and asked him to take them under his protection and exempt them from the authority of the bishops. The popes agreed easily to this, because it was useful for them to have more people who were directly dependent on them in the cities, and because it would increase their power over the bishops. It was of great consequence that an important body like the monks, who at that time were almost the only men who studied, should be completely dependent on the See of Rome.

Once these exemptions had begun, it was not long before all monasteries had left their bishops and put themselves under the Pope.

In France, the bishops appointed by the kings—and still more, those appointed by the mayors of the palace when royal authority had diminished—gave themselves up entirely to temporal matters. The abbots did the same. They contributed soldiers to the king's army and went to war in person, not as religious men to do the duty of servants of Christ there, but armed, and fighting with their own hands. They were no longer satisfied with a quarter of the goods of the Church, but took everything for themselves. The poor priests, who taught the people the word of God and administered the sacraments to them in the churches, had nothing to live on. The people, out of devotion, gave them part of their own goods. In some places they were more generous, in others less, so there were sometimes disputes. The question of how much one should give to one's rector frequently arose, and it became generally accepted that it was proper to give him a tenth, or tithe, following the example of the law of God in the Old Testament. Since God had ordered the Jews to do this, it was easy to make out that it was still obligatory, although Our Lord and St. Paul said no more than that the people owed the minister enough to live on, that the minister or laborer is worthy of his hire, and that whoever serves at the altar should live from the altar, without laying down a precise amount, because in some situations a tenth would be little, and in others, a hundredth part would be sufficient. But this is clear enough, and we will have to discuss it in more detail below, so we will say no more now except that at that time and for some centuries after, sermons which were not about matters of faith were always exhortations to pay tithes. Parish priests had to do this

out of necessity. To make a good piece of rhetoric out
of it, as happens, they often went so far as to reduce
Christian perfection to the paying of tithes. They were
not satisfied with tithes levied on land, but they began
to claim personal tithes as well, that is, tithes levied on
what a man earns by his effort in hunting, in crafts,
and even in military service. Many of these sermons
have been discovered without an author's name, and
some people have (either by mistake or deliberately)
attributed them to St. Augustine and other ancient writers. However, the style shows that they were written
around 800, and the histories are clear that in Africa
and in the East tithes were never paid, and that they
began, as I said, in France.

I will move on to Italy, where for hundreds of years no
one was ever ordained without immediately being assigned a particular office, except in the case of a man
who was famous for learning or sanctity, who in order
for him to be able to carry on his studies, was not given
a specific task, but was ordained a priest without a
parish of his own. St. Jerome was ordained a priest in
Antioch, and St. Paulinus in Barcelona. But this exception apart, in early times the distinction between the
order and the office was unknown. To ordain someone
was the same thing as to give him an office and the
right to be maintained by the common property of the
Church. But in the disorder that wars caused in many
states, many excellent clerics were driven from their
posts, and they turned up at some other church, where
they were welcomed and treated like the other clergy,
maintained at the common expense. Sometimes when
there was a minister lacking in that church, as a result
of deaths or for some other reason, his office was given
to the newcomer, and he was then said to be *incardinato*
[hinged] in the same way as a man who took an office
for the first time was said to be ordained to it. Whoever
lost his own office and was provided with another was
called *incardinato*.

This custom began in Italy about 600, when as a result of the invasion of the Lombards many bishops and
other clergy were driven from their posts. And so they

23

became *incardinati* in other churches, and the bishops were called *episcopi cardinales*, and the priests, *presbyteri cardinales*. Most of those who were driven from their own churches went to the church of Rome or to the church of Ravenna, which were the chief ones, the richest, with the most ministers and the most vacancies. These churches, because they were more rich, took in most strangers, and so they had the most *cardinales*. And these churches positively welcomed the situation, because by this means they obtained the most distinguished men from all parts, as happens at the present time. Sometimes they ordained them, but usually they made them *incardinati*, and so it happened that in these two churches all the clergy were called cardinals. In the church of Rome, the name still endures; in that of Ravenna, it lasted until 1543, when Paul III issued a bull abolishing the title of cardinal in the church of Ravenna. Thus the name of cardinal, which meant an inferior position, changed its meaning and became a sign of higher status, and it came to be said that cardinals were so called because they were *cardines orbis terrarum* [the hinges of the world]. But whoever looks at the councils held in Rome, in which Italian bishops and cardinal-priests of Rome took part, will see that the cardinals always signed after the bishops. Nor was any bishop ever made a cardinal-priest, even in later times. The first bishops who were made cardinals were certain important ones who had been driven from their churches, like Conrad of Mainz, who was expelled by the Emperor Frederick I for rebellion and was welcomed by Alexander III and made Sabine cardinal. The Roman cardinals had no distinctive dress or marks until Innocent IV, who gave them red hats on Christmas Eve, 1244. Paul II added the red berretta, but not for members of religious orders; but Gregory XIV in our time let them wear it, too. This digression was necessary because it was concerned with a rank which at the present is very high in the church and which does not seem to have adequate foundation.

From the beginning until just before 500, as I said, every cleric was ordained to a specific office and lived at the common expense. After the institution of benefices, he was ordained and assigned an office and a benefice; without a benefice no one was ordained. But as time passed, there were sometimes cases of suitable candidates for the priesthood when there was no office or benefice vacant, and in order not to lose them, the bishop used to ordain them without any office or title, and even without a benefice, to wait for a vacancy. Those who were ordained in this way helped the clergy who did have benefices and were maintained by them. But in the progress of time, there came to be so many of this sort of clergy ordained without office or benefice, and the holders of benefices had become so mean about maintaining them, that there were many situations which gave scandal, so that it became necessary to make some legal provision and to force those bishops who ordained men without an office to maintain them themselves At first, these provisions were successful, but not for long. Many attempts were made to combat this evil, but it has always recurred. There are two reasons for this. First, the desire of many men to become clerics in order to enjoy their exemptions and their freedom from subjection to princes. Second, the ambition of prelates who want to have many subjects whom they can command. And so this abuse has never been properly remedied, and many scandalous things have happened in different kingdoms which have made the people lose respect for religion.

The bishops themselves have not escaped from this abuse, for titular bishops have been ordained, or as they are contemptuously called, *nulla tenenti* [have-nothings]. However, they have not done so badly as other clerics without benefices. Although priests, deacons, and other lesser ministers have been ordained without an office in fact or in name, up to now it has not been customary to ordain a bishop without a diocese from which he can take his title. He is assigned an ancient city which the infidel now holds, and takes its name. As there are no Christians there, he has no flock, nothing but the name; and he lives by serving some great bishop, who is unable, or thinks it beneath his dignity, to exercise his episcopal functions himself. There were many such titular bishops before the Council of Trent; but their number is much reduced now. The Jesuits have raised the question whether the Pope can ordain bishops without any title at all, real or imaginary, just as priests and deacons are ordained, and they have decided that he can. Please God that he does not exercise this power, for then bishops will lose their respect, too! Once, all the clergy were held in great respect, at the time when they were not ordained without being given an office, as I said. All of them resided in their parishes, because they could not leave them vacant, nor could they find anyone to do their job for them, because each man was busy with his own. So the abuse of nonresidence was unknown. Similarly, the distinction between benefices which require residence and benefices which do not was unknown. Whether the benefice was rich or poor, whether its duties were light or heavy, its holder had to serve in person. But after men began to be ordained without offices, the officeholders had someone to put in their place, so they left the job to someone who would do it for just a small part of the proceeds, and they themselves did something different. So the French bishops served at court, and so did the parish priests, leaving some poor priest in their place. A beginning was made in remedying these abuses, not by laws or constitutions, but by condemnations and deprivations, so that at the time of which we are speaking, that is the years just before 800, they were checked by this means. But the division of benefices, like ordinations without office and provisions for residence, was not uniform everywhere. Even in the same church there were some variations, as a result of the different ideas of successive bishops, or the action taken by rulers from time to time to remedy the abuses caused by the avarice of some ecclesiastic, or the impatience of one of the people, who was not prepared to see himself totally excluded from church affairs.

There continued to be much variation up to the time of Charlemagne, who brought France and Germany under his control and also reformed the Church, introducing uniformity where there had been local variation, and renewing many of the old canons of the councils which had ceased being observed. He made various Church laws for the distribution of benefices according to the needs of the times. He restored to the parish priests part of the property which the bishops, as I have said, had taken for themselves, ordering that every priest with a cure should be given a certain quantity of land, which in those days was called *manso* [glebe]. At this time there passed into Italy the custom of paying tithes to the parish church, which had been introduced into France long before. Charles added that the bishop, as general overseer and pastor, could distribute tithes as seemed best to him. So the bishops, who were numerous and rich, disposed of them in their different ways. They took some themselves, gave some to the priests of their cathedral, and gave some to the monasteries, instructing them to appoint a curate and give him a sufficient maintenance. Apart from the distribution made by the bishop, churches which were not parish churches sometimes appropriated tithes and, later on, claimed a prescriptive right to them. The princes also gave tithes to the churches to which they were most devoted. Charles restored the freedom of the people to choose bishops, allowing the clergy and the people to choose someone from the diocese and present him to the ruler. When he was approved and invested with the crozier and the ring, he was to be consecrated by the neighboring bishops. Charles also restored to the monks the power of electing their own abbot. In addition, he laid it down that the bishops should ordain as priests men who were presented to them by the people and by the parishes.

Charles also issued instructions how the pope was to be elected. It was to be as it had been when the Eastern emperors dominated Rome, that is, the pope was to be elected by the clergy and the people and the decree of election sent to the emperor. If he approved of the chosen candidate, that man was to be consecrated. It is true that, after the death of Charles, when the emperors, his descendants, were either powerless or weak in the head, the popes chosen by the people had themselves consecrated without waiting for the imperial decree. This is what Paschal did in the time of Louis, son of Charles, although he afterwards sent his apologies on the grounds

27

that he had not wanted this, but the people had forced
him to do it. There are some who say that Louis had
renounced his right of confirming the papal election, and
in support of this assertion, they point to the canon
*Ego Ludovicus,* which other men of great learning with
more reason claim to be a forgery. Anyway, it is unnecessary to trouble about this, for it is certain that Lothair,
son of Louis, and Louis II, his nephew, confirmed all the
papal elections in their time.

In these times, as in those before and after, a few
months sometimes passed before the pope-elect was consecrated, because of the need to wait for the confirmation
of the absent ruler. In such cases, the pope did not act
as such before his consecration, unless there was some
urgent necessity which no one else could deal with, as
happened to St. Gregory. He did not call himself *episcopus* [bishop], but *electus* [the chosen one]. He did not
take the first place, but the archpriest did, to whom this
title was given, *servans locum sanctæ Sedis apostolicæ*
[he who is in charge of the affairs of the Holy Apostolic
See]. After the secular rulers had been excluded, as will
be mentioned in its place, the consecration always followed soon after the election. All the same, it was not
said that it was only the election that made a man pope,
but the consecration. If any man who had been elected
died before he was consecrated, he was not counted
among the popes. This happened to a certain Stephen
elected after the death of Zachary, in 752, who was not
consecrated, and therefore not added to the list of popes.

It seems that Pope Nicholas II was the first to declare,
in 1059, that if the pope-elect could not be enthroned by
reason of war or the malignity of men, he nevertheless
possessed the true papal authority to rule the Church of
Rome and to dispose of its goods. Yet certain remains
of the old procedure have survived to the present day. If
the pope issues a bull before his consecration, he does
not say *pontificatus nostri anno primo* [in the first year
of our pontificate], but *a die suscepti a nobis apostolatus
officii* [from the day we took up the apostolic office].
There have not been lacking, on occasion, people to
argue that the pope should not call himself *episcopus,* or

*electus*, nor should he issue bulls. Such objections were made to Pope Clement V, so, in 1306, he issued a bull in which he forbade anyone to raise these difficulties on pain of excommunication. And so at present it is firmly believed, contrary to the opinion of ancient times, that the pope obtains all his authority from his election by the cardinals alone. Writers of the present time have carefully inserted into the list that Stephen we mentioned before, and so they have altered the numbering of the later Stephens, calling the second one the third, and the third the fourth, and so on up to the ninth, whom they call the tenth, causing much confusion when one looks at ancient and modern writers, and all simply to support this belief.

The government of Holy Church was democratic in the beginning. All the faithful took part in important deliberations. Thus we see that everyone took part in the election of Matthew as apostle and in the election of the seven deacons. When St. Peter received Cornelius, the Gentile centurion, into the faith, he gave an account of it to the whole Church. Similarly, at the Council of Jerusalem, the apostles, the priests, and the other brethren all took part; and the letters were written in the name of all three orders. In the course of time, when the Church increased in size, the faithful gave up the affairs of the Church to look after their own, leaving the administration to the ministers alone. The government of the Church become aristocratic, except for elections, which were democratic. Everything was decided by means of councils. The bishops of a province met together with their metropolitan at least twice a year, making a provincial synod. The clergy met with their bishop in the synod of the diocese, and there was an almost daily assembly which was called the consistory, in imitation of the assembly of imperial counsellors, which was given this name. In the ecclesiastical consistory, the bishop and the heads of the churches in the city took part. After this custom fell into disuse everywhere, the shadow of it remained in Rome. In this consistory, all church business was proposed, discussed, and decided. But after the foundation of benefices, the priests, having something of their own to live on, lost interest in the affairs of the community and no longer went to the consistory, and so it fell into disuse. In its place, the bishops held meetings of all the clergy in their cathedral church to make use of them for advice and administration. As these clergy received their maintenance from a common stock, whether every year, every month, or every day, they were called canons, from the word *canon*, which in the Western empire meant the measure of grain sufficient for an individual, a family, or a city. This establishment of canons happened a little before Charlemagne, and he gave it a still firmer foundation.

It is also necessary to note here that at this time, since benefices were extremely rich, the chief men of court and city were made bishops, and the secular ruler gave them much political power, at first on special occasions, and then, seeing that the arrangement worked well, permanent authority. This did not happen in the same way in every city, but according to the needs of the particular place and the quality of the bishop, and also according to the quality of the court, whose defects could be remedied by having recourse to the bishop. This was why, when the descendants of Charles had degenerated and had finally drowned in the depths of ignorance, the bishops thought it would be to their advantage to cease to recognize that their authority had come from the prince and to claim it as their own and exercise it as belonging to the bishopric, calling it "ecclesiastical jurisdiction." This was the beginning of that jurisdiction about which we now see constant contests with secular rulers, which sometimes cause confusion in the administration of the State.

The arrangements made by Charlemagne did not last long because of the poor quality of his descendants and successors. So on the far side of the Alps, the first abuses easily grew up. In few places and on few occasions did the people have a share in the election of the bishops, and still less in that of other ministers of the Church. It was the bishops who ordained and gave benefices to whoever they pleased, except when the prince put someone forward, in which case they did not fail to do his will. The pope was always elected by the people, and his election was confirmed by the emperor before he was consecrated. The other Italian bishops were not consecrated until they had been approved by the emperor, nor were the bishops of France and Germany. When the pope wanted to appoint someone to a bishopric near Rome, he went to the emperor and begged him to be pleased to bestow the bishopric on this man. If the pope was asked to consecrate anyone who did not have letters of approval from the emperor, he refused, insisting that he first obtain them. However, after the descendants of Charlemagne had been driven from Italy in 884, Adrian III made a decree to the effect that the pope should be consecrated without waiting for imperial approval.

In a book about benefices, it was not irrelevant to discuss the papacy, and it will become still more relevant, for the papacy is one kind of benefice and was particularly named as such by Clement III, at a time when it had not only reached the height of its greatness, but even had its own name, to distinguish it from others. It is very well known that in ancient times the names *santo*, *santissimo*, *beato*, and *beatissimo* [holy, most holy, blessed, most blessed] were common to all the faithful, at a time when everyone aspired to perfect saintliness. After the laity became much more interested in worldly things, these names became confined to the clergy. After the decline of the lower clergy, they became restricted to the bishops. At last, the bishops gave themselves up to the things of this world, and only the bishop of Rome was left, and he retained the titles, not in their original meaning, as a description of his qualities, but as a sign of status. The name of pontiff [*pontefice*] was and is common to all bishops. Canons still exist in which all the bishops are called supreme pontiffs. The name of *papa* [pope], which seems the most specific, used to be given to every bishop. St. Cyprian, Bishop of Carthage, was called "pope." St. Jerome gave that title to St. Augustine. In later times, Sidonius Apollinaris called many bishops "popes," and he was called "pope" by them. There remain many canons in the *Decretals* of Gratian, in which Martin, Bishop of Braga, in Portugal, is called "pope." Gregory VII, in 1076, was the first to decree that the name of "pope" should be used of no one but himself. This became such an established opinion (not to say prejudice) that Anselm of Lucca, one of his followers, said that it was as shocking to use the word "God" in the plural as the word "pope."

Let us turn to the period after the line of Charlemagne had become extinct. In France, something was invented which seemed to favor the laity, but which caused the Church to increase vastly in riches. This was a contract which was called *precario* [corrody]. If someone gave his property to the Church, the Church gave him the same in return for his lifetime, or even double. If he wanted to give up the usufruct as well, he was given three times as much from other Church property. This custom then passed to Italy. This contract was useful to someone who thus trebled his income, or to those who had no children or who did not care about them; but the real gainer was the Church, which received the entire property after the death of the donor.

Between 884 and 963 there were great disorders in Italy, political and ecclesiastical, which affected the papacy in particular. In this eighty years, no true form of church government can be found. All was change, chaos, and scandal. Popes were excommunicated by their successors, and their actions annulled, and even the sacraments they administered. Six popes were driven out by men who wanted to take their place, and two were even killed; and Pope Stephen VIII was so badly injured in the face that he never let himself be seen in public. Theodora, the famous Roman courtesan, had her official lover made pope through the efforts of her faction; he was called John X. John XI was made pope when he was twenty years old; he was the illegitimate son of another pope who had died eighteen years before. So many awful things happened at that time, that historians say that there were not popes then, but monsters. Cardinal Baronio, unable to excuse any of this, says that the Church at that time was for the most part without a true pope, but not without a head, because Christ in Heaven remained its spiritual head, and He never abandoned it.

It is certain that Christ has never abandoned His Church, and that He will never abandon it, or break His divine promise that He will be with it to the end of the world. Every Christian ought to agree with Baronio about this. But he should also consider that what happened then has happened on other occasions, and that just as in those times it was only the help of Christ that preserved the Church, so He has always preserved and will always preserve it in similar crises, even if there should be no pope at all.

Everyone can imagine the state of the other churches in Italy by considering what is the state of the body when the head is seriously ill. It was no better outside Italy, where nobles gave bishoprics to soldiers, and even to little boys. Count Eribert, uncle of Hugh Capet, made his five-year-old son Archbishop of Reims, and Pope John X confirmed the election. In those times, no one visited Rome out of devotion, but if anyone wanted to do anything contrary to the canons and customs of the Church, then he went to Rome, where dispensations from everything were given. Ambition and avarice were covered up by dispensations. The popes, being as we have described them above, made no distinction between what they could or could not do, believing that to grant whatever powerful men wanted added to their own greatness. These men, out of self-interest, defended the popes who granted their desires. The people, out of innocence and fear of the powerful, approved what it could not prevent, and so the opinion became established that no matter what it was, every past mistake could be covered up as soon as confirmation came from Rome.

One might think that, since the clergy cared little for spiritual things, the fervor of the laity would have cooled and they would have given less to churches, so that there would have been an end to the new acquisitions of the clergy. But this did not happen. The less the prelates cared for spiritual things, the more interested they became in maintaining their worldly goods. They made use of the spiritual weapon of excommunication, which was formerly used only for the correction of sinners, to defend their temporal possessions, and even to recover them

33

if the negligence of their predecessors had allowed some to be lost. The people were more afraid of the censures of the Church than of anything else. It was extraordinary how officers and soldiers who were otherwise without any fear of God, and who took their neighbor's goods without worrying about offending His Divine Majesty, treated the property of the Church with great respect, for fear of excommunication. For this reason many men of little power, anxious to protect their property from violence, gave it to the Church, on condition that the Church give it to them to hold in fee for some small service. This made sure that their property was not taken by the powerful, any more than the Church's own. If the male line of the vassal later failed, as often happened as a result of the frequent wars and rebellions, the property fell to the Church.

So far, we have explained how the Church acquired landed property and why tithes were levied on the property of the laity. Before going any further, it will be convenient to discuss and resolve the problem which has been discussed in our own times, and that is whether the goods of the Church are owned *iure divino* or *humano* [in virtue of divine or human law] and who has the power to administer them. The common opinion distinguishes the goods bequeathed or given to the Church by the faithful from tithes, firstfruits, and other offerings. So far as the first class of goods is concerned, everyone agrees that they should be considered as temporal goods, and that the Church possesses them *iure humano*. It is certain, as we have described above, that all colleges were once forbidden to acquire landed property, but that the Church later obtained the power to acquire it, first by the permission, later by the concession of the emperors. The canon *Quo iure* dates from about this time, where it is affirmed that the saying "this property is mine, this slave is mine" is founded simply on human laws, and that if the laws made by secular rulers were done away with, neither the Church nor anyone else could say that anything was his. No one can doubt that the division of property is a civil law matter, and equally that the transfer of ownership from one man to an-

other—gifts, wills, all contracts, and all other dispositions—are matters of human law. There exist in the
world republics and kingdoms where wills are unknown.
*Iure romano* [under Roman law], only a Roman citizen
was allowed to make a will. But it is impossible for the
acquisition of property to be by human law, and its
maintenance to be by divine law. When anything is given
or bequeathed to the Church, if there is doubt about the
title to it, the matter is judged by human laws; and if
the Church has a valid claim, it possesses the property
in virtue of that claim, so its possession is founded on
this and not on anything else. However, everyone agrees
about this, and so I shall say no more about it, except
to add the corollary that this clearly and easily solves
the problem about whether the exemptions possessed by
the property of the Church are *de iure divino* or *humano*,
because the fact and the manner of possession are always subject to the same laws, and jurisconsults say that
the freedom or bondage of property comes from the
same source as the title to it. It would be a great contradiction to say that the Church owned a piece of property *iure veneto* [by Venetian law] which possessed a certain privilege *alio iure* [by virtue of another law]

However, there are two opinions about tithes. One is
the opinion of the canon lawyers, the other is the opinion
of the theologians and of those canon lawyers who study
the Bible as well. The canon lawyers say that tithes are
*de iure divino,* because in the Old Testament God gave
the tenth part to the Levites, as the Bible says. It is in
no way odd that they should say this, because they are
not versed in the study of the Bible, and because it is not
their job to understand the mysteries of the Christian religion. Else they would discuss the article of the Christian religion which says that God, through Moses, gave
laws to the Jews which would apply to that nation in
ritual and in judicial matters until the coming of Christ,
who would take away their binding force. The law relating to tithes is indeed the law of God and of Moses,
but it is not a natural law of God, nor a Christian law.
It was binding on that people at that time, but now it
is not binding on anyone. A man who rules a state may

well make similar laws, but they are not binding in the way that the laws of God are, nor should they be referred to as such; they are civil laws, laws of the ruler who made them. It was a law of God and Moses that blasphemers should be put to death. This is no longer binding, and whoever does not kill them does not commit a sin. The ruler could make blasphemy a capital offense, and this would be just, and it would have to be obeyed. But it would not be called a law of God, although God had once given this law to the Jews; it would be a law of the secular ruler. In this and in many other cases, where these men quote the Old Testament on their side and add that it is *de iure divino*, it is necessary to distinguish the equivocation. What is part of the natural and Christian law of God is binding, but what is part of the law of God and Moses is not binding; and if a ruler makes a statute like it, this is a matter of human law.

I cannot help saying that these men do not put these views forward out of ignorance, but to deceive rash people and to support their own case and increase their own reputation by appealing to the law of God. But I have an argument here to convince them and to close their mouths. In the same part of the Bible, God commands that a tenth be given to the Levites, and also that they should not have any earthly goods, but should content themselves with that tenth. If this command obliges the people *iure divino* to pay them the tenth, they are obliged not to own any property. But God commanded the payment of tithes of the fruits of the earth alone, while the canon laws say that they are to be paid on trading, on fighting, on hunting, and on whatever human activity which brings in money. If God only commanded the Jews to pay tithes on land, then personal tithes must be paid in virtue of human law. The theologians (I do not mention any in particular because none of them are excluded) and many canon lawyers, too, say in unison that it is a precept of the natural law of God that the minister of religion should live by serving the people in godly things, and that it is a special precept of Christ Our Lord in the

Gospels that the minister who serves the people by preaching the word of God and in the ministry of the Church should be given enough to live on. How much should be given is not laid down. It is a great deal at some times and a little at others, according to the number of people and the particular place and time. To give something to the minister of Christ is *de iure divino*. Whether this something is a tenth or a twentieth, greater or less, is laid down by human law or by custom, which comes to the same thing. When one reads in certain decretals that God has instituted tithes, and that tithes are *iure divino*, they interpret an indefinite share as a definite, the necessary share as a tithe; or, they mean that God instituted tithes in the Old Testament, and on this model the law of the Church has instituted the same thing in the New. In general, we can say that the goods of the Church, of whatever sort, are possessed by their owners in virtue of human laws. No one should raise the issue of the indeterminate share which is owed the clergy by the natural law of God and by the Gospel, because, as the lawyers explain very well, it is one thing for something to be owed, another for it to be owned. If a man owns something, he can demand it in law, as they say, *actione rei vindicationis* [by an action in claim of the thing], and he cannot be satisfied by any equivalent. If a man is owed something, he can only bring a personal action and demand the debt, and the debtor is obliged to give him something of that value, but not one thing rather than another. From this it is easy to decide whether benefices are held *de iure divino* or *de iure positivo* [in virtue of human law], because property and tithes are held by the Church *de iure humano,* and so the benefices founded upon them are, too. There is an even easier way to show this, and that is that if the Church held its goods in common, not divided into benefices, for so many years, as was described above, it is clear that benefices were created by men as time went on. Since everyone agrees about this, I shall say no more, except that although these considerations may appear rather subtle ones, they are necessary, as will be shown by what is to come.

From the solution to the first problem it will be clear how to solve the second; who it is that owns the goods of the Church (I speak here of the landed property, because the fruits will be discussed in their place). If this property is held by virtue of human law, it only remains to see to whom the law granted it. Some people say that this property belongs to God; and there is no doubt that they are right, because the Scripture explicitly says that the whole earth and whatever is sustained by it belongs to His Divine Majesty. But everything belongs to God in this way, and these goods no more than any other. One kind of universal ownership is God's; another is that every ruler possesses in his state, which following Seneca may be called the ownership of an overlord [*dominio d'imperio*], or, according to the doctrine of the jurisconsults, a protectorate or ownership of jurisdiction. Another kind of ownership is possessed by every individual, which is private ownership, and it is this of which we speak and for which we are now searching. It cannot be said that God has complete ownership of everything, but He owns everything, just as the king owns everything in his kingdom, and yet also owns some things in particular as a private individual. To the universal ownership of the prince can be added his private ownership, which increases and enlarges the former. But the ownership of God is universal and infinite, so that it cannot be added to, and it refuses to be detailed, just as it refuses to be communicated to any creature whatever. No one can say: God owns these goods and so do I, because I have the same court as He. He is rather a servant of the least of us.

Others openly say that the pope is the owner, and this they prove by the decretal of Clement IV, to the effect that the plenary disposition of all benefices belonged to him. St. Thomas opposes this view, saying that the pope may be called the principal administrator, but that he can by no means be called the owner. Cardinal Cajetan explains this, adding that the pope cannot give away the goods of the Church, nor dispose of them in any other way, but only do what may be done according to the terms of the gift. Cajetan's argument is extremely clear and compelling. These goods belonged originally to an owner who transferred his ownership by gift or by will. But he never intended to give or to bequeath anything to the pope; therefore the ownership has not passed to him. And so Cajetan and Pope Adrian VI say that the ownership belongs to the Church, that is, to all the faithful in the place to which the goods were bequeathed, so that the ownership of the goods of the church of Rome belongs to all the Romans. Everyone knows that *in iure* [in law] "everyone" is like a person, capable of ownership, just as something may be described as being "public property" or belonging to the city, that is, it belongs to no one in particular, but to everyone together. Many wills make bequests in these terms, to the *scuola* [guild] of St. Rocco, to the monastery of the Frari, and so on. This doctrine fits in very well with the ancient custom of the Church and with the terminology of the canons. There is no doubt that if goods have to be named after someone, they are named after their owner. All the canons and ancient customs speak of the goods of the Church; so it is the Church that owns them. Those who say that these goods belong to Christ are saying the same thing, because all Christian churches from the most ancient times have been called not only by the name of the city, but also by the name of its first and most famous bishop, as the Roman is called "of St. Peter," the Alexandrian "of St. Mark," that of Ravenna "of St. Apollinaris," whence the goods of those churches took the names of the same saints, and the goods of the Roman church are called the goods of St. Peter. And so one comes across this manner of speech in all the ancient writers; the patrimony of St. Peter, the lands of St. Peter, the goods of St. Peter, the patrimony of St. Apollinaris, the income of St. Apollinaris, and so on. Christ being the universal head and protector of all the churches, whatever belongs to the whole Church or to any part is called the patrimony of Christ, the goods of Christ, and so on, meaning that it belongs to the Church whose head is Christ, just as the goods of the republic of Venice are called the goods of St. Mark; that is, the goods of the republic which bears the name of St. Mark. Everything that was acquired when the goods of the Church were in common in each diocese was owned by the whole Church, because all gifts and all bequests were made to it. It is certain that these goods were acquired and could only be acquired by those whom the law allowed to acquire them; but the laws of Constantine allowed them to be given to Christian colleges, that is, to all the Christians of a city, and so the goods are owned by those colleges. After the property was divided and benefices were set up, bequests and donations were made to particular churches, and for the most part, for a particular purpose in those churches, so that one cannot say who is the owner of something without consulting the terms of the gift or bequest. Since we want to make well-grounded statements, we can say no more than that the prelates and other churchmen are the governors, administrators, and dispensers of church goods in order to do what those who gave them or left them intended, and nothing else. The owner is that person, individual or collective, in whose favor the gift or bequest was made. And so every rector of a church should be careful to find out what obligations he has to execute. If he does otherwise, it should be put down to human weakness, and no one should persuade himself that the length of time gives him a prescriptive right. This supposes an innocence which no one possesses, because everyone knows in his conscience that those goods were not bequeathed in order for him to do what he is doing.

Who is the owner of those church goods of which the terms of the gift are unknown? The natural and civil law says that where a private owner is completely lacking, the community succeeds, and so in this case the Church remains the owner. To sum up: The incumbents are the administrators of the property of the benefice, but its owner is he in whose favor the gift or bequest was made, and if he is not known, the Church is the owner. This is still true, even if there are secular or ecclesiastical laws which forbid the alienation of the property, because a ward is a true owner of his property, and yet he cannot alienate it. Ownership is the right to do whatever one likes with something, so far as the law permits, and the law imposes conditions on some kinds of people who need a guardian, as communities do.

No one should be surprised if so many modern writers on questions like this (as in the case of making the pope the absolute owner of all benefices and of all the goods of the Church) defend opinions which are contrary to antiquity and to the arrangements made by the apostles themselves, because, as St. Cyprian laments with great feeling, it is one of the imperfections of man that whereas human actions should conform themselves to good doctrine and good laws, the contrary occurs and the doctrines conform themselves to men's interests. It may be observed that for many centuries there was no innovation introduced, especially so far as religion was concerned, which did not immediately find defenders. Is it surprising, then, that this happened in cases where the innovations agreed with men's interests, convenience, and riches, to which many people could aspire? But let us proceed.

In Italy, there was great disorder in political affairs because there were so many kings and emperors at this time. This was the cause of great confusion in the affairs of the Church in other cities, because bishops and abbots were sometimes appointed by rulers and sometimes intruded themselves by their own power; and the other ministers were similarly appointed, sometimes by those who ruled the cities, sometimes by the bishops, and sometimes benefices were even seized by those who had power or popular favor.

In the year 963, Otto of Saxony invaded Italy and conquered it. In order to reorganize the administration, he assembled a small council of bishops and deprived Pope John XII, who, although he came from the greater Roman nobility and had a great following in that city, had been made pope when he was less than eighteen, and his manner of life when pope included adultery, perjury, and other not very religious habits. Otto made the people and Pope Leo VIII (appointed by him in place of John) renounce their right of appointing the pope and the other Italian bishops. He and his son and

41

nephew of the same name kept this right for thirty-eight years, till 1001. There were twelve popes in that time, of whom two were appointed peacefully by the ruler, and the rest with great disturbances. Otto I took one to Germany as a prisoner, and Otto III took another. One was strangled by the man who had wished to be appointed in his place; another fled, taking with him the treasures of the church; another retired into voluntary exile. And so in these years, too, we meet popes that, as Baronio says, are in the list simply to fill it up, and for the rest, the Church had no head but Christ. The other bishops and abbots were appointed by the emperor without any opposition. What happened was that when a bishop died, his ring and crozier were taken to the emperor, who chose his successor and invested him by giving him these insignia. The new bishop would then go and be consecrated by his metropolitan and the neighboring bishops. This custom still survives in France and in Germany. The other minor benefices were bestowed by the bishops and abbots under whom they came, unless the prince nominated someone to a vacancy, in which case he received it without dispute, or unless the prince recommended someone to be given a benefice when there was a vacancy, in which case the bishop would appoint him to the first benefice that became vacant. Thus the Ottonians governed the Church without opposition from the popes, although the second of them remained in Rome for a long time, died there, and was buried there.

After the death of the Ottonians, the emperors who succeeded them retained the power of appointing to bishoprics and abbeys, and even minor benefices, and of giving expectatives for benefices that were not yet vacant. Then the authority of the emperor over Rome decreased and the affairs of that church fell into confusion again. The people regained their right of electing the pope, and after three quiet elections, Benedict VIII and John XX, brothers, were elected one after the other with a certain amount of disturbance. After John's death, Benedict IX, their nephew, was elected, when he was twelve years old. He, besides many other excesses, sold part of the papacy to a certain Sylvester III and another part to Gregory VI. All three reigned in Rome at the same time, and there were many disturbances. In particular, Gregory raised infantry and cavalry and seized St. Peter's by force, with much loss of life, in order to increase his share. So the Emperor Henry the Black came to Italy, put Benedict to flight, sent away Sylvester, took Gregory back to Germany and deprived the Roman people of their right to make popes. He appointed three popes in succession, all of them Germans. Having been chosen by the emperor, they assumed the insignia and costume of popes without more ado. The third, Bruno, Bishop of Toul, began to wear the papal robes at Freising on the emperor's instructions, and he travelled like this to Cluny. But Hildebrand the monk, who had formerly been at St. Peter's, Rome, an extremely subtle man, had a plan for restoring to the Romans their right of election. He advised Bruno, who now that he had put on the papal robes, called himself Leo IX, to enter Rome dressed as a pilgrim, because this would please the Roman people. Leo agreed and entered Rome in pilgrim dress, and Hildebrand persuaded the people to acclaim him as pope. But after the death of Leo, this device did not prevent the emperor in Mainz from choosing Gebhard of Eichstädt, who immediately put on the robes and called himself Victor II. At this time, the emperor not only distributed benefices, but also made a law against those who obtained them by simony, pardoning those who had done so in the past, and imposing penalties for the future.

Henry the Black left the empire to his son Henry IV, who succeeded him while still a boy. During his minority, popes were appointed by agreement between the emperor's guardians, and bishops and abbots were invested with the ring and the crozier by him. However, the popes took this opportunity to free themselves little by little, by attaching themselves to some of the guardians and setting them at odds with the others. So Nicholas II made a law about the election of the pope, laying down that the choice should go first to the cardinal bishops, then pass to the other cardinals, then to the clergy and people, and in the fourth place, the emperor should be asked to consent. Alexander II, his successor, was elected in this manner. The emperor refused both to confirm the election and to accept the excuse offered by a cardinal on behalf of the rest, to the effect that they did this to avoid a bitter conflict. The emperor's refusal was extremely courteous, because the successful candidate was a friend of his. All the same, he appointed the Bishop of Parma as pope, at the suggestion of his chancellor, Gerard of Parma. But three years later, when things had changed at the imperial court and Gerard, the chancellor, had been deposed, the Bishop of Parma was deposed as well, and Alexander became pope. In 1072, when the Bavarians and Saxons made a league against the emperor, the Pope joined them. The following year, he summoned the emperor to Rome on a simony charge for having taken money for appointing bishops. This action of the Pope's was quite extraordinary, for no pope had ever gone so far, but it was soon forgotten because of the death of the Pope. After him, Gregory VII became pope, a monk and a Sienese, who was elected by the Romans and approved by the emperor. But in 1076, after he had been pope for three years, realizing that the emperor was still extremely young, and that he had many troubles in Germany, Gregory decided to exclude him completely from the appointment of bishops and abbots. He issued a letter of warning, advising him not to meddle in these matters in future. The emperor put up great resistance. The Pope excommunicated him, absolved his subjects from their fealty, and suspended him from ruling Italy and Germany. He excommunicated the bishops who served the emperor, made a league with the rebels against him, turned the emperor's own mother against her son, and between that time and 1085, when the Pope died in exile in Salerno, he excommunicated the emperor four times and issued a general decree to the effect that if any cleric took a bishopric or abbey from a layman, he would not be considered to be a cleric and would not be allowed to enter any church. The same penalty would apply to anyone who accepted other benefices and to the emperor and to any king, duke, marquis, count, or any secular authority who dared invest anyone with a benefice.

The emperor made war on the allies of the Pope, and he was supported by the majority of the bishops, so the Pope was in very serious danger. He had once excommunicated the Normans for usurping the kingdoms of Sicily and Apulia: Now he turned to them for help. He absolved them from excommunication and granted them the kingdoms on account of which he had proceeded against them. If Robert, King of Naples and Sicily, who had been the Pope's enemy, had not joined him for this reason and so counterbalanced the power of the emperor, the latter would have won a complete victory. But thanks to Robert's aid, the Pope held out, although he went into exile. After Gregory's death, the same conflict was continued by his two successors, both monks of the same order, with the help of Robert and of three Rogers of the same family. The second of his successors, Urban II, to reward the services rendered by the Normans, gave one of them the bull of the kingdom of Sicily, giving him in fact more power over church affairs than he was trying to take away from the emperor. He excommunicated the emperor several times, encouraged rebellions against him, making even his eldest son rebel; and by these means virtually drove the emperor out of Italy. After Urban's death, his successor repeated the excommunications and encouraged many rebellions, including that of the emperor's other son. Father and son went to war, the father was defeated once and victorious once. At length they came to an agreement, in which the emperor was tricked and forced into private life, leaving the empire to his son, who was also called Henry.

After the death of Henry IV, Paschal, as the Pope was called, the fourth of those who, starting with Gregory VII, had fought with excommunications and other spiritual weapons to take the power of investiture from the emperor, held a council in Guastalla, and then at Troyes in France. In both councils he renewed the decrees of Gregory VII and Urban II to the effect that no layman should meddle in collations to benefices. In

France, the king did not accept the decree, but continued to act in the customary manner. The Emperor, Henry V (the son), also opposed this, and at length in 1110, he came to Italy with an army to be crowned emperor. The Pope refused to crown him on account of the disputes between them, but it was agreed that Henry should go to Rome to be crowned, and that the investiture controversy should not be mentioned by either side. Henry went to Rome, where Pope Paschal, who thought he was in the stronger position, broke the agreement and asked the emperor to give up his claims to invest. Henry, confident in his forces, demanded, on the contrary, that the Pope revoke his decree, saying that he did not want to be inferior to Charlemagne, Louis the Pious, and other emperors, who had invested bishops in peace and quiet. The conflict became more bitter, until the emperor made the Pope prisoner and most of the cardinals, too, and left the city taking them with him. An agreement was negotiated. At length the Pope agreed to crown him, to allow him to collate the benefices, and not to excommunicate him, and swore to observe the agreement. The Pope said Mass and broke the Host in two, and with one half he received Communion himself and administered it to the emperor with the other. He laid horrible curses on whichever of them violated the agreement. The Pope returned to Rome, saying that he would observe it, but his legates excommunicated the emperor; and two years later, in 1112, he held a council and confirmed the decrees of Gregory and Urban against accepting investiture from laymen and had the council annul the agreement with the emperor. Finally, in 1116, he excommunicated him again.

After Paschal's death, Gelasius II succeeded him, and then Calixtus II, and the controversy went on. Both of them excommunicated the emperor. These three popes not only used the weapon of excommunication, but they encouraged many rebellions against the emperor, led by Lothair of Saxony, who won various victories. At last, in 1122, Henry, seeing the difficulties that he was in, gave up his claims to investitures. That was the end of disorders which had lasted fifty-six years under six popes, which had led to the excommunication of an infinite number of laymen and clergy belonging to the emperor's party, and which had led to the death of innumerable men on both sides in sixty battles fought by Henry, the father, and eighteen fought by Henry, the son: *tantæ molis erat* [such an effort it was] to lay the foundations of that edifice which we have seen reach its full height and about which we are going to speak!

Various opinions were held on the subject of the agreement between Paschal and Henry. Some said that the Pope's consent was void because he gave it out of fear (since he and many cardinals were in the hands of the emperor), so that Paschal was right not to observe it. Others said that if the Pope's consent was valid because it had been extorted, so was the consent of the emperor, which was forced from him by the fear of so many excommunications and anathemas, rebellions and plots. On what grounds is one man free to break a promise he made from fear of imprisonment, but not another man who promised from fear of anathemas and of seeing his state and his people thrown into confusion and embroiled in civil wars? At the council, some men confronted Paschal with this dilemma: If the decree and the bull by which he granted investitures to the emperor was legitimate, he was bound to observe it; if it was not legitimate but, as some said, heretical, then the Pope himself was a heretic. It is certain that a just action done out of fear is valid; and that no one, whoever he is, can be excused for breaking the laws of God on the grounds of fear.

This investiture controversy between popes and emperors was not restricted to Italy and Germany, the imperial territories. In France, at the same time, certain bishops, stimulated by this example and their own self-interest, opposed the king on the same grounds. But they were not all in agreement about supporting the pope against the king, so the king was victorious for the most part, and the popes contented themselves with taking little by little what it was impossible to take all at once. In England, the king had always conferred bishoprics and abbeys, till in 1102, Anselm, Archbishop of

Canterbury, refused to consecrate the bishops appointed by the king, on the grounds of the papal decrees. The conflict lasted for many years, the king maintaining that he had the right to appoint and the Archbishop defending his refusal with the help of the Pope. The king believed that he could persuade the Pope of the justice of his case and sent him an ambassador, whom the Pope answered harshly and with threats, so that in order to restrain him, the ambassador was forced to say that the king would not give up his rights, even if he were to lose his kingdom. The Pope, equally warmly, replied that he would not give up his rights, even if he were to lose his head. The king remained firm, and Anselm had to leave the kingdom, unable to return until he submitted to the king's will. But the king died without male heirs and civil war followed, so that it was easy for the clergy to introduce into England what had been introduced into the empire. And so, after the death of Henry (which was the king's name), the Pope got what he wanted. In 1132, Lothair of Saxony, the successor of the Emperor Henry V, who was asked by Innocent II to recognize him as pope and not his rival, refused to do it unless the Pope restored to him the rights to invest which Henry had renounced. The Pope might have agreed, but St. Bernard, who was a great friend of Lothair's, persuaded him to desist, reminding him that he had made war on Henry, his predecessor and feudal superior, at the instance of Pope Paschal for this reason, so that to defend Henry's claim now was to declare that he had been a rebel who had made war on his lord when he was defending a just cause.

What usually happens after great victories is that the defeated side has not been completely destroyed, and the survivors often reappear and make their old claims; and the victor, if he is prudent, will play a waiting game, rather than oppose them openly and so renew the war. This is what happened now. The papal victory was not so great that some benefices did not remain in the power of the laity in some places, or that some princes, sometimes, out of some political necessity, did not appoint some bishop in the old manner without consulting the pope. In France, there remained the *régale*, the king's right to fill all simple benefices which fall vacant between the death of a bishop and the appointment of his successor. In Germany, there remained the emperor's right to appoint one of the canons in each of many churches. Various special powers like this continued to be exercised by some princes. The popes did not want to fight these customs for fear of renewing the conflict and losing everything. Nor did they want to allow them to continue, in case they prejudiced the papal claims in general, so they decided to oppose them by subtle and diplomatic means. They hit on a compromise, which was to tell the canon lawyers and other writers dependent on them to declare that these princes exercised this power by virtue of a papal privilege. This compromise increased the pope's standing by making it appear that the princes exercised these rights only because of papal favor, and it also gave them a basis for further claims in the future; and it was easily accepted by the princes, to whom it seemed a defense against possible papal aggression, adding ecclesiastical authority to the power they already exercised in practice, thus making it more secure. But the future was to show that what they had thought medicine was in fact poison. About 1300, Boniface VIII had a violent conflict with Philip the Handsome of France to make him give up the *régale* that I just mentioned. He went so far as to put that kingdom into grave danger by his excommunications and interdicts and by depriving the king of his kingdom and granting it to the Emperor Albert, if he could take it by force. Originally, when it was agreed to preserve the rights of the prince by means of a grant from the pope, men did not think that the popes might claim to be able to revoke the privileges granted by their predecessors, and even to do this without a reason when they could not invent one. They did not consider that a man who has rights of his own and yet agrees to hold his property by the favor of another is like a man who leaves his own ground and begins to build on someone else's.

The other side of the matter was that whenever any prince lost patience and appointed to some important benefice, as the kings of England and Sicily often did, the pope did not say anything in order not to start a conflict. But in order not to prejudice his position, he would ensure, by means of monks, that the successful candidate gave up his benefice to the pope, promising him that he would be invested by the pope and would thus have quietly what the pope would otherwise oppose, thus causing much trouble. This method, which the popes made great use of at this time, is described at length by Florence of Worcester and by Yves of Chartres, writers of that time, as something which was regularly done in Germany and in France, with this form of words, "that the popes took with one hand and gave with the other." This arrangement was easily accepted because it avoided trouble. The king himself, if he came to hear about it afterwards, dismissed it as something which made no practical difference, without thinking that it might be important in the future. The same means was used against the Catholic bishops of Germany who did not obey their reservations, a matter which will be discussed in its place.

In Spain, the quiet and prudent nature of that nation, together with the good government of its kings, ensured that it remained in peace in the midst of the general disturbances. Perhaps the existence of the Saracens also helped, which made the Spaniards unite with their kings and live in peace. The kings had never tried to keep down the clergy more than was fitting; and the clergy never allied with outsiders to exempt themselves from royal control more than they should. When the kings saw that the popes had obtained something in the other kingdoms by means of force, fear, and skill, they accommodated themselves to the situation, so that their rule would be affected as little as possible. Although it had formerly been the custom that bishops and other ecclesiastics should be ordained according to the ancient manner, after the changes we have described in other states, the Spanish kings did not want to provoke a conflict with the popes, and so they made a prudent compromise. They were satisfied if no bishop was ordained without their consent. To be sure of this, Alfonso VI asked for the approval of Urban II, who granted him the *iuspatronato* of all the churches in his kingdom. These kings proceeded in a very different manner from the Germans, French, and English. The Spaniards were content to accept as a favor from someone else what was actually their own in order to keep it in peace; the others went to war in order not to do this. All, however, were prudent. The others saw that there was a danger of losing everything and of becoming slaves, because what the popes had demanded was not their final aim, but only a beginning. They considered how their subjects, especially the clergy, were lovers of liberty (not to say licence) and would therefore be ready to make an agreement with the outsider to weaken the authority of their prince; and so they thought it was necessary not to open the door to these possibilities. But the Spaniards, confident in the peaceable nature of their subjects, had no reason to fear that they would decide to call in any outsider. Considering how small their territories were in those times, they had good reason to fear that he who was able to provoke rebellions against princes much more powerful than they were would use the same methods against them; and so, most prudently, they decided to accept of their own free will what greater princes than they had been forced to allow after many wars.

To conclude, between 1122 [Henry's renunciation] and 1145, it was virtually established that when a bishop died, his successor would be elected by the chapter of canons and confirmed by the metropolitan. When an abbot died, the monks would elect his successor, and the bishop would confirm it, unless the monastery was exempt. If it was exempt, the pope would confirm it. The other benefices which were *de iure patronatus* [which had patrons] would be conferred by the bishop, but the patron would present; the others would be at the bishop's disposal. There remained the papacy itself. With the secular ruler excluded, it seemed that the pope would once again be elected freely by the people; but in 1145, Innocent II had a conflict with the Romans, who drove him from the city, and he in return deprived them of the power of electing the pope.

In the disturbances that followed, many cities rebelled against the emperor, led by their bishops, who allied with the pope. The bishops made themselves rulers of the cities, taking over their income and the rights exercised by the emperor. By the time the conflict was over, they had taken such firm possession, that the ruler was forced to give them as a fief what they had usurped. So they acquired the titles of dukes, marquesses, counts; and there are many in Germany who retain the title and the power and many in Italy who retain the title only. This turned much secular property into property of the Church, and there was a great increase not only during these disturbances of which we have spoken, but also in those that followed under the Suabian emperors.

At this time, the monks began to take a leading part on behalf of the popes against the princes. They came to lose their reputation for saintliness, and in fact observance of the rule declined in monasteries because monks took part in politics and in wars. They also ceased to acquire property, apart from some small congregations newly founded in Tuscany, which took no part in these disturbances, and in which obedience to the rule did not decline. The people continued to be devoted to these congregations which acquired new possessions for the Church, but not much, because they were so small.

However, another opportunity occurred for the Church to make great acquisitions at this time, and that was the war for the Holy Land. So great was the enthusiasm to go there or to contribute to its conquest, that people took no account of their property, their wives, and children, but joined the army, sold what they had, and crossed the sea. Even women did not think of their children, but sold their goods to aid the war. The popes by their briefs took under their protection and that of the other prelates the affairs of the "crusaders" (as those were called who took part in this war). This gave the churches the profit that usually goes with being the guardian or manager of widows and minors. The secular authorities could not think of forbidding it for fear of excommunication, a weapon the Church then made use of without pity. Added to this was the fact, which was extremely important, that Eugenius III laid down that anyone could, even for the sake of a pious work, alienate his fiefs. If the feudal superior did not accept this, he could be stripped of these possessions by the churches, even against his will. This made it easy for great acquisitions to be made. It even happened that the popes made use of the crusaders for various enterprises on behalf of the temporal power of the Roman church, and papal legates and bishops of places where crusaders had assembled to make the journey together made use of them to increase the temporal power and riches of these churches in various ways. Much money was collected from the faithful, especially from women and others who were unable to serve in person, whether in fulfillment of vows or to obtain indulgences and other concessions. Not all this money was spent on the war. The princes doubtless took a share, but an important part remained in the hands of the prelates, and so the riches of the Church increased. At this time were founded the military orders of the Templars, Hospitallers, and so on for the defense of the church in Jerusalem and of the pilgrims who went there, and to fight against the Saracens. This was something quite new, to found religious orders to shed blood, but it was received with such enthusiasm that in a very short time they acquired great riches. All these things added greatly to the wealth of the Church.

Another way of increasing the property of the Church was to review the matter of tithes and to lay down that a tenth should be paid not only on the fruits of the earth, but also on the produce of animals and on human labor. To tithes were added firstfruits, which were first instituted by Alexander II, in imitation of the Mosaic law by which the Jews were commanded to pay them. Moses did not lay down the amount, but left it to the donor to decide. Afterwards, the rabbis, as St. Jerome testifies, decided that the amount should be not less than a sixtieth part and not more than a fortieth. This was imitated by our own clergy in the manner most profitable for them; that is, they laid down a fortieth, which in our time is called *il quartese*. Alexander III, about 1170, decided that excommunications should be used to ensure the full payment of tithes levied on mills, fisheries, hay, wool, and bees, and that tithes should be paid before the deduction of the expenses of collection. Celestinus III, about 1295, laid down that the weapon of excommunications should be used to ensure the payment of tithes not only on wine, grain, and the produce of trees, flocks, gardens, and merchandise, but also on wages and the profits of hunting, and even on windmills. All these things can be found in the papal decretals. The canon lawyers went even further, saying that a pauper is obliged to pay a tenth of the alms he receives begging from door to door, and that a prostitute is obliged to pay a tenth of her profits, and other such things which the world has never been able to put into practice.

Tithes used to be paid to parish priests for their services to the people in teaching the word of God, administering the sacraments, and performing other ecclesiastical functions; and so nothing else was paid for these. A man who was both pious and rich used to give something for the burial of his relatives or for his reception of the sacraments, if he wanted to; gradually, the free gift turned into an obligation, and even the amount to be paid was laid down by custom. This matter became controversial. The laity refused to pay anything for the administration of the sacraments because they paid tithes for this. The clergy refused to perform their functions unless they were given the payments that were customary. Innocent III settled this conflict, about 1200, by severely forbidding the clergy to make any sort of bargain for the administration of the sacraments, or to deny them to anyone who refused to pay. They must perform their functions without any more payment. But laymen were constrained by censures to maintain what the Pope called the praiseworthy custom of paying the usual amount. He made out that there was a great difference between demanding money beforehand, or bargaining, and demanding it afterwards, on pain of censures. One he approved as something legitimate, the other he forbade as a case of simony. The name changed, but the practice remained the same.

Another innovation was introduced among the old canons which made the acquisitions of the Church much more easy. The canons did not allow anything to be accepted, whether by gift or by will, from various kinds of public sinner, like those who had committed sacrilege, those who had engaged in family quarrels, prostitutes, and other such people. These exceptions were now lifted, and the Church accepted indifferently the gifts of all. In fact, the most frequent gifts and legacies came from prostitutes and from people who had quarrelled with their relatives and so left or gave their goods to the Church. The popes made great efforts not only to acquire more property, but also to retain the power of control over what they had acquired—power seized from the hand of the ruler with great difficulty and bloodshed, as has been described. Out of self-interest, all the clergy not only accepted, but also helped this process by their preaching and writing, teaching that it was usurpation on the part of the people and tyranny on the part of the rulers to interfere in any way with the distribution of benefices and above all in the election of the pope. In our day, one of the arguments used by Baronio in his *Annals*, at every possible opportunity and in a most irritating manner, is this, that it was an impious and tyrannical usurpation on the part of both rulers and subjects to meddle in the election of bishops and still more in that of the pope. He does not realize that the best popes have been appointed by secular rulers, and that whenever the clergy have made the choice by themselves, there have always been great disorders. But what is more important is that popes of most holy life and emperors worthy of eternal memory have recommended that practice and considered it to be necessary, so that it cannot be criticized now without insulting two dozen saintly popes, and in particular St. Gregory.

If from the beginning the secret aim of depriving princes of investitures had been unmasked, the clergy would never have allowed themselves to be persuaded to accept this innovation. They would have believed this to be a matter concerning their own interests and their own freedom. And so, the practice of giving benefices in the way which we have described began within the diocese, some being elected by the chapter, others collated by the bishop. The pope in the same way distributed the benefices of the diocese of Rome, and he did not meddle in beneficiary matters outside his diocese, except in one case only, when a prelate who had gone to Rome out of devotion or on business died there and was accompanied by an able man of the same nation, in which case the pope immediately appointed him bishop in the dead man's place. Then he would write to the diocese or to the monastery, conveying his regrets for the death of their bishop, and consoling them by sending them a replacement. This was easily agreed to, since it did not often happen, and since it seemed a sign of favor from the pope, nor was there any reason to oppose his choice, since the substitute was able and came from the same country. When the news of the death arrived in the diocese, if the pope had not already made provision in this way, they did not wait, but provided themselves with a bishop in the usual way. Apart from this, the pope did not concern himself with beneficiary matters outside the diocese of Rome.

The pope deserved well of all the clergy, because so many popes had gone to so much trouble and spilled so much blood to acquire authority over benefices in order to exclude the rulers who had for a long time possessed rights over benefices and the people who had possessed them from the beginning. So the bishops had a high opinion of the pope and tried to please him in every way they could; and this inspired the popes to treat the bishops in the same way that the emperors had done, that is, to recommend to them people who should be given benefices. At first these requests seemed extremely odd to the rulers because they opened a door through which foreigners could enter to acquire benefices in their kingdom, but they were welcomed by the bishops, who were intent on excluding the rulers from these matters, and never thought that anyone else would assume the power to collate to benefices. The Curia did well out of the presents it received from those who wanted to be recommended to the pope and the gifts made to cover the expenses of papal bulls. Very quickly, papal requests and recommendations began to multiply to such an extent that bishops came to be deprived of almost all their collations, and they were forced at times to turn the requests down. The popes' answer to this was to command as well as request. At first these commands were carried out, but they were so frequent that the bishops had to disobey them and make collations according to their own interests and those of their church, ignoring the censures of the pope. The pope had to accept the *fait accompli* because there was nothing else that he could do, and he had to pardon the bishops.

This way of obtaining benefices in Rome would have been closed easily had not the Curia thought up another plan. To the requests and commands they added an executor. If the bishop did not confer the benefice as required, the executor would summon him and punish him for disobedience. This method was used sparingly, in cases where the bishop was obstinate. But in the end, to save time, they came to agree to the request, the command, and the execution all together. The churches and bishops felt this to be oppressive, and rulers and nations complained not only because of the loss of their power, but because by this means the benefices which had been given by ancient custom to the men of that country were now always given to foreigners who were at the Curia. Often, it happened that men were made bishops and parish priests who did not understand the language of the people, and they could not even learn it easily because of its difference from their own, as was the case with the many Italians who held English benefices. The situation became so serious that the popes forbade anyone to hold a benefice, especially a parish, unless he knew the language of the people, reserving for themselves the right to make dispensations. This did not remedy the problem, but simply increased the expenses of the suitors and the profits of the Curia, since they did not stop giving expectatives to foreigners, but granted them at the same time a letter of dispensation. This great authority assumed by the Curia displeased pious men, but it was welcomed by a great number of clergy and other benefice-hunters who were subject to impediments in canon law, which made them ineligible. No bishop wanted to appoint such people out of respect for canon law. But what no one else wanted to do, the pope did with ease, dispensing from every law and constitution of the Church, and introducing the phrases *de plenitudine potestatis* [out of our plenitude of power] and *non obstantibus* [not withstanding] which now occur in every bull concerned with benefices. In the good old days, the popes themselves claimed to respect the canon law more than any other bishops when they distributed the benefices of the Church of Rome. And one of the glories of the popes, as can be seen from the example of St. Leo and his successors, was that they observed the canons punctiliously themselves before ensuring that others observed them. It should not be said that these popes had less authority. It is certain that they were superior in goodness and learning, and they did themselves only what they allowed others to do, whereas in Rome, later on, popes did everything that no one else dared do.

St. Bernard, who lived during the first stage of these changes, although they had not gone so far as they were to go later, criticized them severely in a letter to Eugenius III, complaining that the city of Rome was the place to which flocked the ambitious, the avaricious, the sacrilegious, and those who committed simony or incest or kept concubines, and all to acquire benefices, since they could not find anyone to accept them elsewhere, and Rome was the only place which could make legal what was everywhere considered illegitimate.

The popes themselves could not deny that the granting of these expectatives did great harm to the Church. Gregory IX admitted this openly in his decree *Mandatum apostolicum*. So they were restricted by the insertion of the following clause, "if we have not written concerning someone else," implying a custom to the effect that each pope could grant an expectative in each church, and no more. It was also the custom for a pope, when he took office, to revoke his predecessor's expectatives in order to make more room for his own; or rather those who had obtained expectatives were forced to acquire new ones and pay for them all over again. Sometimes popes even revoked their own expectatives, so that the petitioners would have to pay for new bulls in order to get what they wanted. As for elective benefices (that is, bishoprics and abbeys), expectatives were not given for them because this had never been done by secular rulers. But the Curia invented other means to make many of these appointments in Rome, laying down many conditions which had to be observed before the election took place, and others in the course of the election, and demanding various qualifications from the successful candidate, adding that if one of these conditions was not observed, the electors would be deprived of their power to elect, and it would devolve on Rome. Besides this, there were cases in which the electors for various reasons disagreed over the validity of the election, and one side would appeal to Rome, which usually declared that both sides were in the wrong and the election invalid, and then made the appointment itself. Also, when the Curia heard that some good bishopric or abbey was vacant, they would immediately send instructions that the election should not be held without their knowledge, and on the pretext of lending a hand or avoiding possible trouble, they would send someone to take part in the election who would manage to have that appointment made which was most in the interests of Rome.

It came about that for the reasons given above, there were few elections of bishops or abbots which were not examined in Rome, so that the pope concerned himself with almost all of them after they had taken place, on the pretext that this was for the common good because the electors had failed in their duty. The popes then came to think it opportune to intervene in elections even before they had taken place, commanding the electors not to proceed without their permission, or without the advice of someone nominated by them. Thus in various ways they came to take part in the elections themselves. These procedures, which they used as individual situations required, did not have the force of laws, but were considered simply as reasonable customs, until 1227. At this time, Gregory IX reflected how Theodosius had laid down imperial policy by collecting his decrees and those of his predecessors in a book, which came to be known as the Theodosian Code, and how Justinian, adapting ancient laws to the needs of his own age and collecting the decrees of his predecessors, called them the Code of Justinian. So Gregory collected together the decrees and precedents which might serve the power of the pope, abolishing the others and generalizing what had been laid down for a particular situation, or even for an individual case, and called the book the *Decretals of Gregory IX*. This collection was the foundation of the Roman monarchy, particularly so far as benefices were concerned, and it contains much more about the winning of lawsuits than about the winning of souls.

The ancient collectors of canons, particularly Gratian, put together everything that they thought might increase the power of the pope, and they even falsified some of the passages they quoted. They believed that they had raised the authority of the pope to its height, and, so far as their own times were concerned, they were not mistaken. But now things had changed, and that collection was no longer appropriate. And to Gratian's *Decreto* there succeeded Gregory's *Decretals*. Later on, even that collection proved unsatisfactory, and as the popes continued to increase their powers, new rules were made. Particularly as concerns benefices, the rules in force are not those of the *Decreto*, or the *Decretale*, or the *Sesto*, but other rules, as I shall explain.

The distribution of benefices on a grand scale at the Curia attracted every sort of clergy there. Those who lacked benefices went there to acquire them. Those who had benefices went to acquire bigger and better ones. Yet another cause of nonresidence was added to the old ones. The Curia could not hide this because every diocese complained that the churches lacked their clergy and gave the correct explanation of the fact, so it was decided to do something about it. The popes of this period did not consider it a good idea to punish the nonresident, as used to be done, because there were too many, and because this would have the effect of driving them all out of Rome. If that had happened the Curia would have been empty, and everyone would have gone to his own bishop for benefices instead of sending money and messengers to Rome to acquire expectatives. So they made a compromise, which was to pass laws requiring the residence of the sort of benefice-holders who could little afford to hang about the Curia, and making no mention of the rest. So Alexander III, in 1179, ordered all benefice-holders who had cure of souls to reside, and those were added who had canonries or administrative duties. Concerning other holders of lesser benefices, it was never declared that they were not obliged to reside—but they were not ordered to reside either. And so little by little, they came to consider that they were not obliged to, and a distinction grew up between benefices which carried the obligation of residence and "simple" benefices which did not. The lawyers said that everyone was *de iure* [legally] obliged to reside, but that by custom an exception was made for simple benefices.

There was a common saying, *beneficium datur propter officium* [the benefice is given as a return for performing the duty]. Those who did not have to reside had no duty, so it seemed that the simple benefice would be no more than a name. This problem was solved by means of an equivocation. The canonical hours, which had originally been said in church by all the brethren, but which were later permitted to be said in private, around the year 800 acquired the name of *officium divinum* [divine office]. Since this was said by everyone, either in public or in private, the statement *beneficium datur propter officium* was still valid, though "office" now meant the recitation of divine office, not serving the faithful by residing in one's church and doing one's job, as used to be the custom. In this way, the scruples of many benefice-holders about remaining absent from their churches were assuaged. It also seemed necessary to find a means to permit the holders of the other kind of benefice, who were obliged to reside, to remain at the Curia without doing violence to the laws. So Honorius III, around 1220, declared that those who were in papal service were not obliged to reside. All that was left now was to find a way for a man with a rich benefice with cure of souls to avoid residence. This too was found. It was quite normal for the parish priest, when he had a legitimate excuse, to have a deputy serve in his place and pay him a suitable fee. What was now done was to appoint a perpetual deputy by papal authority and to give him a sufficient portion of the income of the benefice, leaving the rest to the rector, and obliging the deputy to reside. The rector received the greater part of the income, and he was free of obligations. His share was treated as a simple benefice; the deputy's share had the cure of souls attached to it. In the primitive Church, it was unknown for any benefice to be given to anyone without duties attached, and everyone was obliged to perform his duties in person. No one was ever given two jobs, not only because this would be impossible if they were in two different places, but because the holy men of those times believed that it was no small matter to do one job well. There are many canons which refer to the ancient rules that no one could be ordained to two functions or serve in two churches.

At this time, when the distinction was made between benefices with the duty of residence attached and benefices without, men went on to say that it was possible to have more than one of those benefices where it was not necessary to carry out the duties in person. This was the beginning of the distinction between compatible and incompatible benefices. Those that require residence are incompatible with one another, because a man cannot be in two places at once. But these are compatible with benefices where it is not necessary to serve in person, and those benefices are compatible with one another.

At first men proceeded with great caution in this matter and went no further than to say that when a benefice was not sufficient for a clergyman to live on, he could have another compatible one. They did not dare suggest a third, or even suggest a second when the first was sufficient. The bishop was never given more power than this, but the pope was later considered to have authority to grant a man still more benefices, when the two were not enough to support him. What the canon lawyers considered enough to live on was an extremely generous amount, because in the case of simple priests, they considered it to include not only his personal expenses, but those of his household, his relations, three servants, and a horse, not counting an allowance for entertaining strangers. When the benefice-holder was a nobleman or an educated man, he was given still more, enough to live in the style to which he was accustomed. It is extraordinary to see how much they allowed a bishop. As for cardinals, it is enough to quote the common saying of the Curia: *æquiparantur regibus* [they are the equivalent of kings]. This does not count dispensations, for every canon lawyer holds that the pope can allow someone to hold as many benefices as he wishes. And in fact, dispensations for pluralism went so far that about 1320, John XXII revoked them all and restricted dispensations to two benefices only. He reserved to himself the distribution of the others (as I shall explain when I discuss *reservations*), so that people believed that he did this not to reform an abuse, but for profit, all the more because this pope was a subtle inventor of methods for filling the treasury. And time proved them right, for he indulged in pluralism on an even greater scale than before. Up to our own day we have seen, and see, dispensations without measure.

All the canon lawyers and casuists agree that such dispensations must be given for a legitimate reason, and that the pope commits a sin if he grants them without such a reason. They do not agree about whether the man who receives the dispensation is excused. Some say that the dispensation is an excuse in the eyes of God and men, others, that it excuses from the penalties of the canon law, but from the point of view of conscience and in the eyes of God it was worthless. This latter opinion is followed by the more pious; the former is more pleasing to the Curia, which does not want any law or anything else to limit the authority of the pope, especially where benefices are concerned. Some of them even argue (though others violently disagree) that the pope can grant dispensations to hold several benefices with cure of souls in plurality. However, they have not made use of this argument because they have found other means of giving a man several benefices with cure of souls, under the pretext that they are really one benefice. These devices began to be used at the time we are discussing. One of them is the *union,* the other is the *commendam,* and it will be useful to describe them here.

It was a most ancient practice that when a congregation was so reduced by war or plague or floods that it could no longer afford to maintain a minister, the bishop would put the neighboring parish priest in charge of them and give him what little income there was. This was to unite the two parishes. Similarly, when cities diminished in size, so that they could no longer maintain a bishop in a fitting manner, the metropolitan and the bishops, assembled in council, would give two or more cities to a single bishop, which they would call "uniting" them. The opposite occurred when the population increased, and one priest was not sufficient, so that one parish was divided into two. These procedures are still used at present, and they are praiseworthy, being for the service of God and the spiritual benefit of the people. The next stage was to make unions for the convenience of some poor bishopric, or monastery, or hospital. By virtue of this union, it would seem that the recipient has two benefices, but in fact he has one. The stage after was the invention of human subtlety. In order to give a man two incompatible benefices, they were united during his lifetime, so that when he was given the main one, it followed that he was given the other, too, so that nominally the law against having more than one benefice was not broken. In fact the letter of the law was obeyed, but the law was really broken; lawyers call this "finding a loophole." This device was also used to give a benefice with cure of souls to a child or to someone uneducated without obliging them to be ordained. The benefice with cure of souls would be united with a simple benefice for life, and the simple benefice would then be conferred on the child, who would then own both properties, but without technically breaking the law. The power of uniting benefices *ad vitam* [for life] was never granted to bishops for whatever reason, but was reserved for the pope alone. Some lawyers call it union in name, but relaxation of the law in practice, and they condemn it, so in some kingdoms it has been forbidden. It was long practiced by the Curia, but is so no longer, like many other devices (not to say deceits), for reasons which shall be given when we reach our own times.

The *commendam* too has an honorable and ancient ancestry. When an elective benefice, a bishopric or abbey, was vacant—or a benefice which had a patron—so that the bishop could not fill it at once, someone was appointed to take charge of it until the appointment was made. This man did not have the right to touch the income, but only to administer it. An excellent man would be appointed, usually a man who had a benefice already, and the appointment would simply be an extra burden for him, which he shouldered simply for the service of the Church. It could not be said accurately that he had the benefice in *commendam*, because in fact he did not have two benefices. All the same, not to press this point, the maxim became established among canon lawyers that a man could have two benefices, one in title, the other *in commendam*. The *commendam* lasted only until the vacancy was filled. In practice it lasted for some time, occasionally for a long time. So the pope forbade bishops to allow *commendams* for more than six months, though he did not forbid himself to do so. Through the work of the Curia, the *commendam* came to be used in a way which was not altogether praiseworthy. When the pope wanted to give someone a benefice and was unable to do it because he was too young or because the benefice was a monastic one, and he was not a monk, or for some other reason, he gave it to him *in commendam* until he acquired the necessary qualifications to possess it officially. But at length, about 1350, the popes put all these considerations aside and (keeping the other bishops to their six months) began to give *commendams* for life. If a *commendam* was given to someone who officially possessed another, incompatible, benefice, he kept the letter of the law against granting a man two benefices. However, in fact the law was broken, because to hold a benefice *in commendam* for life was like possessing it. Again, to give a benefice *in commendam* to someone who lacked the qualifications required by canon law did not go against the words of the law—but the benefice was given not just in words, but in fact. *Commendams* of bishoprics and other benefices have almost fallen into disuse in Italy, except for abbeys, for reasons which will be given when we reach our own times. By these means the popes gained control of a great part of the distribution of benefices in all Western Christian kingdoms. In the Eastern Churches, they were not allowed to dispose of an atom, not only in the last centuries of the Byzantine Empire, when the Greeks had completely broken away from Rome, but even in the first centuries, when we were all united. The only exceptions are in certain areas in Soria and in Greece when they were under the rule of the French and the Venetians. The papal letters which disposed of benefices in these ways were usually obeyed, but not without complaints and frequent arguments about whether the pope had the power to do this or that.

In Italy, there was no opposition to the pope except on the part of some pious men for reasons of conscience and the service of God, because the great power of the pope was convenient for the Italians, who alone were courtiers in Rome, since by this means they received incomes from the other side of the Alps. In Spain, the business skill of that nation was a match for the arts of the Curia. In England, an area where benefices were numerous and rich, the Roman courtiers made great acquisitions, which is why, in 1232, a league was made there between the English clergy and the English knights against the Roman clergy who held benefices in that island, whose goods and incomes were taken away from them. The pope commanded the king, on pain of excommunication, to punish the offenders, and he commanded the prelates to excommunicate them. However, there turned out to be so many of them that neither the king nor the prelates dared proceed against them. Things remained quiet for a few years, so Pope Innocent IV (a Genoese) took heart and sent a certain Martin, a relation of his, to restore the former situation. The English appealed to the king, complaining that the Italians were seizing all the benefices. The king drove Martin out of the kingdom. He had it calculated how much the Pope gained from England and found that it was an amount equal to the king's own income, that is, 60,000 marks. The king raised this matter at the Council of Lyons, complaining of the burden just mentioned, but the Pope replied that the Council had not assembled to discuss this, and that it was not the time to attend to it. In the same city of Lyons, during the council, the Pope tried to give some prebends of some churches there to his relations. There was such a great tumult as a result, the Pope was warned that they would be thrown in the Rhône, and so he made them depart in secret.

This did not make the Curia give up its schemes. In 1253, the same Pope commanded Robert, Bishop of Lincoln, a man famous at that time for his goodness and learning, to give a certain benefice to a Genoese, contrary to the canons. The bishop considered this improper and injust, and he replied that he respected the Pope's commands when they agreed with the teaching of the apostles, but that this was a breach of faith and a disturbance of the peace of Christendom; that it was a grave sin to defraud the flock of its shepherd; that the Apostolic See had full powers for building things up, but none for pulling them down. The Pope was furious when he received this reply. But Cardinal Egidio, a prudent man and a Spaniard, tried to calm him down, pointing out that to proceed against a man with such a high reputation and for such an unpopular reason could have no good effect. While the Pope was considering what he would do, Robert fell ill. At the end of his life he did not change his opinion, and he died with the reputation of a saint, and it was said that he performed miracles. When the Pope heard of his death, he had the king told to have the corpse disinterred; but the following night the Pope had a vision, or a dream, in which he saw Robert, dressed in pontifical robes, who scolded him for this persecution and struck him on the side with the foot of his crozier. The Pope woke up with great pain in that spot, which afflicted him till his death—a few months later. In 1258, his successor, Alexander IV, excommunicated the Archbishop of York for a similar reason. The Archbishop did not go back on his decision, and he endured papal persecution with great patience. When he was close to death, he wrote the Pope a most sensible letter, exhorting him to imitate his sainted predecessors and to abolish innovations which did great harm both to the Church and to his own soul. He died with the reputation of a saint and martyr.

In France, too, there was need to do something at this time, and I shall explain what after saying that whatever obstacles kings and bishops placed in the way of the schemes of the Curia, they never thought of giving up. On the contrary, in 1266, Clement IV resolved to lay foundations so that he or his successors would be able to declare themselves absolute masters of all collations to benefices all over the world and not have to keep on finding devices for attracting collations to Rome. He issued a bull, which referred to nothing but the reservation of vacant benefices at the Curia, saying that collation to these benefices was by ancient custom reserved to the pope, and so he approved this custom and wished it to be observed. However, in order to reach this conclusion, he made a hypothetical prologue, saying:

Although the plenary disposition of all benefices pertains to the pope, so that he not only has the power to confer them when they become vacant, but can grant rights to them before; nevertheless ancient custom has particularly reserved to him vacancies at the Curia, and so we approve this custom.

If the Pope had made an edict declaring that he had the power to dispose of all benefices, the whole world would have risen up, and the clergy as well as rulers and other patrons would have claimed their rights; but this proposition, inserted into a conditional clause and leading to no conclusion, passed by with ease, without anyone noticing how important it was. Two years later, in 1268, without taking any notice of this bull, St. Louis, King of France, seeing that the provisions made by the queen his mother, regent during his minority and his absence in the Holy Land, had not remedied the confused state of matters concerning benefices, issued his celebrated Pragmatic, in which he ordered cathedral churches and monasteries to hold their elections freely. All other benefices, he declared, should be conferred as the law demanded, and the Curia was to lay no impositions on benefices without his consent and that of the French Church. However, the French allowed the Curia to recover its powers with ease because the king went to Africa to fight the Moors and died in 1270, and the house of Anjou needed the favor of the Pope to consolidate the Kingdom of Naples and to recover the Kingdom of Sicily, and the Pope allowed the king to impose tithes on the pretext of the Crusade. In 1298, Boniface VIII placed the constitution of Clement among the decretals, and made what had been said hypothetically and by the way into a serious assertion, and to give it greater authority attributed it to Clement without making it clear whether it was Clement III or Clement IV, for some copies have one reading, and others the other. This was when men began to believe that the plenary disposition of all benefices belonged to the pope. This statement could be interpreted to mean something that was not in fact perverse, that is, that the pope had full powers, subject only to law and legal rights. However, Clement V shortly afterwards made this interpretation impossible by saying that the pope had not only full, but absolute power over all benefices. This absolute power was interpreted by the canon lawyers to mean power exempt from all laws and legal rights, so that the pope could, in spite of the rights or interests of whatever church or individual, even a lay patron, do whatever he pleased. This proposition was inserted into bulls on every occasion, and there was no canon lawyer who did not approve of it and even declare it an article of faith, saying that the pope could, in the collation to any benefice, compete with the bishop and even forestall him; and even, if he wished, give anyone he wanted the power to compete with or to forestall the bishop. This power has since been given to papal legates by a general constitution.

It is as clear as the light of midday that the election of ministers was originally by all the faithful. Then it passed to the secular rulers (after they had received the Christian faith and began to think about the affairs of the Church). Finally, it passed to the clergy, and the laity were excluded, thanks to the management of Gregory VII and his successors (but elections and collations to benefices still took place within the diocese till, little by little, the popes assumed these powers for themselves in the way which we have described). But nothing is more extraordinary, so far as benefices are concerned, than to see how the canon lawyers, out of bias, or because it is not their job to know anything which is not contained in the decretals, have said and still say in our own day, without taking notice of the well-known facts which contradict them, that the pope originally appointed to all bishoprics and other benefices, and that later, as a favor, he granted chapters the right to elect and bishops the right to collate to benefices. There is no doubt that one day this matter will be made an article of faith, to make the Church accept a doctrine directly contrary to that which had formerly been preached. At this time, Anselm, Bishop of Lucca, wrote three books against Gilbert, the antipope, in favor of Gregory VII, books which still exist; in the second book, he proves by means of the authority of the popes, the Fathers, the general councils, and of custom from apostolic times to his own day (about 1080) that the election of bishops (whom he called "pontiffs") belonged to the clergy and people of the diocese. He argues that the pious emperors Constantine, Constans, Valentinian, Theodosius, Arcadius, Honorius, Charlemagne, Louis, and others outstanding for their faith and religion have never violated this custom observed by Holy Church from the time of the apostles. He exhibits a constitution of Charlemagne and Louis the Pious in the *Capitulary*, to the effect that bishops are elected by the clergy and people of their own diocese according to the canons, and he says that this constitution is in agreement with the Fathers, with the Council of Nicæa, and other general councils, and that it was put into the mouths of these emperors by the Holy

Ghost. So it can be seen that to take elections out of the hands of the secular rulers, the popes appealed to a tradition contrary to that which they now want the canon lawyers to affirm and us to believe. Either the canon lawyers must be wrong, or the authorities cited by Anselm of Lucca. But if the ordination of bishops in their dioceses as we have described was in the hands of all the churches, as the Fathers and the councils teach, and if it was Our Lord Jesus Christ who granted them this right, then the men who say that the Curia has enslaved all the churches on the pretext of defending their liberty do not say such scandalous things after all.

Having spoken in various places about the different means used by churches to acquire property, it is now necessary for me to discuss how it was preserved, which was by prohibiting its alienation in any manner, something diametrically opposed to the practice of the primitive Church. When churches were allowed by the laws of the land to acquire landed property, they used to keep what had been given or bequeathed them. However, the bishop was free not only to make use of the income from such property, but to sell the property itself to obtain money for the maintenance of the ministers and the poor, or to give it away, if that was necessary. The power of the bishop was not limited to what the property brought in, as it is now, but extended to the capital. In the beginning, this property was honestly administered and nothing improper happened. This situation lasted a long time in poor churches, where there was no occasion of sin, because the property was small, and the bishops did not have much power. However, in large and rich churches, whose prestige encouraged the bishops to attempt something that not everyone would have been allowed to do, and whose property was extensive enough to allow them room for maneuver, the bishops began to pass from moderation to excess, from charity to extravagance, so that it became necessary to do something about it. The measures that were taken were initiated not by the clergy, but by the laity, who were the real victims; because when the property of the Church diminished, it was not the clergy who suffered—they were the first charge on the funds—but the poor, who had to wait till last. It was in the most important churches, Rome and Constantinople, that something had to be done first. The Emperor Leo, by a law of 470, forbade all alienation of property by the church of Constantinople. In 483, Basil Cecina, Prætorian Prefect of King Odoacer in Rome, made a decree while the See was vacant, to the effect that the property of the church of Rome could not be alienated. The three popes who followed Simplicius did not find this extraordinary. But in 502, after the disappearance of Odoacer and his power, Pope Symmachus assembled an all-Italian council, in which he suggested that it was a great absurdity for a layman to have made a constitution for the Church, and with the assent of the council, he declared it null and void. However, not to make it appear that they did this because they wanted disorder, the council made a decree to the effect that the pope and the other ministers of that church could not alienate their property, specifying that the decree would affect only the church of Rome.

The following period showed that all churches were in need of the same laws, so Anastasius extended Leo's law to all the churches subject to the Patriarch of Constantinople, forbidding them all to alienate property. The Emperor Justinian made a general constitution in 535, affecting all the churches of the East, the West, and Africa, and all other pious foundations, forbidding them to alienate their property except to feed the poor if there was an acute famine and to ransom prisoners, in which cases it would be permissible, as was the ancient custom mentioned by St. Ambrose, that not only property, but also church plate used to be sold for these reasons. Justinian's law was observed in the West as long as Rome remained part of the Eastern Empire, and there are many letters of St. Gregory which mention goods alienated to ransom slaves. From the time of Pelagius II till Adrian I, two hundred years, an incredible amount was spent by the church of Rome to ransom slaves from the Lombards and to persuade them not to besiege cities or to lay waste to the countryside. St. Gregory bears witness to this in his time. In those days, no one believed the doctrine now current, that the goods of the Church are exempt from contributions to meet general needs. On the contrary, the goods of the Church were the first to be spent on such purposes, before contributions were levied upon private property.

After Charlemagne refounded the Empire, the Roman laws lost their authority and abuses returned. Various councils issued various prohibitions, especially in France, where the squandering of church goods was very great. After the popes came to take more part in the administration of other churches, they saw that a general prohibition had little effect, because prelates did not lack pretexts for making an exception out of each individual case. So they made various decrees between 1000 and 1250, laying down certain solemn formularies which helped to restrain the abuses. However, in the time of which we speak, Innocent IV began to declare null and void the alienations made without observing these conditions; and Gregory X, in the Council of Lyons in 1274, laid down that no property should be alienated except in case of necessity, and then only by permission of the pope. This ordinance has remained in force up to our own day, and no alienation has been permitted unless its usefulness has been obvious. The practice of selling church property to feed the poor in times of great famine or to ransom slaves has been given up because these activities have been interpreted as harming rather than helping the Church. So much have times changed, that where once it was a work of Christian perfection to sell one's goods and give to the poor, it is now something to be condemned! Christian perfection is now to hold on to the property of the Church, and it cannot even be exchanged unless this is obviously profitable; and the laws against alienating property, which were made at the expense of the clergy and in favor of the laity, have come to operate at the expense of the laity and in favor of the clergy.

Let us return to the declaration of Clement IV and Clement V and to the common opinion that the pope can compete with or forestall anyone who has the right to collate to benefices. This was not of great profit except in the case of benefices which fell vacant in places near the Curia, so that they could hear about the vacancy immediately. So far as vacancies in distant parts were concerned, the pope's powers were of little use, because before the Curia heard of the vacancy it would have been filled by the bishop. This is why the *reservation* was invented, which is a decree by which the pope, before a benefice becomes vacant, declares that when it does become vacant, no one can grant it to anyone, and any such collation is to be null and void. This is something odious, as even the gloss admits, and to make people swallow it easily, it was used sparingly from the first. The absolute reservation which Clement IV had made of all vacancies at the Curia seemed too much, so Gregory X restricted it to a month, and after this, appointments could be made in the normal manner. Clement V added the reservation of the cathedral church and monastery of Holy Cross of Bordeaux on one occasion. Pope John XXII, his successor, went a step further and made a constitution to reform pluralism. He forbade anyone to hold more than one benefice with cure of souls and one without (with a dispensation), except for cardinals, and commanded everyone with more to resign them. In future, he ordered anyone who had a benefice with cure of souls and received another to resign the first, and the resigned benefices would be reserved for the pope to distribute. The bull, with its apparent aim of abolishing pluralism, seemed a very good thing. The reservations, although their only aim was the profit of the Curia, passed as something subordinate and which, at first sight, seemed not to have dangerous consequences because it had not yet been discovered in which direction they were tending.

It is necessary to halt here for a little because this pope gave his successors many examples of how to collate to benefices and accumulate wealth. He divided many large bishoprics and made bishoprics out of abbeys. When a rich benefice fell vacant, he would give it to someone who had a benefice worth slightly less, and that benefice he would give to another, so that sometimes for one vacancy he would make up to six provisions, moving everyone up from a poorer benefice to a richer one, and giving the bottom man a new benefice. Consequently, everyone was happy, and everyone paid the pope.

He also invented *annates,* taxes on benefices previously unheard of, which for some time caused grave scandals. When emperors and kings granted benefices, if those aspiring to receive them offered any gift, or bargained with the ruler or his ministers to give them part of the income of the benefices in order to obtain them, this was most severely condemned by the popes. They said this was illegal, and quoted the Gospel, *"gratis accepistis, gratis date"* [accept freely, give freely] and called the acceptance of gifts or part of the income a sale of spiritual things, a simoniacal contract, and some went so far as to call it heresy. However, there were also those at that time who excused it on the grounds that the ministry of Christ was something quite distinct from the power of binding and loosing, as regards the possession of the temporal goods attached to the benefice, and that therefore it was not improper for the prince to receive a share of the temporal goods for the needs of the commonwealth. There was a solemn disputation about this.

This reply did not satisfy pious and learned men. If the income from benefices is temporal, the right to them is spiritual. It seemed to them all, and still seems to them, that there was good reason to condemn this practice of the popes and to call it simony. The original pretext for the adoption of this practice was to take the power to collate to benefices away from secular rulers. However, after the pope had gradually gained a large part of the power which the emperors had lost, John XXII, in 1316, ordered that for three years, everyone who obtained a benefice worth more than twenty-four ducats should pay a year's income at the time the bulls were issued. After the three years were up, he continued the practice, as did his successors. In various places there was resistance, and in some it was accepted that only half the income should be paid, and in other places only a certain sort of benefice was obliged to pay, and the others were exempted. This innovation was regarded most seriously by private families because the benefice-holder paid his annates with his family's money, and there was a danger that he would die before repaying it. Rulers also regarded this as a most serious matter because it meant so much money was leaving the kingdom without any advantage to the state. It was all the more serious because it was added to the former expense of bulls, dispensations, and presents, all of which take money, which is a kingdom's true strength. And this money never returns, as it does when it leaves by way of trade.

When this innovation was introduced by the Pope, ordinary people did not see what was the difference between this payment and that which had been criticized in the days when rulers conferred benefices; but educated men in those early times universally condemned this practice as simony. Later, some studied how to justify it, and learned men became divided, some condemning it as something illegitimate and simoniacal and prohibited by the laws of God and man, and others praising it as something necessary and legitimate and as something to which the Pope had a right. These latter went so far as to defend the proposition that the Pope could not only demand a year's income, but even more, as if he were absolute owner of all the fruits of the benefice, not just some of them. They also said that whatever contract the Pope made in collating to benefices, it was impossible for him to commit simony. It is certain that if he was the owner, as they claimed, this consequence would follow, because everyone can enter into contracts with his own goods just as he pleases, without doing wrong to anyone. But it seems that neither God nor the world accepts this. This Pope was so intent on making money out of everything, that in twenty years as pope he accumulated an incredible treasure. It is certain that he spent and gave away as much as his predecessors, yet he left twenty-five millions at his death. Giovanni Villani relates that a brother of his was charged by the College of Cardinals, after the Pope's death, to count the money, and he found eighteen millions in coined money and seven millions in plate and bars, which he weighed.

When Pope John XXII invented annates, they affected only benefices newly conferred and were paid when the bulls were issued, and this practice continued in his time. Afterwards, all the benefices which are united to monasteries, hospitals, and pious foundations, and so never become vacant, were obliged to pay annates every fifteen years, and so this was called the *quindennium*. Paul II, about 1470, applied this rule only to benefices united after 1417, and by the pope; but Paul IV extended it to all benefices united by the pope before this; and Sixtus V included not only benefices united by the pope, but those united by legates, nuncios, bishops, and others.

Let us return to the origin of annates. Those men who opposed John XXII's invention, eager to prevent things from going any further, not only failed in their aim, but caused the extension of annates, just as those who opposed reservations had an effect the opposite of what they intended. After this, Benedict XII, in 1335, on the pretext of wanting to provide suitable people to benefices, reserved for his own disposition (during his own lifetime only) all the vacancies occurring at the Curia (as had been done before) and also, all vacancies occurring because the holder was deprived or translated; also, all benefices resigned at the Curia and all the benefices of cardinals, officials of the Curia, legates, nuncios, and other administrators and treasurers of the papal states; also, the benefices of those who went to the Curia on business, if on the way there or back they died about forty miles from the Curia; and also, all benefices which became vacant because their holders had received another benefice. These reservations affected quite enough benefices and greatly restricted the authority of the bishops and gave quite enough benefices to foreigners. All the same, because they were for the Pope's lifetime only, they were accepted. But one must never believe that anything useful to a man in power which is instituted for a short time is going to last no longer than that. On the death of Benedict XII, Clement VI, his successor, made the same reservations. Edward III, King of England, seeing that because of these reservations and expectatives all the benefices of the kingdom were going to foreigners, commanded on pain of death that these papal provisions should not be accepted in his kingdom. The Pope wrote to the king, complaining of this and urging him to cease. The king replied, begging the Pope to reform those things that were a shame to the Church and a scandal to the people, adding that his ancestors had made gifts to churches which, as a result of papal provisions, had been seized by foreigners and unworthy men, which was contrary to the intention of the testators. This was harming the kingdom. The pope was there to feed the sheep, not to shear them. Kings had formerly made appointments to benefices; at the popes' request they had allowed the clergy to elect, and now the popes wanted to abolish the elections and usurp the power themselves. It would be a good thing to return to the original system, which was for the ruler to confer benefices. This dispute, which lasted as long as the Pope lived, was the reason that Innocent VI, Clement's successor, revoked all his reservations in a constitution that began with the word *Pastoralis*, which is no longer extant, but is mentioned by many famous canon lawyers.

A few years later, reservations were revived, so Edward, in 1373, sent an ambassador to Gregory XI, in Avignon, asking for them to be abolished. Two years of negotiation followed, and at length, in 1375, the Pope annulled them completely. But on his death, in 1378, the Great Schism began, and there were two popes and two curias and double expenses, which were also much higher than usual because of the popes' need to spend money on attacking or defending themselves from one another. And so both of them tried out every means of making money, and in both curias simony was open, benefices were sold freely, and appointments were taken away from the bishops as often as possible.

Up to this time it had not been manifest that the Curia aimed at nothing but money. Whatever they did, there had been some pretense of doing more for the Church than the bishops could, or of providing some deserving person to a benefice. But Urban VI made it clear why

he concerned himself with benefices when he laid down
that requests for benefices which did not mention their
value were invalid. Formerly, benefices were conferred
primarily for spiritual considerations, and the temporal
ones were secondary. Now, spiritual considerations were
not mentioned at all. The duties were not considered, but
only the profits. This arrangement has lasted until our
own days. When nuncios are given the authority to confer some minor benefices, the distinction between greater
and lesser benefices is made on the basis of their income.
Monastic reservations are made without any care for
spiritual things; those worth more than two hundred
scudi are reserved, and the rest are left free. Everything
is done to make sure that the papal treasury receives
the highest possible amount of annates. If two men are
granted a benefice, and one estimates its value at higher
than the other, the bulls of the man who estimated less
are void, and the man with the higher estimate receives
the benefice. Some people say that this is to auction benefices and sell to the highest bidder; others say that it is
to prevent the papal treasury from being defrauded of its
dues. However, this matter pertains to the section about
annates.

Let us return to the time of the schism. No one denies
that there were great disorders in the two curias, and
this became worse when some kingdoms and provinces
were so scandalized that they refused to recognize either
claimant, so that the popes had to extract their normal
income from those that remained.

Germany refused to have reservations and expectatives
imposed any longer. Bishops conferred benefices without
any regard for instructions from Rome. For this reason,
in 1359, Innocent VI sent a legate to Germany to issue
new bulls to those who had been collated to benefices by
bishops, provided they paid a fee, and to make a bargain
about firstfruits, which they could keep if they paid part
to the papal treasury. This would have caused a large sum
of money to leave Germany, and so the Emperor Charles
IV refused to allow it, saying that what needed reforming was the way of life of the clergy—not their purses.
All these confusions increased greatly with the addition

of a third pope in 1409; and although the French joined his party and gave him their obedience, they still kept to an edict made by their king three years before, by which reservations and other exactions of the Curia were prohibited unless and until they were imposed by a genuine general council. The king was not really capable of ruling, but Louis, Duke of Orléans, who dominated him, was responsible for all the edicts; and after he had been killed, it was easy for Pope John XXIII to regain the power of conferring benefices in France by giving the king and queen and the dauphin and the house of Burgundy the power to appoint their servants to benefices, and keeping the rest for himself. The Curia retained this power until the king's death, because his successor, Charles VII, his son, renewed the edicts against reservations and the rest.

In Italy, too, various states made various kinds of provision which all tended to remedy the abuses. Baldus is witness that the people of Bologna made provisions concerning benefices and, in particular, ordered that they should only be conferred upon natives of the city. The popes did not enjoy much honor at this time. When John XXIII and his court were in Florence, a conflict arose about the appointment to a benefice, and the republic deprived him of the power of conferring benefices within their territories for five years.

At this time unintelligible clauses were invented for insertion in bulls, clauses like those distinguishing between petitions signed *concessum* and those signed *fiat*; between bulls containing the clause *motu proprio* and others with the clause *anteferri,* which was better. The result of these inventions was that different bulls were issued granting the same benefice to different people, and annates were paid several times over, so that there were lawsuits which had to be heard at Rome, to the further profit of the Curia. If the litigant died they would put another in his place, so that his end did not mean the end of the suit, but only another payment of annates and the continuation of the suit. As lawsuits multiplied, the clauses *si alteri, si neutri, si nulli* were invented, by means of which the benefice would be given to a third party during the conflict between the other two. This forced rulers to give cases about the ownership of benefices back to the secular courts in order to remedy the confusions, conflicts, and lawcases afflicting their subjects. These cases belonged to the secular courts, but the rulers had connived at their being taken away and given to the church courts.

The provisions made by various rulers to restrain the introduction of innovations concerning benefices into their states gave the Curia occasion to invent still more, to achieve the same ends with different pretexts, to multiply the means of doing what they could do already, and to find means of doing what they could not.

At this time they discovered resignations. Not good and praiseworthy ones, which are most ancient, but another kind, which the world does not praise at the present time. A man who had been given a post in the Church was never allowed to leave it on his own authority. It was fitting that a man who had undertaken a task and had received a reward for it (the benefice) should carry on with the job. Nevertheless, because some legitimate occasion might arise which made it necessary or convenient from the private or public point of view that a man should give up this career, the custom of resignation was introduced, provided that this was with the permission of one's superior and for some good reason. Good reasons were the hostility of local magnates, which made residence dangerous, or old age, or infirmity of mind or body, which made it impossible. When the bishop accepted a man's resignation, the benefice was taken as vacant, and it would be conferred in the same way as if the previous occupant had died. Now, however, resignations were introduced which were not for any good reason, but were simply a means to confer the benefice on a nominee of the previous occupant. A novelty should be given a new name, and this was called *resignatio ad favorem* [resignation in favor of . . .] because it was done simply to favor the successor, to give him the benefice. The superior had the power to accept or refuse the resignation, but he could not accept it without giving the benefice to the occupant's nominee. This was a means of making benefices hereditary and so was harmful to the good government of the Church, but it was useful to the Curia because it meant that benefices changed hands (and annates were paid) more often.

Avarice and other worldly passions led many men to apply for benefices not because they wanted to continue to hold them, but with the intention of enjoying them until they found something better, or until their plans to marry or take up another way of life were successful, or until some child was old enough for them to give it up in his favor. Pious men never condoned this, and it was generally held that whoever accepted a benefice with the intention of resigning it could not receive its revenues with a good conscience. Some people, more broadminded, did not want to say this in general, but only about those who took benefices when they had the intention of becoming laymen. Those who accepted resignations *ad favorem* obtained some profit from this, so the Curia, in order that the profits should be entirely theirs, forbade bishops to accept such resignations and reserved this power to the pope alone. Many benefice-holders, feeling that death was close at hand, took this means of choosing their successor; so the papal chancery laid it down that resignations made by a sick man in favor of someone should not be valid if the man resigning died within twenty days of the agreement.

At this time the offerings of the faithful seemed to grow less. While the Crusades lasted, and afterwards, while there was hope that they would begin again, the clergy were given a great deal of money for this reason; but when all hope was abandoned, offerings stopped. However, this example was followed, and indulgences were introduced, that is, remissions and concessions to anyone who contributed to any pious work. Every day there were new pious works in every city for which indulgences were granted from Rome, to the great profit of the clergy and the Curia, which took a share. This went so far that in 1517, in Germany, came the revolution known to everyone. In our time, Pope Pius V issued a constitution, annulling all indulgences which included the clause about helping hands, that is, all which involved the obligation to pay money; but this has not yet put an end to this harvest. Although nowadays indulgences are granted without this condition, the collecting-boxes are still displayed in the churches, and the people believe that their sins will not be forgiven unless they make an offering.

Let us return to the years of the schism. It seemed that hope was quite lost of acquiring more income and property for the churches. The monks had a reputation for sanctity no longer; enthusiasm for a Crusade had not just cooled, it was quite extinct; the mendicant friars, who were all founded after 1200, owed their reputation to the fact that they had given up the power of acquiring landed property and vowed to live on alms alone. It seemed that the property of the Church would increase no longer, but a happy solution was discovered. This was for the pope to grant the mendicant friars the power of acquiring property, which was forbidden them by their vows and the terms of their foundation. There were many people who were devoted to them and most ready to enrich them—all that was lacking was a way to do it. Once this was found, the houses of the mendicants in Italy, Spain, and other kingdoms quickly received a considerable amount of property. Only the Frenchmen opposed the innovation, saying that they had entered the kingdom vowed to poverty, and it was fitting that they should continue that way, and up to the present they have never allowed such acquisitions. In some other places, the gains have been very great, particularly at the time of the schism, when the rest of the clergy had fallen very low in reputation.

The schism was ended at the Council of Constance. One of the popes resigned, and the other two were deprived, and in 1417, the Council elected Martin V. Everyone hoped that the Council and the Pope would do something about the abuses relating to benefices. In fact, the Council proposed to the Pope articles of reform concerning reservations, annates, graces, expectatives, commendams, and collations. However, the new Pope and the Curia wanted to go home, and all the Fathers of the Council were also tired of their long absences, so it was easy to postpone the discussion of such a difficult and time-consuming matter to a future council, which was announced for Pavia five years later. The French did not want to wait for the next council. An *arrêt* [ordinance] of the Parlement declared that they would not give the Pope their obedience until he accepted the royal edict forbidding reservations and the extraction of money. And so, when Martin sent a nuncio to the king to tell him of his election, the king replied that he would accept it on condition that elective benefices were conferred by means of elections, and that reservations and expectatives were abolished. At the time, the Pope agreed, but in 1422, having acquired the support of some of the universities, he tried to have reservations accepted. He could not obtain what he wanted, and his supporters were imprisoned. The Pope laid Lyons under interdict, and the Parlement ordered that it not be observed. The conflict lasted until 1424, when the king and the Pope agreed that His Holiness would accept as legitimate the collations made up to that time, but that in future all his commands would be obeyed. However, the procureur and the avocat-général and many nobles opposed this, telling the king how much the kingdom would suffer, so the agreement went up in smoke.

Meanwhile, the Council of Pavia was held, which was quickly transferred to Siena and brought to an end. Nothing important was discussed, but men were led to hope that everything would be reformed at the council which was to be held in Basel seven years later. At the end of that seven years, Martin died, and he was succeeded by Eugenius IV. Under Eugenius, at the Council of Basel, the necessary and much-desired reform of abuses concerning benefices was made. Reservations were prohibited except in the case of vacancies occurring at the Curia. Expectatives, annates, and all other exactions of the papal court were also forbidden. The Pope could not bear to see his power and wealth so limited, and he opposed the Council. First, he tried to transfer it elsewhere, to a place where he could bring pressure to bear on the prelates. They resisted this, and he was unable to get his way. There were many conflicts between the

Pope and the Council, and pious men intervened each time to make a compromise. In the end, the breach was irreconcilable because the Council was resolved to do something about the extortions of money, and the Pope was equally resolved to preserve his authority and his income. The Pope annulled the Council, and the Council deprived the Pope and elected another, so there was schism in the Church. The Council was accepted in France and in Germany, and in 1438, that famous Pragmatic Sanction was published in France which restored to the chapters their power to elect and to the bishops their power to collate, and which prohibited reservations as the Council of Basel had done.

In Italy, the Council was not accepted, but everyone supported the Pope. Reservations gained a footing, and each pope renewed them without difficulty, and even introduced new abuses into collations to benefices, none of which ever disappear unless an easier means is found to achieve the same results. Julius II and Leo X introduced mental reservations, as they were called, or reservations *in pectore*, which were not published like the others, and no one knew about them. But when a benefice became vacant and the bishop conferred it, or someone went to ask for it, the datary would reply that the pope had reserved it mentally. This system lasted a few years, and then it fell into disuse because it turned out to be inconvenient for the Curia itself. All the other devices were extended to excess. To resignations *in favorem* were added resignations of the title of the benefice only, so that the man who resigned it kept its fruits; this was essentially to retain the benefice but to appoint a successor who might have the title before the death of the man who had resigned it, but in practice had no rights. In order that the new man might not obtain anything by collecting the fruits and assigning them to the former occupant, it was added that the latter not only retained his rights to all the fruits, but that he could collect them on his own authority. There was nothing to distinguish him from the patron of a benefice but the fact that if his successor died first, although he continued to enjoy the fruits of the benefice, he could not appoint another successor, and the title could be given by the collator to whoever he pleased, and this man would then succeed after the death of the man who had resigned. However, the Curia found an excellent remedy for this, too, which was the *regress*.

In the time of the primitive Church, it was a holy and praiseworthy custom that a man who was ordained to serve in a church never left it to take up a benefice with greater income or prestige. Everyone thought it sufficient to do their duty as well as they could. Sometimes, out of necessity, the superior, when he could not find anyone suitable for some important task, took someone occupied in something less and transferred him by virtue of his vow of obedience. Later, some men asked for this for their greater convenience or profit, and so translation, from being something rare, became very common indeed. So much did everyone want to rise in position, it often happened that a man would give up his benefice and apply for another and, being unsuccessful in his application, lose both. To avoid this situation, the custom grew up that if the application for the second place was unsuccessful, then the applicant could return to the first one without more ado. This was called the *regress*. On this model, a man who resigned his benefice was given the power, if the man in whose favor he had resigned it died or himself resigned it, to return to the benefice and take possession of it as if he had never resigned it. Even if he had never taken possession of it before resigning (in which case he could hardly "regress" or "return" to it) he could still enter and take possession of it by his own authority, without going to a judge; and this was called *regress*. The pope never allowed anyone else to accept resignations on these terms, but reserved this power for himself. This device was condemned by all writers, especially in the French universities, and it was forbidden by the Parlement. It cannot be made honest by any fine ancient precedent. Some men had scruples about it and were ashamed to use it. To satisfy them, another device was found, of ancient origin but, as usual, adapted to present needs. This was the coadjutor.

It was a most ancient and praiseworthy practice in

churches that when some minister or prelate had become unable or less able to perform his duties as a result of old age, infirmity of mind or body, or whatever, he could ask for a helper, and his superior would give him one. This man was only concerned with the office or benefice during the lifetime of the man whose coadjutor he was. On his death, a new appointment was made. Later, it was thought that if the coadjutor was to succeed, this would be better, because he would be more diligent, being engaged in something which was to become his, and others would treat him as the genuine article, rather than as an outsider. So the coadjutor was appointed with the right of succession—an arrangement which had opponents and defenders. The opponents argued that all succession to benefices ought to be condemned, and that it provided a motive for bringing about or desiring the death of someone else. The defenders quoted the famous example of St. Augustine, who was made coadjutor with the right of succession by Valerius, his predecessor. This was not too good an example, because St. Augustine himself later criticized it and did not want to follow it, and he was not ashamed to say that he and his predecessor had done this out of ignorance. However, during the times of which we speak, coadjutors with the right of succession were given not only to prelates and other administrators, but even to the holders of simple benefices, where there were no duties for which assistance was needed; the coadjutor was purely nominal—the only thing he did being to succeed, which was the very thing abhorred by the canons.

At this time, a man who held a benefice and wanted to appoint a successor did one of the following things according to taste. Either he took a coadjutor with the right of succession, or he resigned in favor of someone, reserving to himself the fruits of the benefice and the regress; but this last method was reserved to the pope alone and under no circumstances granted to other collators.

In Germany, the Council of Basel was accepted by some and not by others. Cases about benefices were also interpreted in different ways by different people. In order to remedy these differences and conflicts, in 1448, Nicholas V and the Emperor Frederick made an agreement as follows. Benefices which fell vacant at the Curia were to be reserved to the pope, and in the other elective benefices, elections should be held. As for the others, those falling vacant during six months of the year should be filled by the pope, those in the other six should be filled by the other collators. In addition, it was laid down that if within three months the pope had not conferred the benefices which were in his gift, the right to collate would go to the bishops. This concordat was not accepted all over Germany, and some dioceses up to 1518 still observed the decision of the Council of Basel, which abolished all reservations. In the progress of time, even those who had accepted the concordat in the beginning ceased to observe it, defending themselves by saying that the concordat was not generally accepted, or that it had fallen into disuse and so lost its force, so that (we are not concerned with those cities where bishops and chapters had left the Church of Rome) even in churches which still obeyed the pope, it was little observed or not at all. Clement VII, in 1534, issued a severe bull about this, but it had little effect. Gregory XIII made another in 1576, without better success. At the Diet of Regensburg, in 1594, Cardinal Madruzzi, Pope Clement VIII's legate, made a serious complaint in the Pope's name about this, but it had no result. At present, the same variety and confusion remains. The Curia has only two remedies. One is by means of the confessions of the Jesuits, who work on consciences to the effect that men given benefices by bishops should still ask for bulls from Rome, and some do do this. The other means used by the Curia, in the case of important benefices and of men partly dependent on them, is that when an election or collation is made contrary to the terms of the concordat, the Curia annuls it, but then the Curia itself gives the benefice to the same person. This remedy was formerly much used on other occasions, too, not because it helped at the time, but because the documents are kept in later times to show that they had obedience.

In France, the Pragmatic Sanction was strongly attacked by Pius II, but the French clergy and the University of Paris firmly defended it. The Pope therefore addressed himself to King Louis XI and persuaded him that it was unseemly for him to accept the decrees of the Council of Basel, since when he was Dauphin and had quarrelled with his father, Pope Eugenius IV hired him to attack the Council. Persuaded by these arguments, King Louis gave way and revoked the Pragmatic Sanction in 1461. There followed protests from the University and remonstrances from the Parlement, which still survive, in which they explained to the king the burdens this would lay on the kingdom and on the clergy, with a careful calculation that in three years four millions had gone to Rome for beneficiary matters. Three years later, the same king revived the Pragmatic Sanction. Sixtus IV then opposed it and made a concordat to abolish it, which still survives; but this was not accepted, and the Pragmatic Sanction remained in force. Innocent VIII, Alexander VI, and Julius II did all they could to have it removed, but they were never able to succeed.

Finally, Leo X made a concordat with King Francis I which abolished the Pragmatic Sanction. It laid down that the chapters of cathedral churches and monasteries should lose their power of electing bishops and abbots. When vacancies occurred, the king would nominate a suitable person, and the pope would give him the benefice. The pope would not have the power to grant expectatives, or general or special reservations. Benefices that fell vacant for four months of the year would be conferred by the bishops on University graduates, and those falling vacant in the other eight months would be conferred freely by them. Every pope, once in his lifetime, would have the right to make every collator to benefices, if he had between ten and fifty in his gift, confer one as His Holiness wanted, or two if he had fifty or more in his gift. There were many difficulties in the way of accepting the concordat, and the University appealed to a future legitimate general council, but the authority and interests of King Francis were successful, and the concordat was published in France and put into execution. And so, after so many popes from 1076 to

1150 had had so many people excommunicated and killed in order to take from the rulers the right to confer bishoprics and give it to the chapters, Pius II and five of his successors fought, on the contrary, to take it from the chapters of France and give it to the king, and Leo X was at length successful. This is how changes of interest bring with them changes and contradictions in doctrine!

King Francis made many more laws to regulate the possession of benefices, and the concordat was observed by him. His son Henry II, when he was at war with Pope Julius III over Parma, did not observe it for some years. In 1550, he forbade the acceptance of any papal provision to benefices and ordered that all of them should be conferred by the bishops. When peace returned, however, an agreement was made and the concordat was again observed. Then, in 1560, the Estates-General met at Orléans while Charles IX was still a minor and made regulations about collations to benefices and abolished many of the provisions of the concordat. There followed great disturbances and wars in the kingdom. The Cardinal of Ferrara was sent to France as legate, and he obtained the suspension of the decrees of Orléans by promising that the Pope would issue a brief, remedying the abuses concerning which the ordinances had been made. After this, nothing was done—so at present, the concordat remains in force. So much for German and for French affairs.

The Italian situation, which we have described last, was greatly changed by the holding of the Council of Trent. The Council made many decrees on this subject to remedy the abuses mentioned above, which were very serious. From its beginning, which was in 1545, the Council began to take an interest in these reforms and to make many decrees, but they were not executed until the Council came to an end, which was in 1563, so that it can be said that all the provisions refer to this time. The Council's intention was to reform three abuses. The first was pluralism, the second hereditary benefices, the third was nonresidence. To root out every case of pluralism, it was laid down that even a cardinal might not have more than one benefice. If a benefice was so poor that it did not suffice for the expenses of its holder, then he could have another, but without cure of souls. The Council forbade commendams *ad vitam* [for life] of benefices with cure of souls, which was a covert way of possessing two; they laid down that, in future, monasteries should not be given *in commendam,* and that those which had been should be conferred in the normal way when vacancies occurred; they also forbade unions of benefices for life, which was another pretext for pluralism. In order to abolish hereditary succession, they quite forbade regresses and accesses. They absolutely forbade coadjutorships with the right of succession except in cathedrals and monasteries, and in those cases, they declared that the pope should not allow them without good reason.

For the last fourteen months, they discussed residence, with a certain amount of disagreement. Shortly before, the question had arisen among the Doctors as to whether the residence of bishops and others with cure of souls was *de iure divino* or *canonico* [whether they were obliged by the law of God or the law of the Church]. The Council was divided on this issue, and in April 1562, when a ballot was held, there were sixty-seven who held that it was an obligation by the law of God, thirty-three who thought that it was an obligation by the law of the Church, and thirty who believed that they ought not to decide this question without first discussing it with the pope. The first group was composed of the bishops from outside Italy and others who were rejected, the second and third groups included were composed of the bishops dependent on the Curia. If the obligation to reside was a matter of the law of God, it followed that the pope did not have the power to dispense from it, and also that the authority of bishops derived from the law of God, and that no one had the right to restrict it. That would have weakened the power of the Curia, which is why both sides were so involved in their points of view. They passed on to what steps were to be taken, and after fourteen months, the clergy were ordered to reside, without a declaration concerning which law obliged them to do so, but simply the provision of penalties for the nonresident. Otherwise, things were left as they had been.

The Council did not discuss reservations, a most important matter, because they had increased to excess. This was because the matter touched the Pope nearly. Reservations remained, in fact they increased.

It seemed that to have done away with unions and commendams for life, regresses, and coadjutorships, was to have reformed most of the abuses, even if not all of them. But a device was soon found which was even more effective than these four, and that was the *pension*. To charge benefices with pensions is not a modern innovation. What is new is the method, and the frequent use made of it. When the goods of the Church were in common, the word pension was unheard of; and after the foundation of benefices, the rule observed by everyone was that benefices should be conferred whole and without diminution. Later, when clerics began to go to law with one another, in doubtful cases, one man would give up his rights in return for receiving part of the income, called a pension. Again, if two men with benefices exchanged them, for some good reason and with their superior's permission, if the incomes from the two benefices were unequal, the man who gave up the richer benefice would receive a pension. Later, when someone resigned his benefice with the bishop's permission, the bishop would give him a pension to support him. About 1200, papal decretals can be found concerning these three kinds of pension. Even the French were prepared to accept these kinds legally, but refused to accept the others, which are given to one man simply to give him something to live on, to another because he deserves well of the Apostolic See, to another because he is well-educated or virtuous, or has done a service for the Church or for a prelate, or just because he has the pope's favor. The canon lawyers say that all these are good reasons for granting pensions, and they are not ashamed to add that even without any reason, the pope has the power to grant a pension upon any benefice to anyone he wants. And the man who accepts it without any reason other than that is the will of the pope can do so with a good conscience. And so, whereas formerly a man might hold two benefices with cure of souls, but one nominally and the other *in commendam,* or two benefices which were united for life, so that he was obliged to pay someone to perform his duties in one of them, nowadays he is given one nominally and the remainder of what he wants in the form of a pension. It is the same for him, in fact it is to his advantage, because he used to be responsible for the mistakes of his substitute, and so he had to pay some attention to this, whereas now he has no responsibilities, but the advantages are the same. Similarly, the man who took a coadjutor or resigned with powers of regress had to take some thought for the benefice he shared which might become completely his again; but in resigning it and receiving a pension, he is free from all cares. If his successor dies or gives the benefice to someone else, it does not matter to him, his pension is safe, and he has nothing to worry about.

It is much more convenient to have a pension than a benefice. In the first place, many benefices require that the holder be ordained and also be of an age to be ordained, whereas for a pension it is sufficient to have received the first tonsure and to be seven years old. Pensions are also given to laymen; for example, it is customary to give them to the knights of St. Peter, founded by Leo X, to those of St. Paul, founded by Paul III, to other pious orders of knighthood founded by Pius IV, and to the knights of Loreto, founded by Sixtus V, who can be given pensions of one hundred fifty or one hundred twenty scudi, and they can also be given to whoever the pope pleases. In the case of benefices, even at the time when it was possible to hold more than one, there was always something that went wrong. Dispensations were necessary, which was an expense, and even then, the Doctors raised a doubt about whether a man could in good conscience possess them. But one can have any number of pensions without scruple; they are never incompatible with one another. A pension can be granted, together with the power of transferring it to someone else at one's pleasure, which cannot be done with benefices without submitting to the conditions and going through the ritual of resignation, and resignations are only valid if the man who resigns survives for twenty days more, whereas one can transfer a pension on one's deathbed.

What matters above all is that the pension can be "extinguished," which is to make of it what in Italian is called *pecunia numerata* [ready cash], whereas every contract concerning a benefice is considered to be a case of simony. To "extinguish" a pension is simply to accept a lump sum which frees the donor from paying it any longer. The amount of compensation is fixed by agreement according to the age of the pensioner. Before our own time, there was no way of turning a benefice into ready money; that would have given great offense to God and man. But now it is done legally. I have a benefice worth two hundred scudi, I resign it to Antonio, reserving for myself a pension of a hundred scudi, and then I immediately "extinguish," that is, resign it, for seven hundred scudi. By this means I have made seven hundred scudi in cash out of my benefice without committing any sin. There are some people, not very penetrating, to whom it seems that this procedure is the same as selling my benefice for seven hundred scudi; this shows how they lack judgment. There are many other ways in which the pension, as it is now used, is much more convenient than unions, commendams, coadjutorships, and regresses. Some people, exaggerating the pope's powers of making money for the needs of the Apostolic See, say that if he were to extend regresses, he would get all the money he wanted; but they show that they do not understand beneficiary matters. He would not get a penny by this; pensions are much more useful and convenient. And so, it was easy to execute the provisions made by the Council because they were actually profitable. However, the abolition of monastic commendams, which the Council also recommended, has not yet been implemented. Many which were officially abolished have returned *in commendam* because they could not find a means to escape. Pensions cannot be levied upon benefices by anyone but the pope, a matter of great profit to the Curia.

This change has taken place in Italy as a result of the Council of Trent. The Council did not deal with reservations, which increased and every day still increase, so that a good five-sixths of Italian benefices are at the pope's disposition, and he has good reason to hope that he will acquire the other sixth as well.

By the rules of the chancery, there are reserved to the pope all the benefices which John XXII and Benedict XII had reserved. Also reserved are all the benefices obtained by any official of the Curia, even after he has given up the office; also all the patriarchates, archbishoprics, bishoprics, and monasteries which are worth more than two hundred gold florins; and all the benefices which are waiting to be conferred by someone, but which remain vacant by reason of the resignation, deprivation, or death of the collator until his successor takes peaceful possession; the higher ranks after the bishop in cathedral churches and the highest ranks in collegiate churches; priorates, headships [*prepositure*], and other monastic ranks; the preceptorships of all orders except military ones; the benefices of everyone in the household of the pope or of any cardinal, even if they are no longer in his service, either because they have left it or because the cardinal is dead. Also reserved are all the benefices of members of the Curia who die while the court is travelling, as well as all the benefices of chamberlains and runners. Besides all these benefices, which include all the important ones and a great part of the rest, the pope reserves all benefices of whatever kind that fall vacant for eight months of the year, leaving only four months for others, and this only in the case of benefices which have not been named above. Besides this, by a constitution of Pope Pius V, all the benefices which fall vacant because of heresy or for confidential reasons are reserved, and all those that are not conferred according to the decree of the Council of Trent. If all these reservations are added together, it will be found that at least five-sixths of all benefices are filled by the pope, and one-sixth by all the other collators together.

Praise should be given where it is due, and I must not omit to mention how conscientious the popes have been to ensure that bishops and other collators do not fall into any abuses. They have never allowed them the power of uniting or commending benefices for life; they have never allowed them to give dispensations to hold incompatible benefices in plurality, or to grant regresses or coadjutorships with the right of succession. With the same conscientiousness, they have not allowed them to impose any pension, even a tiny one, upon a benefice. Similarly, they have not allowed them to accept resignations *ad favorem*, and even in the case of absolute resignations, which were a most ancient custom in the Church, Pope Pius V, in 1568, forbade all bishops under severe penalties to give a benefice which had fallen vacant by resignation to any friend or relation of the man who had resigned, warning them that they should not allow anyone to be mentioned or pointed out to them as the man whom the man who had resigned would like to be given the benefice.

It is constantly affirmed by all the canon lawyers and casuists that every bargain concerning benefices is simoniacal, when the pope is not party to it; but his consent makes it all legitimate. Their assumption, which is not very edifying, is that the pope, in matters beneficiary, cannot commit simony. The more moderate canon lawyers limit his power, distinguishing between one sort of simony which is prohibited by the law of God and another which is prohibited by human law, and adding that the simony which the pope is unable to commit is only that prohibited by human law. In spite of this qualification, they come up against the same stumbling block, because what is neither evil of its own nature nor prohibited by God does not deserve to be called simony, and it is unnecessary to make a human law against it. Whoever looks deep into the matter and does not use words to hide the truth will see that all simony is prohibited by God. Certainly, it cannot be said that the pope has failed to make the other bishops do their duty, and God has given the popes much grace in that they have been able to keep the rest of the Church free from simony, even if they have not been able to extend this benefit to themselves and to the Curia. And if one day, as is hoped, some good pope will think of reforming the Curia, it will be something most easy to do simply by applying to himself the laws which he has imposed on the other bishops. We could expect this most useful reformation to happen soon, were it not for the adulation of the Curia, who suggest to the popes that since they are in a position, at least in Italy and in other small places, to be free from all restrictions, it is not good for them to give up this freedom—a renunciation which would be to the prejudice of the Apostolic See. However, from what has been said above it is quite clear that whether or not the pope has such complete authority over the property and the benefices of the Church, he is subject to no rule in their administration. Let us reason things out. If the church in a certain place is the owner of the property which it possesses because the authority was transferred to it by the previous owner with the permission of the ruler who gave it the property by law, then the property ought to be administered by those who are appointed to do so, in the first place by the law, in the second place according to the conditions laid down by the donor who was the previous owner, and in the third place according to the arrangements made by the church itself, the new owner, as long as these are not contrary to the other conditions. This is so clear and so obvious that it cannot be doubted except by someone who lacks common sense, or by one who in speech and action does not follow what he feels within him. The clergy were made the administrators of these goods by virtue of laws which granted to the Christian colleges the power of acquiring landed property, and by virtue of the wills and the gifts of men who left them their goods, and by virtue of the authority that the Church has given to these clergy in the canons. Therefore they are obliged to look after and to dispose of these goods according to the terms of the laws, gifts, and wills and according to the canons. If they do anything to the contrary, it can only be called injustice, injury, and usurpation.

Now, the canon lawyers say that the pope has full authority over the goods and benefices of the Church, so that he can unite them, divide them, abolish them, diminish them, turn them into new ones, give them *ad nutum, ad tempus, sub conditione* [at his pleasure, for the time being, conditionally], reserve them, change them, confer them before they fall vacant, impose on them rents, taxes, and pensions. Wherever benefices are concerned, the will of the pope is in the place of justice. This is not enough for them, but they even add that the pope can divert what is bequeathed *ad pias causas* [for pious causes] to other works and can alter testamentary dispositions, applying to one purpose what was intended for another. Martin Navarro and some of the more moderate canon lawyers qualify this proposition about the power of the pope to alter a last will and testament, restricting it to those cases where there is a legitimate reason to do so, which would otherwise be to deprive a man of his own property and of the power which is his in virtue of natural and divine law. They even descend to details and say that the pope cannot without good reason give to one church what has been bequeathed to another. Navarro also says that the saying of the gloss which the canon lawyers like to quote, that is "in beneficiary matters, the will of the pope is in place of justice," is meant to apply only to matters which are *de iure positivo* [matters of human law] and not to what cannot be done without breaking either divine or natural law. Those who do not give the pope absolute power would also allow him to be subject to the canons of the Church. The above-mentioned Doctor Navarro also adds that where it says in the *Clementine Decretals* that the pope has the power to dispose freely of benefices, "free" means without permission, without consultation, and in spite of the opposition of whosoever, but also without prejudice to any third party. If we accept this interpretation, and it seems right to do so, then here we see a serious argument both against reservations, because they are to the prejudice of the bishops, and against giving benefices to foreigners, because this is to the prejudice of natives of the country, in favor of whom the wills were made. And this argument would not be too favorable to the claim to be able to alter a last will and testament, because this is to the prejudice of the memory of the dead man. I well know that the others will reply to this that it is all true when there is no legitimate reason; the point is, who is to be the judge of what counts as a legitimate reason, because if it is the same man whose authority is to be restricted, one might just as well give him absolute power as power limited by a "legitimate reason." What Navarro adds is to be noted carefully, and that is that in our time the opinion of lawyers who so greatly enlarge the power of the pope in beneficiary matters is gladly believed by men who want to acquire many benefices, and they accept it because it suits their ambition and avarice. He relates that he heard a famous theologian and a canon lawyer say openly that they would gladly take all the benefices in the kingdom, if they were given them by the pope. Pius V, on the contrary, told him that lawyers are accustomed to attribute to the pope more power than is fitting. He replied that there are also some who take too much away, but that it is proper to take a middle course, paying due respect to the laws of God and man, and not doing like modern lawyers who enlarge the laws of man so much that they clash with the laws of God. Out of the reverence which I owe to the pope, I do not want to contradict the opinion which gives him so much power; I shall simply raise a few difficulties, and when they are resolved, the truth of this matter will be quite clear.

The first difficulty is whether the pope has such great authority as has been given him. Not by Christ, because the authority He gave was simply authority in spiritual matters, that of binding and loosing, that is, of forgiving or retaining sins. But the property of the Church is held *iure humano* and not *divino* [by human, not by divine law], as we decided above; therefore the pope did not receive this power from God. Still less did he receive it by virtue of the laws of secular rulers, the testamentary dispositions of individuals, or the canons of the Church, because all these gave the administration of the goods of each church to the clergy of that church and laid down definite conditions which could not be changed. So he could not have acquired it from them. But there were no other owners, and no one could have authority unless the owner granted it. It remains to see by what other means it was given him.

To this difficulty, a second can be added. If the pope possesses this authority, how is it that his predecessors did not exercise it for over a thousand years? It cannot be argued that they had no need of it in those days, because for the three hundred years from 800 to 1100, so great were the disorders all over Europe, that those of the present time are comparatively tolerable. Yet no pope interfered with the property of other churches, although they badly needed looking after. And even after the popes had begun to interfere, none of them exercised full and absolute power until Clement IV. Even Clement himself did not openly claim such power, but mentioned it more or less by the way, and this does not fully prove the point, because very often what is said in one way casually is put very diffierently when it is considered carefully and expressed explicitly. Still less can it be said that this authority was for a good purpose, because it seems that it was by this means that almost all the abuses were introduced. This is how commendams came in, and pensions, regresses, unions, resignations, expectatives, reservations, annates, *quindennia,* and other devices, which no one can defend except by alleging the general corruption of the times.

There remains a third difficulty which is no less serious, and that is that Christian kingdoms have always complained of this absolute power, ever since the popes began to exercise it, and they have opposed it, as was described above, so that the popes were compelled to limit it. This limitation did not come about by their condescending to give up the authority they claimed, but by the sort of bargain which is made when one's rights are not clear, making concordats with different kingdoms, and deciding by contract how far their power is to extend. They could not have done this to the prejudice of their successors, had the papal power been so very great. Pope Leo X made the concordat to get rid of the Pragmatic Sanction. He calls it a "concordat" himself in the bull. But a man with absolute power does not make concordats; he treats with his subjects as a superior, and he makes concessions. I am not twisting the sense of the words, but describing exactly what happened. Leo not only asked for *concordia*, but said: *"Illam veri contractus et obligationis inter nos et Sedem apostolicam prædictam ex una, et præfatum regem ex altera partibus legitime initi."* [It was a genuine and binding contract between the Apostolic See and the aforesaid king.] Someone will ask for an explanation here. There was a conflict between the Pope and the king of France because the Pope claimed to have absolute power over benefices (to reserve them, and so on), whereas the king claimed that this authority belonged to the prelates of the kingdom. They were the two parties at law, and to end the dispute they made a genuine and binding contract which declared what their respective powers were. How can anyone say that the Pope's claim was a legitimate and clear one? I cannot say that I know the answer to any of these difficulties, and I leave it to wise men to judge whether there is any answer. I will simply say that by carrying on in the way in which men carried on for more than a thousand years, and administering the goods of the Church in each diocese by means of the ministers of that diocese, every difficulty is avoided. If it is possible to learn from examples, it follows that they would in that case be better and more fruitfully administered than they are now.

The first three questions considered the wealth and property of the Church. There remains the fourth, which relates to their fruits, revenues, and incomes. The Holy Fathers, who wrote before the division of church goods into four parts, all agreed that the goods of the Church were the goods of the poor, and that the clergy in charge of them had no other power than that of administering them and dispensing them according to the needs of the poor. Ministers who used these goods for other purposes they called not only thieves, but also sacrilegious. Not all the clergy administered these goods (although they all lived on them, like widows, the poor, and other unfortunate people), but just the deacons and subdeacons and some others. They were responsible to the bishop and in some places to the priests as well. After the division had been made and benefices had been instituted, although it might seem that the bishop and the priests and the other clergy might do whatever they liked with the income from the benefices as it was their own property, all the same the writers speak of it in the same way, saying that a cleric might only spend as much of the income as his needs demanded, and that he was obliged to spend the rest on pious works. They were quite right to say this because the division could not change the essence of the matter, and if property subject to an obligation is divided, the same obligation falls on both the parts. Among others who wrote after the division, St. Gregory, who was more than a hundred years afterwards, and St. Bernard, who was nearly a thousand years afterwards, cried out against those who put to ill uses the income from benefices, treating them as usurpers of the property of the community and murderers of the poor, who should have been supported by this income. So wrote all the Doctors until 1250, when things began to be discussed in a more subtle manner. They held firm to the traditional view that it was a sin to put to bad use money that surpassed the needs of the individual cleric, and they discussed whether a benefice-holder who did this sinned in the same way as a man who puts his own money to ill use, or whether besides sinning they were also obliged to make restitution, like a man who puts to ill use the property of others. If they were the owners of the fruits of the benefices (or, as the laws say, if they had the "usufruct" of the benefices) then however much they sinned in maladministering the property, they did injustice to no one and were not bound to give anything back because they had maladministered their own property, not that of someone else. If, however, they are simply administrators with nothing but the power of providing for their own needs (what the law calls "usuari") then they are obliged to make restitution of whatever they did not spend in a proper manner; and those who receive free gifts from them are obliged to give them back because they have accepted them from someone who is not the owner. Conscience constrains me to raise this difficulty, which has been discussed these three hundred and fifty years and is still unsolved, with an equal number of authors on each side. Lately, there has been a sharp controversy on this subject between Martin Navarro, a canon lawyer and a casuist of great reputation, and Francisco Sarmiento—Navarro holding that the clergy are not the owners but only the administrators, and that they not only sin, but are also obliged to make restitution. Cardinal Cajetan holds a middle opinion, arguing that it is one thing to speak of bishops and rich abbots, and another to speak of those who have only enough to live on or a little more. These latter, having no more than their share, are owners of it, but the richer ones have the share of the Church and the share of the poor included in their income, and so they are obliged in justice to give alms and to do other pious works as an act of restitution. He even argues that men who are given Church property by the pope in order to make them rich or ennoble them are obliged to restore it, since every gift of such goods which is not a work of piety or a case of necessity is dissipation and usurpation.

I believe that it is possible to resolve all the doubts arising from this subject without subtle disputation. And firstly, to speak separately of the income which by will or other original foundation is dedicated to some pious work, I believe that the income is so tied to that purpose, to take it for oneself or for some other worldly use can freely be called usurpation of the goods of another. If any benefice-holder ceases to execute the wishes of the donors, keeping the income for himself or giving it to others, I do not believe that he can by means of any pretext or bull differentiate himself from any executor of a will who takes for himself what was bequeathed to others. I believe that everyone who is not indulging in self-deception will hold this to be true. On the other side, justice requires that whoever receives service should give the servant his reward, and he can spend it how he pleases. There is no doubt that the cantor, the organist, and other such servants of the Church have a right to the payments that they receive. It is not inappropriate to say that the priests, too, and other clergy, for their services to the Church, should have their reward, to which they have a right. When a benefice is created with an obligation to serve the Church in some specified way, as is the case with many canonries, mansionaries, theological prebends, and other such benefices, then it is not improper to say that they are the payments for these services.

There remain the benefices which are so old that all memory of their foundation has been lost, and so it is not known whether obligations are attached or not. Here, too, the man of conscience can decide by considering the size of the income and the service which he renders to the Church. If these two are equal, he can consider the benefice as his salary; but if the income is much greater, he will never be able to delude himself into believing that so much money was left to him to do as he pleases, nor can he ignore the fact that the foundation must have carried some obligation with it, because it is implausible that so large a sum should have been assigned to him alone. The controversy among the Doctors which is difficult to resolve in the abstract is quite easy to resolve in practice in individual cases. Conscience, for everyone who is not so evil that theirs has suffocated, resolves all difficulties in particular cases with ease, and God has left uncertain no one who wishes to keep His commandments.

As for new acquisitions, every prudent man would have thought that they were finished, or at least that there would not be many more, and those would be acquired slowly. Secular priests, monks, and military orders have no one devoted to them any longer. The mendicants, who have already been empowered to acquire property, cannot hope to succeed where they have been unsuccessful up till now; and where they have been successful, if they have not lost their support, they can still hope for something more, but not very much. The others, like the Capuchins, who had had themselves excluded from the privilege granted by the Council of Trent which permitted all religious orders to acquire property, continue to be well thought of on account of their poverty; and so, as soon as they were to change their constitution in the slightest, they would not acquire property, and they would lose their alms. So it seems that there is no way of going forward. If anyone were to want to found an order with the power of acquiring property, no one would believe him; if he were to found a truly mendicant order, he could not hope either for property while their poverty lasted, or for trust if it changed. All the same, our century has not lacked a method of its own, which is not inferior to all the methods of the past, and that is the foundation of the Jesuits, who profess a mixture of poverty and riches, and by their poverty gain trust and devotion, while with the other hand they are able to own property and to take whatever the Society is given. They have founded professed houses which are forbidden to possess landed property, but also colleges which have the power to acquire and possess. They say, and say well, that no simple form of government in this world is perfect, but a mixed government is useful in any situation. They say that the state of evangelic poverty borrowed from the mendicants has this defect: that in this way one can only support those who are already on the right road, which cannot be a large number. But in their colleges they accept and instruct young men, and teach them, besides other virtues, how to live in evangelic poverty. And so, poverty is their aim and their essence; property is simply an "accident." All the same, it is better to base one's belief on what men practice than on what they preach. Up to the present time, they write that they have had twenty-one professed houses and two hundred and ninety-three colleges, from which proportion everyone may conclude which is their substance and which their accidents. It is certain that their acquisitions have been very great, and that they are still increasing.

Just as all the temporal goods possessed by the Church come from the alms and offerings of the faithful, so the ancient sanctuary in the Old Testament was raised by means of alms and offerings. When the people had offered enough, but the offerings continued to come in,

those in charge of the building went to Moses and said
that the people had brought too much for the work which
the Lord had commanded. And Moses issued a procla-
mation that no more offerings should be made for the
sanctuary, because enough and more had been offered.
It can be seen that God does not want superfluity in His
temple. And if in the Old Testament, which was worldly,
He did not want everything for His ministers, He wants it
still less in the New. Where are these acquisitions going
to end? When is it to be said amongst us: "The people
have offered more than enough"? When the ministers of
the temple were the thirteenth part of the people, they
were given a tenth part, and it was not allowed to go
beyond this. Now they are a hundredth part, and they
have perhaps more than a quarter. It is not fitting that
the goods of the Church should increase infinitely, and
that the whole world should become their tenants. Among
Christians, the secular laws have not determined the
quantity of goods which each man is to possess, because
what he acquires today, he alienates tomorrow. But here
is a corporation which never dies, and which can always
acquire property but never alienate it. In the Old Testament, the Levites were given the tithes because they were
the heirs of God, and so they were forbidden to have any
other share. It is right that anyone who wants to take
advantage of their privileges should take them all, and
not only those which are to his own profit.

I have described in detail how the goods of the Church
were acquired, who was put in charge of them, and how
they were distributed. But I have not said anything about
what happened when on the death of a benefice-holder
some of the income was found not yet spent, whether he
disposed of it by will, or whether it passed to other people *ab intestato* [because he died intestate]. While the
goods of every church were in common and administered
together, it is certain that whatever was found in the
hands of a minister remained part of the common stock
and was administered in the same way as before by his
successor. But when benefices were instituted, at the
same time canons were made to the effect that whatever was found in the hands of a benefice-holder be-

longed to the Church, meaning by the Church the college, if it was run as a college and had a common table. If the benefice-holder did not have colleagues, then "Church" meant his successor, who was obliged to administer this leftover income in the same way as his deceased predecessor had done, from whom the income came. This was the custom until the year 1300. However, clerics with benefices very often possessed patrimonies of their own, or acquired goods by their own skill and industry, and it was also said that this was absolutely their own, and that they could bequeath it to whoever they pleased, whereas they could not dispose of the income of the benefice in this way. It followed that clerics with small benefices which did not exceed their expenses bequeathed their entire property, and if by economizing they had saved something from the income, they considered it to have been acquired by their industry, and they disposed of it in the same way. And so the custom grew up in many Christian kingdoms that the holders of lesser benefices could bequeath the income from the benefice as well, and if they did not, their heirs *ab intestato* would succeed to it just as they succeeded to the patrimony. What was bequeathed by bishops remained subject to the ancient canons of the Church. After this, in some kingdoms, the bishops also obtained by custom the power of bequeathing the income of their bishoprics, so that around 1300, there were three different customs in different countries. One was where no cleric could dispose of the surplus income from his benefice; another, where the income from benefices was treated in the same way as the patrimonies of the clergy; and a third, where the lesser clergy disposed of their surplus as their own, but that of the bishops went to the Church. In the period following 1300, when the popes had more need of money than usual, they sent their stewards to the kingdoms where it was customary for the churches to inherit from the deceased benefice-holder, and before his successor was appointed, they took all the surplus and put it into the papal treasury. This was easy to accomplish, because when the benefice was vacant, there was no one in whose interest it would be to stop them, and when a successor had been appointed, he easily acquiesced in a *fait accompli*. They began to send such stewards wherever they could and to call all the income left at the death of an incumbent "spoils," and the papal officials sent for them were called "collectors." The popes seized these spoils in silence, where they could, without there being any law to grant them to them. There was always murmuring on the part of the heirs of the dead priest and of others on account of the extortions of the collectors and subcollectors, who included even the church ornaments in the spoils, and they gave the heirs much trouble by trying to make the goods which the priest had acquired by his industry or had taken from his patrimony appear to be taken from the benefice and by deciding in doubtful cases that the property belonged to the pope, excommunicating anyone who opposed them.

In France, it had become customary that the spoils of bishops and abbots should go to the pope. In 1385, Charles VI forbade this, laying down that the heirs should succeed to these goods just as to patrimonies. In many areas, the custom of spoils has continued up to the present century, when the extortions of collectors so aggravated men's complaints that some dared oppose the custom openly and deny that the spoils of deceased clerics should go to the treasury of the pope. So, in 1544, Paul III became the first to issue a bull on this subject, in which he said that certain overcurious people, in order to usurp the rights of the apostolic treasury and defraud it, were raising a doubt as to whether the goods of prelates and others, called spoils, belonged to the treasury, since there was no apostolic constitution laying down that they did. However, from the fact that they had sent collectors to various places, it clearly appeared that the intention of the Apostolic See was to reserve them and take them for the treasury. Therefore he declared and ordained that the spoils of all clerics who died in whatever kingdom or dominion, on both sides of the Alps, and on both sides of the seas, belonged to the papal treasury, even if collectors had never been sent for them. And so, because some overdiligent people tried to liberate a few small provinces from this burden, they caused it to be imposed on the whole world. The bull has only been implemented in the customary places; but this is how things have always happened. Bulls have been issued and then, while the world wonders at the novelty, they have been left for some time without being executed. Then, when a good opportunity presents itself, they are put into execution with censures and other penalties for nonobservance, as if they had been in force before but the malice of certain individuals had so far prevented their execution.

Until 1560, spoils only included what was found left over from the income of the benefice on the death of the incumbent. In that year, Pius IV issued a bull which included under the title "spoils" (which all over the world, on both sides of the mountains and the seas, belong to the papal treasury) everything that the incumbent acquired by illegal trade or by any other means contrary to canon law. This includes quite enough, because it is called "illegal trade" whenever something is sold in the same state in which it was bought. Afterwards, the canon law forbade the clergy many kinds of customary activities which brought in a considerable amount of money, and so, the treasury made considerable gain, which would bring in a large income if the bull concerning spoils could be executed in half of Italy, where it is still not executed, and in Germany and in France and in other kingdoms, which have not yet accepted it. In the kingdoms of Castille, too, they do not take the spoils of all the clergy, but only of the bishops, by laws of Charles V and Philip II.

The canon lawyers defend the right to spoils with the argument that the pope is the owner of all church revenues. Those who speak more moderately call him the administrator. As a result of this doctrine, the custom has been introduced in Rome that if anyone has usurped a benefice or has robbed the Church in some other way, he then makes an agreement with the papal treasury to give it a share and keep the rest with a good conscience. When the agreement has been made and he has paid the stipulated amount, everyone says that he can legally keep the remainder as his own, because the pope, as was said, is the owner or administrator of all church revenues.

# History of the Council of Trent

*(Istoria del Concilio Tridentino)*

## Sarpi's Aim and Method

I am not ignorant of the laws of history, nor of how histories differ from annals and memoirs. I know that a plain narration of events of the same sort is dull for both the writer and the reader, and that to include details of little importance deserves to be called foolish pedantry. Nevertheless, I notice frequent repetitions and narration of details in Homer, while Xenophon, in his *Persian Expedition*, holds the attention more and is more instructive when he describes the talk of the soldiers, serious and amusing, than when he deals with the actions and opinions of princes. I believe that every subject needs its own appropriate form, and that mine cannot follow the usual rules. I am sure that this work will be read by few and will soon be forgotten, not so much from its formal defects as from the nature of the subject. There is evidence of this from what has happened to similar works. However, I am not looking for notoriety now, nor for eternal fame hereafter. It will be enough if I can be of use to one man, to whom I shall show it because I know that he will profit from it. As for the future, I know that this book will have whatever fate circumstances bring. [Book Three, opening.]

I thought about giving some form to the materials that I had collected, which would not be beyond my powers, and which would be appropriate to the subject. It occurred to me that of all that had happened to Christians in this age (and perhaps of all that would happen in the years to come), this Council is the most important. Men find it useful and pleasant to understand the details of matters they consider important; so I judged the form of a day-by-day narrative to be appropriate. There were two arguments against this opinion of mine. The first was that this form was not appropriate to tell the story of the happenings of the twenty-nine years that preceded this Council and those of the other fourteen years in which on two occasions it seemed to be sleeping—possibly alive, possibly dead. The second objection was that all the material necessary to a continuous narrative did not and could not exist. Following nature and fitting the form to the matter (and not like the schools, which fit the matter to the form), I thought it not absurd to write a year-by-year account of the years leading up to the Council and between the sessions and a day-by-day account only of the period when the Council was sitting in the cases where I have sufficient information, trusting that if anyone ever reads this piece of work, he will forgive my omissions of those things about which I was unable to find out. For if an important part is quickly lost, even those matters which the persons concerned make every effort to completely preserve in their memories, how much more will be lost of this, where a great number of extremely able people have done all they can to cover up the affair altogether! Of course, important matters deserve to be kept mysterious as long as it is to the common good to do so; but when not to know the whole story is extremely harmful for some people, and useful for others, it is not surprising if men with contrary ends proceed by contrary means. Much to the point is the common and celebrated maxim that he who tries to avoid loss has more right on his side than he who tries to make a positive gain. And so, this essay of mine, for the reasons I have given, is somewhat uneven in its treatment. Such unevenness can also be found in some famous writers. However, this will not be my defense, but that whoever has not written in this uneven way has not written the history of the Council of Trent, or anything of like nature. [Book Seven, opening.]

I have often included in my account various details which I am certain many will consider not worth mentioning, just as I used to think myself; but finding them preserved and noted in the memoirs of those who were present at these events, I am persuaded that there is something which I have not noticed which makes them worth remembering, and I have decided to include them, following the opinion of my sources, rather than my own. Some sharp mind will perhaps discover in these details something important which I was not aware of, and those who do not, will have wasted but little time in reading them. [Book Seven, Chapter Five.]

# BOOK ONE

## Chapter One

My plan is to write the history of the Council of Trent, because although many famous historians of our time have touched on details of it in their writings, and Johann Sleidan,[1] a most diligent writer, has with great pains told the story of the events leading up to it, there has not been any general work collecting it all together.

As soon as I had acquired a taste for studying human affairs, I become extremely curious to know all about the Council. After reading carefully both the books written about it and the official documents (whether published or circulating in manuscript), I made further researches. I went to a great deal of trouble and looked at the surviving writings of the prelates and others who had taken part in the Council, at their memoirs and their publicly expressed opinions (preserved by the authors themselves or by others), and at the letters written from Rome. I was lucky enough to see whole collections of notes and letters written by men who had played a great part in those proceedings. Having collected material abundant enough for a narrative, I have now decided to organize it.

I will describe the causes of the Council and the management of an ecclesiastical assembly, which for twenty-two years was demanded by some men, while others postponed it and put obstacles in its way for various reasons and by varying means. For another eighteen years it was sometimes in session, sometimes dipersed. It was held for many different reasons, yet what emerged was quite contrary to the plans of those who had fought for it and the fears of those who had done

[1] German historian (1506–56), author of *Commentaries* on the reign of Charles V.

their best to hinder it. A fine example to make one trust in God and not in the wisdom of men.

For this Council, which pious men desired and procured to reunite the Church (which was beginning to split apart), has, on the contrary, made the split a permanent one and the parties to it irreconcilable. It was planned by the princes to reform the Church, but it has brought about the greatest corruption of the Church since the name of "Christian" was first heard. The bishops took part in it to recover their episcopal authority, which the pope had come almost to monopolize, but it has made them lose what little authority they had and has given them a vested interest in their own slavery. On the other hand, feared and avoided by the Curia as an effective means of limiting the papal power, once so small and now grown so unlimited, this Council has so strengthened and confirmed it over that part of the Church which is still subject to the pope, that it was never so great nor so well rooted.

It would not be inappropriate to call this story the Iliad of our age. As I unfold it, I shall follow truth closely, since I have no prejudice to make me deviate from it. The reader who notices me linger over some periods, and pass quickly over others, will realize that not all fields are equally fertile, and not all crops are worth keeping. Of those that are worth keeping, some ears will escape the reaper; as in every harvest, there will be something left to glean.

But before anything else, I ought to point out that it was a most ancient custom of the Christian Church to settle religious controversies and to reform corrupt discipline by means of synods. For example, the first controversy, which arose while many of the apostles were still alive, was whether converts to Christianity were bound to observe the Mosaic Law, and it was settled by a meeting in Jerusalem of four apostles and of all the faithful who were in the city. This example was followed for more than two hundred years. When problems arose in each province, even while persecution was raging, the bishops and the most important members of the churches met to solve them, this being the only way to reunite the divisions and to reconcile contrary opinions.

After it pleased God to give peace to His Church by the conversion of Constantine, communication between churches improved—and splits became more common and now involved the Empire instead of a city, or at most a province, as before. So councils, the customary remedy, had to be enlarged as well, and Constantine having called a council of the whole Empire, it became known as the great and holy synod. Some time after, it was also called a general and ecumenical council, although it did not include the whole Church (much of which was outside the frontiers of the Roman Empire), just as it was customary at that time to call the Emperor the ruler of the whole inhabited world, although the Empire did not contain a tenth of it. Following this precedent, on the occasion of other religious disputes, similar councils were called by Constantine's successors. Even when the Empire was divided into East and West, councils continued to be called for the whole Empire.

However, after the split between East and West, and after the eastern part had been invaded by the Saracens and the western part had been divided among many different princes, the name of general and ecumenical council was no longer thought to refer to the unity of the Roman Empire. Both the Greeks and ourselves now thought it meant the unity of those states which obeyed the Roman pontiff in ecclesiastical affairs. These states continued to meet in council, not primarily to settle religious disputes as before, but to organize Crusades, or to settle divisions within the Roman church, or to deal with disputes between the popes and Christian princes.

At the beginning of the sixteenth century after the birth of Our Lord, there seemed no urgent reason for holding a council, nor did it seem that there would be one for a long time. The objections of many churches to the dominance of the Curia seemed to have died down, and the whole of Western Christendom belonged to the Church of Rome. The only exception was a tiny one— where the Alps join the Pyrenees there remained some of the old Waldensians, or more accurately Albigensians, but they were so uncivilized and illiterate that they could not communicate their doctrines to anyone else, and anyway, they had such a sinister reputation with their neighbors for impiety and obscenity, that there was no danger the plague would spread.

In a few corners of Bohemia there were also small numbers of people with the same beliefs, the remains of the Picards, but there was no question of their numbers increasing, for the same reason. In the same kingdom of Bohemia there were the followers of Jan Hus, who called themselves Utraquists, but they hardly differed from the Roman Church except in giving the chalice to the congregation at Holy Communion. These were not important either because their numbers were small, because they lacked education, and because it did not seem either that they wished to teach their doctrines or that others wished to learn them.

There had been, however, some danger of schism. Julius II, who was more interested in military than in religious affairs, and who as pope had treated princes and cardinals with too little consideration, had forced some of them to separate from him and to call a council. Add to this the fact that Louis XII, who had been excommunicated by the same pope, had withdrawn his obedience and allied himself with the separatist cardinals, and it seemed that this would have been the beginning of some important developments. But Julius died in time, and the skillful diplomat Leo succeeded him, and he quickly pacified the cardinals and the kingdom of France, so that a fire which seemed as if it might consume the Church was put out with remarkable ease and speed.

Leo X, as one might have expected from a man of good birth and education, brought many accomplishments to the office of pope. He had a remarkable humanist learning; he was extremely pleasant to deal with; he had an almost supernatural charm; he was very generous and much inclined to favor artists and men of letters, qualities which had not been seen for a long time in a man in his position. And he would have been a perfect pope if he had added to these qualities a slightly greater piety and a little knowledge of religion, but he was not much interested in either. Although he was good at giving, he was not self-sufficient at acquisition, but relied on Lorenzo Pucci, Cardinal of Santiquattro, who was able enough at this.

So Leo found himself without problems and, one might say, without enemies, for the schism was ended, and those few Waldensians and Utraquists are not worth considering. He spent easily and gave generously to his relations, to the courtiers, and to literary men. When the other means by which the Roman court was accustomed to attract the riches of other regions were exhausted, he thought he would try that of indulgences.

This method of raising money began to be used after 1100.[2] A short while before, Pope Urban II had given a plenary indulgence and remission of all sins to whoever went on Crusade to conquer the Holy Sepulchre from the Mohammedans, and this was followed for centuries by his successors. Some of them extended the indulgence (as always happens with new inventions) to those who paid for a soldier, being unable or unwilling to serve personally. And then, in the course of time, it was also extended to wars on Christians who were not members of the Roman Church. Much money was raised under these pretexts, all or most of which was then used for other purposes.

Following these precedents, Leo, on the advice of the Cardinal of Santiquattro, issued an indulgence for the whole of Christendom, applicable to whoever contributed money, and including even the dead, who would be freed from the pains of purgatory, he claimed, when the payment was made. He added permission to eat eggs and dairy produce on fast days, to choose one's own confessor, and so on. If it is true that, as people say, the execution of this plan was in some respects not very pious or honorable, and that this gave scandal and caused innovations, it is also true that many similar concessions made by popes previously had less honorable causes and were administered still more extortionately. But there

2·See pp. 82-83.

are many times when opportunities occur sufficiently to produce important effects, and they are lost through lack of men who know how to make use of them; and more important still, for something to be achieved it is necessary that the time come in which God is pleased to make up the deficiencies of man. All these forces coincided in the time of Leo, of which we are speaking.

In 1517, he proclaimed the indulgence and also spent part of the proceeds before the crop was harvested (or even sown), giving the revenue of various provinces to various people, and keeping some for his own household. In particular, he gave the revenue from indulgences for Saxony and the area from there to the sea to his sister Maddalena, the wife of Franceschetto Cibò (illegitimate son of Pope Innocent VIII), as a result of whose marriage Leo had been made cardinal at fourteen years of age, which was the beginning of the great ecclesiastical career of the Medici family. Leo's generosity was not so much the result of family feeling as it was a repayment of the expenses of the Cibò family at the time when he had taken refuge in Genoa, being unable to stay in Rome while Alexander VI was allied with the enemies of the Medici, who had driven them from Florence. Maddalena, to make sure of her profits, entrusted the administration of the indulgences and the raising of the money to Bishop Arembaldo, who on becoming a bishop had given up none of the qualities of a precisely calculating Genoese merchant. He sold the power of proclaiming the indulgence to the highest bidder without taking notice of the kind of man he was. In fact, the whole affair was so commercialized that no small man could make him an offer, but had to go to intermediaries like himself, who were only interested in making money.

It was the custom in Saxony that papal indulgences were proclaimed by the Augustinian friars. Arembaldo's men did not want to make use of the Augustinians because they were accustomed to the job, and so they might be able to make a secret profit for themselves, and also because, being used to the job they would not try to raise more than usual. They went to the Dominicans instead. The Dominicans gave scandal in proclaiming the indulgences by their attempts to make them out to be more valuable than usual. Add to that the way of life of the preachers of indulgences, who spent in taverns and in other places, in gaming and in other activities of which it is best to be silent, the money which the people saved from their substance to acquire indulgences.

It was this that incited Martin Luther, an Augustinian friar, to attack these preachers of indulgences. At first, he criticized only the newest and greatest abuses; then, he began to study the subject and tried to find out the foundations and roots of indulgences; and having passed from new abuses to old ones and from the building to its foundations, he published ninety-five theses on the subject, which he proposed for a disputation in Wittenberg. He found no one to oppose him in open disputation (if I have done my research properly), but the Dominican Johann Tetzel put forward other and contrary theses to his in Frankfort-on-Oder.

These two sets of theses were like a declaration of war. Martin Luther wrote in his own defense, and Johann Eck attacked him. The theses and other writings were sent to Rome, and so the Dominican Silvestro Prierio wrote against Luther. This controversy forced both sides to leave the original topic and pass to others more important.

The question of indulgences had not been properly examined in the previous centuries. No thought had been given for their defense any more than for their attack; their nature had not been properly considered. Some thought that they were simply an absolution (by episcopal authority) from the penances which in early times the Church imposed on penitents for discipline's sake (penances which in later centuries were imposed by a bishop alone, then delegated to the penitentiary, and finally to the confessor), but that they did not dispense one from paying one's debts to the justice of God. It seemed to others that this did more harm than good to the faithful who, being freed from the penances of the Church, were careless about satisfying God with voluntary penance; but they were divided. Some thought that this was a simple freedom without need of com-

pensation; others disliked this and argued that since
the Church was one body, one man's penance could be
passed on to another and free him in this way. But
then this seemed more a matter for men of saintly and
austere life than for the authority of prelates, and so,
a third opinion arose, which made indulgences partly
absolution, for which authority was needed, and partly
compensation. However, the prelates' way of life was
such that they were not in a position to give many of
their merits to others, so they invented a treasury of
the merits of all those who had a surplus of them. The
pope was in charge of the treasury, and with his indulgences he paid the debts of sinners with corresponding amounts from the treasury. That was not the end
of the difficulties. It was objected that the merits of the
saints were finite in number, so that the treasury might
be exhausted; and to avoid this they added the infinite
merits of Christ, thus raising the problem of why there
was any need of any drops of the merits of others when
there was an infinite sea of Christ's merits available.
This made some people argue that the treasury contained Christ's merits only.

All this was very uncertain and rested only on the
foundation of Clement VI's bull for the jubilee of 1350;
it did not seem enough to oppose or to convince Martin.
And so Tetzel, Eck, and Prierio, seeing that they were on
shaky ground, raised the question of the authority of
the pope and the consensus of the Doctors of the Church.
They argued that, since the pope could not err in matters
of faith, the Doctors of the Church were on his side,
and as the indulgences had been proclaimed to all the
faithful, it was necessary to believe in them as an article
of faith. This gave Martin the opportunity of passing
from indulgences to the authority of the pope. The
others argued that he was supreme head of the Church,
but Martin that he was subject to a legitimate general
council, for which, he said, there was urgent necessity.
The dispute became more and more heated, and the
higher the others raised the authority of the pope, the
more he lowered it, though to hide his true opinion he
continued to speak respectfully of Leo. The Romans,

in their effort to defend indulgences, also raised the questions of the remission of sins, of penitence, and of purgatory.

More to the point were the writings of the Dominican, Jakob Hoogstraaten, inquisitor, who dropped these arguments and exhorted the pope to convince Martin with steel, fire, and flame.

The controversy grew more and more bitter, and Martin kept on raising new points, whenever opportunities were given him. And so, Pope Leo, in August, 1518, had him summoned to Rome by Girolamo, Bishop of Ascoli, his judge; he wrote to Duke Friedrich of Saxony not to protect Luther; he also wrote to Tommaso de Vio, Cardinal Cajetan, his legate at the Diet of Augsburg, to do all he could to make Luther a prisoner and send him to Rome. The Pope arranged to have the case examined in Germany by his legate, with instructions that if he found there was any chance of Martin's admitting that he was wrong, he should promise him an amnesty for the past, and even honors and rewards, if he thought good. But if he found him to be incorrigible, then he should join with the Emperor Maximilian and the other princes of Germany to punish him.

Martin went to meet the legate in Augsburg under an imperial safe-conduct, and they discussed the matters at issue. The Cardinal found that he could not convince Martin by means of scholastic theology, in which he was an expert; Martin always based himself on the Bible, which the scholastics do not use very much. So the Cardinal said to him that he did not want to have a disputation with him, but to exhort him to retract, or at least to submit his books and his theories to the judgment of the Pope, and he showed him the danger that he would be in if he persisted, and promised him the favor of the Pope. Martin did not contradict him, and the Cardinal thought that it was better to wait for the threats and promises to make an impression, rather than to force an immediate decision which might be a refusal; so he sent him away. He also had Johann Staupitz, the Augustinian Vicar-General, help him persuade Martin to conform.

Martin met him again, and the Cardinal had a long discussion with him about his principal ideas, listening to him rather than arguing with him, in order to gain his trust to arrange a compromise. At the end he exhorted him not to miss such an excellent opportunity. Luther replied, with his usual effectiveness, that no agreement could be made to the prejudice of the truth; that he had not offended anyone and did not need anyone's forgiveness; that he had no fear of threats; and that if anything unlawful were attempted against him, he would appeal to a council. The Cardinal (who had heard that Martin had the support of some important people who wanted to put a bit in the Pope's mouth), disliking his tone of conviction, fell into a rage and hurled abuse at him, saying that princes have long arms; and he told him to get out. Martin, remembering what had happened to Jan Hus, left Augsburg immediately. Then he reconsidered the matter and wrote a letter to the Cardinal, admitting that he had been too sharp, and alleging in excuse the importunity of the preachers of indulgences and of his adversaries. He promised to be more moderate in the future, to satisfy the Pope and not to say any more about indulgences, provided that his adversaries did the same. But neither side was able to keep silent. They provoked one another, and the controversy grew more bitter still.

In Rome, the Curia was extremely critical of the Cardinal, blaming him for everything that had gone wrong because he had abused Luther, and because he had not promised him riches, a bishopric, and even a cardinal's hat. Leo feared disturbances in Germany, not so much against indulgences as against the authority of the pope. On November 9, 1518, he issued a bull in which he declared that indulgences were valid, and that as the successor of Peter and the vicar of Christ, he had the power to issue them to the living and the dead; and that this was the doctrine of the Church of Rome, the mother and the leader of all Christians, which ought to be accepted by all who wished to be members of the Church. He sent this bull to Cardinal Cajetan, who was at Linz, in Upper Austria. The Cardinal published it and had many copies made, sending them to all the bishops in Germany, with instructions to publish it and to command everyone to believe it under pain of serious punishment.

Martin saw from this that he could expect from the Pope nothing but condemnation. Before the bull, he had spared the person and the authority of the pope, but after, he decided to attack them. He published an *Appeal*, in which he said first that he did not want to oppose the authority of the pope when he taught the truth, but added that he was not exempt from the common condition of sin and error, quoting the example of St. Peter, who was seriously rebuked by St. Paul. But as it was easy for the Pope (he went on), with all his riches and power, to persecute those who did not agree with him, there was nothing for it but to appeal to a council, for there was every reason to hold that a council was superior to the pope. This *Appeal* was distributed throughout Germany, and it was read by many and thought to be reasonable, so that Leo's bull did not put out the fire kindled in Germany.

In Rome, however, the Curia was encouraged and thought that the fire had been put out. The Franciscan, Sanson da Milano, was sent to preach the same indulgences to the Swiss. He proclaimed them in many places and collected about one hundred twenty thousand scudi. At last he arrived in Zurich where Huldrych Zwingli, Canon of the cathedral, was teaching. Zwingli attacked the doctrine of the preacher of indulgences, and a serious dispute began, passing from one topic to another in the same way as had happened in Germany. And so, it came about that many people went to hear Zwingli, who acquired a reputation and was able to attack not only the abuses of indulgences, but the indulgences themselves as well, and even the authority of the pope who granted them.

Martin Luther, seeing his ideas become popular and spread to other areas, became more confident and began to examine other articles of faith. On the subjects of confession and Communion he departed from the teaching of the scholastics and of the Roman Church, supporting Communion in both kinds as practiced in Bohemia, and arguing that the most important part of penance was not conscientious confession to the priest, but the resolution to amend one's life in future. He went on to talk of vows and of the abuses of monasticism. His writings arrived in Louvain and in Cologne, where they were examined and condemned by the theologians. But this did not deter Martin; on the contrary, it was an incentive to him to clarify and defend his ideas.

So passed the year 1519, with disputes rather than with discussions. News of the troubles in Germany and in Switzerland kept arriving at Rome, gaining in the telling as rumors do, especially those from distant parts. Leo was considered negligent because he was not attempting vigorous remedies for such serious dangers. The friars in particular blamed him for neglecting important matters and for giving himself up to festivities, hunting and other pleasures, and to music, in which he took an inordinate delight. They said that in matters of faith the tiniest thing must not be overlooked, nor the remedy put off for even a moment. Remedies were easy before the evil took root, difficult later on. The Arian heresy was a tiny spark that could easily have been put out, yet it came to set the world on fire. Jan Hus and Jeronym Prazky [Jerome of Prague] would have done the same, if at the Council of Constance they had not been put down from the first. Leo thought just the opposite. He was sorry that he had taken any action at all in this matter, and especially that he had sent to Germany the brief concerning indulgences. It seemed to him that it would have been better to let the friars dispute among themselves and have remained neutral, respected by both sides, rather than to have declared himself for one and so forced the other to oppose him. The matter was not all that important. There was no need for him to have staked his authority on it. He would be thought of as lacking seriousness, but few people would think about this, and if his name had not already been mixed up in the business, he would have gone his way, and the troubles would have disappeared.

In spite of this, he decided to yield to the common opinion, as a result of the pressure of the German bishops, the universities (which had condemned Luther and wanted the support of papal authority), and most of all of the Roman friars. He set up a congregation of cardinals, prelates, theologians, and canon lawyers, into whose hands he put the whole affair. They decided easily and quickly that he should fulminate against so great an impiety; but the theologians wanted him to proceed to excommunication immediately, whereas the canon lawyers said he [Luther] must be cited to Rome first. The theologians argued that Luther's doctrines were obviously wicked, his books in circulation, and his sermons well known. The canon lawyers said that the fact that they were well known did not mean that they could not be defended *de iure divino et naturali* [by the law of God and by natural law], citing the usual passages, "Adam where art thou?" and "Where is thy brother Abel?" and in the affair of the five cities, "I will go down and see." They added that the judge's citation of the year before, by virtue of which judgment was confided to Cajetan in Augsburg and would be invalid if anyone else made it, showed this to be necessary. After many arguments, in which the theologians claimed for themselves alone decisions concerning matters of faith, and the canon lawyers made the same claim concerning the form of the judgment, a compromise was suggested, dividing the business into three parts; the doctrine, the books, and the man. The canon lawyers allowed the doctrine to be condemned without citation, but not the man. However, they could not convince the others, who insisted warmly on their point of view and hid behind the shield of religion, so they made a compromise that they would issue a summons to Martin which would be much like a citation. There was more of a dispute about the books, which the theologians wanted condemned absolutely along with the doctrine, whereas the canon lawyers treated them along with the question of the man. They could not agree about which to do, so they did both: condemned them out of hand, and then fixed a date for burning them. And so the bull of June 15, 1520 was drawn up, which was virtually the foundation of the Council of Trent, and so it ought to be summarized briefly here.

The Pope began by asking for the help of Christ, who left Peter and his successors as vicars of the Church; from Christ he turned to St. Peter, begging him in virtue of the charge he was given by the Saviour to attend to the needs of the church of Rome, hallowed by his blood; and passing to St. Paul, he begged him for the same help, adding that even if he had thought heresies necessary as a test of good Christians, it was convenient all the same to suppress them from the start. Finally, he turned to all the saints and begged them to intercede with God for the Church to be purged of such a disease. He went on to relate how he had been informed, and had seen with his own eyes, that many errors of the Greeks and the Bohemians (already condemned) had been revived, and other errors, likely to give scandal, to offend pious ears and lead the simple astray, had been spread in Germany—a country for which he and his predecessors had always had great affection. In fact, his predecessors, after the division of the Empire, had always asked the Germans to defend them, and their princes had published many decrees against heretics which the popes had confirmed. And so, being unwilling to tolerate such errors, he meant to list some of them. And here came forty-two articles concerned with original sin, penance and the remission of sins, Communion, indulgences, excommunication, the power of the pope, the authority of councils, good works, free will, purgatory, and begging for alms; doctrines which were respectively characterized as harmful, pernicious, scandalous, offensive to pious ears, contrary to charity, contrary to the reverence due to the church of Rome, and contrary to that obedience which is the foundation of Church discipline. For this reason, he wished to proceed to condemnation and had examined these doctrines diligently with the help of the cardinals and the heads of the orders of monks and friars, and other theologians, and Doctors of civil and canon law. Therefore he condemned and reproved them respectively as heretical, false, giving scandal, giving offense to pious ears, leading pious minds astray, and as contrary to Catholic truth. It was forbidden, under pain of excommunication and innumerable other punishments, for anyone to dare hold, defend, preach, or support these doctrines. And because the above-mentioned doctrines were to be found in the books of Martin Luther, they were condemned, and he ordered that under pain of excommunication, and so on, no one was to read or to own these books, but that they should be burned, both those containing the afore-mentioned propositions and others. As for the said Martin himself, the Pope said that he had admonished and cited him and ordered him to present himself, with a promise of safe-conduct and traveling expenses; that if he had come, he would not have found so much wrong with the Curia as he was accustomed to say; and that he, the present pope, would have taught him that the popes, his predecessors, had never made a mistake in their constitutions. Since he had been under censure for a year and had dared to appeal to a future council, something which Pius and Julius II had forbidden under pain of heresy, it was possible to proceed to his condemnation without more ado. Nevertheless, the Pope would forget previous affronts and admonish the said Martin and his supporters to desist from their errors, cease preaching, and within sixty days, under pain of similar penalties, give up their above-mentioned errors and burn their books. If they did not do this, he declared them notorious and pertinacious heretics. The same penalties would fall on anyone who possessed other books by the said Martin, even if they did not contain these errors. The Pope ordered everyone to shun Martin and his supporters, and commanded everyone to lay hands on them and bring them to Rome personally, or at least to drive them from their own territories. He laid under interdict all the places to which they went, ordered that his bull should be read everywhere, and excommunicated anyone who hindered its publication. He declared that summaries of it should have credence and ordered that the bull be published in Rome, Brandenburg, Misna, and Mannsberg.

Martin Luther heard about the condemnation of his ideas and his books and published a pamphlet defending himself and repeating his appeal to a council. Besides this, he offered to prove that the Pope had proceeded against him without summoning him to Rome, without convicting him, and without giving the doctrinal dispute a hearing, so that the Pope had put his own opinions before those of the Bible and had not left anything for a council to do. He asked the emperor and all the magistrates to allow his appeal in order to support the council's authority, and he argued that the Pope's decree did not bind anyone so long as the case was not officially discussed at a council.

Judicious men marvelled at Leo's bull when they saw it, for a variety of reasons. So far as its form was concerned, they were surprised that the Pope should use the formulas of the Curia for a matter which had need of the words of Scripture, and especially that he should write in such a complicated and long-winded manner that it was almost impossible to make out the meaning, as if this were a judgment in feudal law. They noticed one clause in particular, which said, "*inhibentes omnibus ne præfatos errores asserere præsumant*" [forbidding anyone to assert the aforesaid errors] was extended with so many amplifications and qualifications that between *inhibentes* and *præsumant* there were more than four hundred words. Others went a little further and considered that doubts were raised rather than allayed by putting forward forty-two propositions and condemning them as heretical, false, giving scandal, giving offense to pious ears, and leading simple minds astray, without explaining wherein lay the heresy, falsehood, and scandal, but attributing an indeterminate quality to each proposition with the word "respectively." This was not to put an end to the matter, but to make it more controversial than ever and show the need of prudence and of a different authority to put an end to it.

Yet others were full of surprise that it had been said that the forty-two propositions included errors of the

Greeks which had been condemned already. To others it seemed unprecedented that the decision on such propositions concerning matters of faith should have been taken in Rome with the advice of the Curia alone, without the participation of the other bishops, the universities, and the learned men of Europe.

The Universities of Cologne and Louvain, however, happy that the Pope had lent support to their judgment, burned Luther's books in public. This was the occasion of Luther's holding a meeting in Wittenberg and solemnly and publicly burning not only Leo's bull, but the papal decretals as well, and then explaining his action to the world in a long manifesto which circulated in manuscript, accusing the Pope of tyrannizing over the Church, corrupting Christian doctrine, and usurping the power of the true rulers.

As a result of Luther's appeal and of these and other considerations, everyone came to think that a legitimate council was a necessity; a council which would not only decide the matters of controversy, but remedy long-standing abuses in the Church as well. The more the dispute grew, and the more pamphlets were published by one side or the other, the more this necessity became apparent. Martin did not fail to write in defense of his position, and as he studied, he discovered more and went back further and raised issues that in the beginning he had not considered. He claimed to do this out of zeal for the house of God—but he was also forced to do so by circumstances. For since the Pope had arranged with the Elector of Saxony in Cologne, by means of Girolamo Aleandro, that Martin should be delivered prisoner to him, or be removed in some other way, Martin saw that he was obliged to show the prince and people of Saxony that he was in the right, so that his prince or another would not assist the papal attempts on his life.

So passed the year 1520. In 1521, the Diet of Worms was held, and Luther was summoned to it to render an account of his ideas under safe-conduct from Charles, who had been elected emperor two years before. He was advised not to attend because Leo's condemnation had already been published, so that he could be sure that the condemnation would be confirmed, even if nothing worse happened. Nevertheless, contrary to the advice of all his friends, Luther said that even if he could be sure of having as many devils against him as there were tiles on the roofs of the houses of that city, he would go all the same; and so he did.

There, on the seventeenth of April, in the presence of the emperor and all the princes, he was asked if he was the author of the books that were circulating under his name, and the titles were read out and copies were shown to him. He was asked if he wanted to defend everything contained in them, or retract anything. He replied that he recognized the books as his, but that as the decision whether or not to defend their contents was such a serious one, he needed time to think about it. He was given that day and had to reply on the next. The next day Martin came to the Diet and made a long speech: He began by apologizing for his lack of education, in case he did not speak in a way appropriate to the dignity of the Diet and give everyone the correct titles. He confirmed that the books were written by him. As for their defense, he said that they were not all of a kind, but that some were concerned with matters of faith and piety, others criticized the ideas of the popes, and a third sort were controversial writings directed against the pope's defenders. As to the first, he said, it would be wrong and unchristian to retract them, and even Leo's bull, though it condemned them all, did not judge all his books to be wicked. As for the second sort, it was all too obvious that the whole of Christendom and Germany in particular had been exploited and groaned under slavery, and to retract what he had said would be simply to confirm the existence of that tyranny. But as for the books of the third sort, he admitted that he had been more bitter and more vehement than he should, saying that he did not claim to be a saint and was defending his ideas, not his way of life, and that he was prepared to explain himself to whoever wished it, saying that he would not be obstinate, but that if anyone Bible in hand were to show him his mistakes, he would throw his books into the flames himself. He turned to the emperor and the princes, saying that for the true doctrine to be revealed was a great gift of God, and that to repudiate it was to draw great calamities on oneself.

When he had finished speaking, he was asked by order of the emperor to give a simple answer to the question, whether he was prepared to defend his books or not. He replied that he could not take back anything that he had written or taught unless he were convinced either by the words of the Scriptures or by self-evident conclusions.

When he heard this, the emperor determined to follow in the footsteps of his predecessors and defend the Church of Rome and to use every means to put out the fire of heresy. He did not want to break his word, however, but to proceed against Martin after he had returned safely home. There were others at the Diet who approved what had been done at Constance and said that faith ought not to be kept with him; but Ludwig, the Elector Palatine, opposed this as something that would make the name of German shameful forever, saying disdainfully that it would be intolerable if for the sake of priests Germany were to get a name for faithlessness. There were yet others who said that one should not rush into condemning Luther so easily, because this was a matter of the highest importance and serious consequences might follow.

During the next few days there was a discussion in the presence of some of the princes, including the Archbishop of Trier and Elector Joachim of Brandenburg, and Martin argued at length in defense of his ideas, and others argued against them. They tried to induce him to submit unconditionally to the judgment of the emperor and of the Diet. But he said that the prophet forbade us to trust in men, even princes, to whose judgment nothing was more repugnant than the word of God. Finally, it was proposed that the whole matter should be submitted to the council that was to be held. He agreed to this on condition that the propositions that were to be placed before the council should be extracted from his books first, and that they should be judged according to the Scriptures. In conclusion, he was asked what remedies he thought were appropriate to this case, and he replied: "Only those that Gamaliel proposed to the Jews": that is, that if the affair was of human inspiration, it would come to nothing, but if it was of God, it would be irresistible; and that this ought to satisfy even the Pope, for everyone should be convinced (as he was himself) that if his plan did not come from God, in a short time it would have come to nothing. On these matters it was impossible to shake him, and he also remained firm in his resolution not to accept any judgment unless it were according to Scripture. He was given twenty days to return home, on condition that he did not preach or write on the way. He expressed thanks for this and left on April 26.

On May 8 at the same Diet of Worms, the Emperor Charles issued an edict, in which the preamble declared that it was the duty of the emperor to support religion and extinguish heresy when it appeared, and which went on to say that Brother Martin Luther was trying to spread this plague in Germany, so that if remedy were not taken, the whole nation would become gravely ill; that Pope Leo had admonished him paternally, and a council of cardinals and other excellent men had condemned his writings and declared him a heretic unless he recanted within a certain time; that the Pope had sent the emperor, as the protector of the church, a copy of the bull of condemnation by means of his nuncio, Girolamo Aleandro, asking for it to be enforced throughout his dominions. But for all that Martin did not reform; on the contrary, he went on writing books full of new heresies as well as those which had already been condemned, and in German as well as in Latin. The edict went on to give details of many of his errors and concluded that every writing contained some deadly sting, so that it could be said that every word was poisonous. The emperor and his councillors from all his dominions had considered these matters, and following in the footsteps of his predecessors, the Roman emperors, he had discussed the whole matter at Worms with the electors and representatives of the estates of the Empire and with their advice and consent (although one ought not to listen to an obstinate, perverse, and notorious heretic who had been condemned by the Pope), in order to remove any pretext for objections (since many people said that it was necessary to hear the man himself before putting the papal decree into execution), he had sent one of his heralds to Luther to tell him to present himself, not to take upon himself the judgment of matters of faith, which was the pope's business alone, but to persuade Luther gently to follow the right path. The edict went on to relate how Martin appeared at the Diet, what he was asked, how he replied (as has been described above), and how he was sent away.

The conclusion was therefore, for the sake of the honor of God and the Pope and the imperial authority, with the advice and consent of the electors, princes, and estates of the Empire, to execute the papal sentence, declaring Martin Luther a notorious heretic and ordering everyone to consider him as such; forbidding everyone to receive him or defend him in any way; and ordering all princes and states under heavy penalties to capture and imprison him when the twenty days were up and to take action against all his followers and supporters and to seize all their goods. Everyone was forbidden to own or read his books, although they contained some good things, and all princes and magistrates were ordered to burn and destroy them. Since pamphlets were being produced, extracted from his works, and also pictures satirizing various people, the Pope included, it was ordered that no one was to print them, paint them, or own them, but they were to be taken and burned by the magistrates, and the printers, vendors, and buyers punished. A general law was attached, to the effect that nothing however small which treated of matters of faith could be printed without the permission of the bishop.

At the same time the University of Paris extracted various propositions from Luther's books and condemned them, partly as revivals of the doctrine of Wyclif and Hus, partly as innovations of his own. But all that came of this condemnation was that Luther replied to it, many books were written on both sides, the dispute grew more bitter, and the curiosity of many people was awakened, who, wishing to inform themselves about the controversy, became acquainted with the abuses which Luther attacked, and so stopped supporting the Pope.

Among the most illustrious opponents of Luther was Henry VIII, King of England, who was not the eldest son and had been destined by his father for the archbishopric of Canterbury, and so given a literary education. But his elder brother died, and then his father, and he succeeded to the throne. And wanting for the sake of show to take part in such an important dispute, he wrote a book about the seven sacraments which defended the Pope and opposed Luther, for which the Pope was so grateful that on receiving the king's book he honored him with the customary title of "Defender of the Faith." But Martin did not let himself be frightened by the majesty of a king and replied with the same violence and lack of respect that he had used toward mere doctors of theology. The fact that a king had entered the controversy made people more interested in it, and as in contests it always happens that the spectators support the weaker side, so the king swung public opinion in favor of Luther.

In the same month that Luther was put to the ban of the Empire, Hugo, Bishop of Constance, in whose diocese the city of Zurich lay, wrote to the college of canons there, which included Zwingli, and also to the council of the same city. In these letters he discussed the harm done to church and state by innovations in doctrine and the disturbance, the confusion, and the threat to souls. He exhorted them to be wary of those professing new doctrines, arguing that they were inspired by the devil and their own ambitions. He forwarded them the papal decree and the imperial ban with advice to follow them, and he drew their attention to the doctrines of Zwingli and his followers, ordering Zwingli to justify his teachings to his colleagues and to the town council. Zwingli wrote to the Bishop, insisting that priests with mistresses should no longer be tolerated, for this brought the clergy into disrepute and encouraged loose living in general—though this could not be remedied without following the doctrine of the apostles and introducing clerical matrimony. He also wrote to all the Swiss canons in his own defense, referring in particular to an edict of their ancestors, to the effect that every priest must have his own mistress in order to protect respectable women and adding that although the decree appeared to be a ridiculous one, it had been necessary and ought not to be changed now, except for the substitution of "wife" for "mistress."

The Bishop's action provoked the Dominicans to preach against Zwingli and provoked him to defend himself. He, too, published theses, sixty-seven of them, which expounded his ideas and attacked the corruption of the clergy and the prelates. There was so much controversy and confusion as a result that the town council of Zurich took action to calm things down and summoned to a conference all the preachers and doctors under its jurisdiction. The Bishop of Constance was invited to send some sensible and learned man to take part in order to lay disputes to rest and come to a decision that would be to the glory of God. The Bishop sent Johann Faber, his deputy, who was later Bishop of Vienna. On the day fixed for the conference, a large number of people arrived; Zwingli stated his theses again and offered to defend them against any opponent. Various Dominican friars and other Doctors made various criticisms of Zwingli, and he replied to them. Faber then said that this was not the time or the place to deal with such matters, but it was the business of the council, which was soon to be held, because (so he said) the Pope and the princes and prelates had so decided. This gave Zwingli the opportunity to say that this promise was just an attempt to nourish the people on empty hopes and to keep them sleeping the sleep of ignorance, and that while they were still waiting for the council to make a statement on the topics of controversy, he could come to clear and certain conclusions based on Holy Scripture and on the practice of the primitive church. He continued to insist on Faber's opposing his theses and reduced him to saying that he did not want to argue with him, but would reply to his theses in writing. The conference ended with the council's decree that the gospel should be preached according to the Old and New Testaments and not according to any man-made laws.

It became apparent that the efforts of the Doctors and prelates of the Church of Rome, the papal condemnation, and even the imperial ban were unable to annihilate the new doctrine; on the contrary, it made more progress every day. So everyone came to realize that these remedies were not the right ones for the disease, and that it was necessary to make use of that medicine which had been effective in similar situations in the past—and that medicine was the calling of a council. Every class of person wanted this as the only possible remedy.

It came to be realized that the origin of the innovations was the corruption introduced in the course of time through the negligence of the clergy, and that the current troubles could not be remedied without remedying the abuses that were their cause, and that there was no other way of remedying the abuses peacefully and in a uniform manner except by a general assembly. This was how pious and disinterested men spoke. There were also various sorts of people for whom a council was useful, provided that it were limited in such a way as not to be contrary to their interests. Firstly, those who shared the opinions of Luther wanted a council on condition that Scripture was the sole criterion on which decisions were to be based, not on papal decrees or scholastic philosophy; they would then be certain not only of defending themselves, but of coming off victorious. What they did not want was a council like the ones of the last eight hundred years, and they made it clear that they would not submit to the judgment of such a one. And Martin was accustomed to say that he had been too timorous at Worms, and that he was so certain that his doctrine was God's doctrine that he would not even submit it to the judgment of the angels; on the contrary, it was this doctrine by which men and angels should be judged. Secondly, princes and other rulers were not much concerned about what the council would decide on doctrinal matters, but wanted it to reform the priests and friars, hoping that this would result in the reversion to them of all the temporal powers and riches of which the clergy had gained control. And so, they said that it would be useless to hold a council at which only bishops and other prelates had votes because it was they who needed to be reformed, and the reforming needed to be done by others who would not be misled by self-interest and forced to come to decisions contrary to the good of Christendom. Thirdly, those men who had some understanding of human affairs wanted ecclesiastical authority to be limited so that the poor people would not be burdened with exactions on the pretext of tithes, alms, and indulgences, nor oppressed by episcopal officials on the pretext of correcting and judging them. Fourthly, the Curia, a most important group, wanted a council insofar as it would encourage people to obey the pope again, and insofar as it would adhere to the precedents of the last few centuries. What did not please them was a council with power to reform the papacy and abolish the innovations from which the Curia received so much profit and by means of which a large amount of the wealth of Christendom found its way to Rome. Lastly, Pope Leo, who was subject to pressures from both sides, did not know what he wanted. He saw that he was obeyed less every day, and that whole nations were leaving him, and he wanted a council to remedy this; but then he thought that the council was the greater evil because it would bring reform in its train, and so hated and feared it. He tried to work out a way of holding a council in Rome or somewhere else in the Papal States, like the Lateran Council which his predecessor had successfully organized a few years before, having by its means put an end to schism, recovered the kingdom of France, and (what was no less important) abolished the Pragmatic Sanction, which was a threat to papal authority in two ways; it was a precedent for taking away from the pope his power of appointing to benefices (one of the foundations of his greatness), and it was a reminder of the Council of Basel, and so of the subjection of the pope to a general council. However, he did not see how a council of this sort could be any use, because the danger came not from the princes and the great prelates, with whom deals could be made, but from the people, whom only genuine reforms would satisfy.

## Chapter Three

*[Sarpi now describes the death of Leo X, the short reign of Adrian VI, and the election of another Medici, Clement VII (1498–1534). Clement joined the League of Cognac formed by Francis I against Charles V (1526), as a result of which the emperor's troops took and sacked Rome in 1527.]*

The Pope, full of fear, as happens in sudden accidents, fled to the Castle with a few cardinals, and although he was advised not to shut himself up there, but to pass immediately into the city and from there to take refuge in some safe place, nevertheless he did not take this good advice, perhaps for some higher reason. The city found itself without a head, and there was such confusion that no one thought of the obvious action to take in that situation, which was to break down the bridges over the Tiber between the suburbs and the city and to put the city in a state of defense. If this had been done, the Romans would have had time to convey important people and valuable goods to a safe place. This was not done, and the soldiers entered the city, pillaging not only the houses but the churches, too, taking ornaments and smashing relics and other holy things of no value. They took the cardinals and other prelates prisoner, and they made fun of them by leading them on mean beasts in their official robes. It is certain that the cardinals of Siena, Minerva, and Poncetta were well beaten and led in ignominious procession, and that the German and Spanish cardinals and those who had taken refuge with them because the army was composed of soldiers of those nations were as badly treated as the rest. The Pope was besieged in the Castle of Sant'Angelo and forced to surrender both himself and it to the imperial captains, and he was closely guarded there. He was already extremely upset by what had happened, when something occurred that he thought even worse: the Cardinal of Cortona, who governed Florence in his name, took himself off and left the city unguarded as soon as he heard the news of the capture of the Pope. The citizens immediately expelled the Medici and re-formed their constitution, and the majority of them showed so much hostility to the Pope and his family that they defaced all their coats of arms, even those in private places, and also the pictures of Leo and Clement in the church of the Annunciation.

When the emperor heard of the sack of Rome and the imprisonment of the Pope, he showed many signs of great sorrow and made a show of this by immediately cancelling the solemn festival that was being prepared at Valladolid to celebrate the birth of his son on the twenty-first of that month. These signs would have convinced the world of his piety and religious feelings if he had as quickly commanded at least the freeing of the Pope himself. But the world, which saw the Pope remain in prison six months more, perceived how great the difference was between appearance and reality.

[*Sarpi describes the reconciliation between Clement VII and Charles V, who met in Bologna in 1530 for Charles's coronation.*]

Many subjects were discussed by these two princes, touching both the peace of Christendom and their own particular interests. The principal subjects were general peace in Italy and the suppression of Protestantism in Germany. The first of these does not concern us here. Concerning the second matter, some imperial councillors proposed that, bearing in mind how tenacious of liberty the Germans were, the best thing would be to dissemble and to persuade the princes to return to the papal fold by gentle means, because once they ceased to protect the leaders of the Protestants, it would be easy to deal with the rest. The best way to persuade the princes was to hold a council, because they had asked for it, and because everyone would respect that majestic and venerable name.

But the Pope feared nothing more than a council, above all if it were to be held on the other side of the Alps, freely and with the participation of those who had openly thrown off the papal yoke. He saw, too, that it would be extremely easy to persuade the others of this as well. He considered besides that if he had some interests in common with all the bishops, whose riches were threatened by the opinions of the reformers, nevertheless there remained some ill feelings between them and the Curia. The bishops claimed that the power of collating to benefices had been taken from them through reservations and priorities, and that a great part of the administration had been drawn to Rome by appeals, reserved dispensations, absolutions, and other such faculties which were once common to all the bishops but which the popes had monopolized. Clement therefore calculated that the holding of a council would result in an enormous diminution of the authority of the pope. And so, he turned all his attention to persuading the emperor that the council would not help allay the troubles in Germany, but that, on the contrary, it would harm the authority of the emperor in those parts. He made him consider two sorts of people, the multitude and the princes and nobles. It was plausible to assume that the multitude would be deceived, but to satisfy their demand for a council would not make them wiser, but rather introduce popular license. If they were allowed to raise doubts or to demand greater clarification of religious matters, they would immediately have an excuse for imposing laws on the government and restricting the authority of princes by decrees. If they were successful in their claims to examine the authority of the Church, they would learn to raise difficulties about the authority of the state. He showed him that it was easier to oppose the first demands of the multitude than to make some concessions and then try to stop. As far as the princes and nobles were concerned, he was sure that their motives were not pious ones; they wanted to possess the property of the church themselves and to become absolute rulers, with little or no regard for the emperor. Many of them were still free from that disease because they had not yet discovered the secret; once it was out, they would all address themselves to the same ends. There was no doubt that the loss of Germany was a great loss for the papacy, but it would be a greater loss still for the emperor and the house of Habsburg. If he wanted to provide against this, his only means was to make strong use of his authority while the greater part of the empire still obeyed him, and he would have to be quick, before the numbers of the disobedient increased and everyone discovered the advantages of holding the new opinions. But nothing would be more opposed to the speed of action which was necessary than the council, because even if everyone agreed to it and there were no hindrances, it would take a long time to meet and to discuss its agenda. He would only mention that case because one would never end a consideration of the hindrances that would arise, as people opposed it for various motives and with various pretexts, using delaying tactics in order to make the council come to nothing. The rumor had spread that popes did not want councils for fear that their authority would be limited. But this argument made no impression on him because he had his authority directly from Christ, with the promise that even the gates of hell would not prevail against it, and because the experience of past times had shown that no council had ever diminished the authority of the popes. On the contrary, following the words of the Lord, the Fathers have always described that authority as absolute and unlimited, as in fact it is. And when the popes out of humility or for other reasons have not made full use of their authority, the Fathers have forced them to do so. This can be seen clearly by anyone who reads history, because popes have always used councils against the new opinions of heretics and in every other case of necessity, and by this means they have increased their authority. And leaving aside Christ's promise, which is the true and only foundation of the pope's authority, and considering the matter in human terms, the council is made up of bishops, but the greatness of the papacy is useful for bishops because it protects them against prince and people. Kings and other sovereigns as well, who understand the laws of politics, will always support the authority of the pope, because they have no other means of keeping their prelates under control when these wish to exceed their powers. The Pope ended by saying that he was so sure of the outcome that he would go so far as to prophesy that if a council were held greater disorders in Germany would follow. Those who demanded the council would use it as a pretext for carrying on what they had begun; when the council condemned their opinions (as must happen), they would find another excuse for deprecating the councils. In the end, the authority of the emperor would be annihilated in Germany and weakened elsewhere, whereas the authority of the pope would diminish in Germany but would be increased in the rest of the world. The emperor should believe him all the more because he was not motivated by his own interests, but by his desire to see Germany united to the Church and the emperor obeyed. This would be impossible unless the emperor went immediately to Germany and used his authority, executing the judgment of Leo and the Edict of Worms without listening to whatever the Protestants had to say (whether they demanded a council, or more teaching, or put forward their appeal, or made some other excuse, which were all nothing but pretexts to hide their wickedness). He must use force as soon as he was disobeyed, which would be easy while their numbers were small, and he would have all the princes of the Church and most of the lay ones on his side in this matter. This and this only was the action befitting his position as emperor and the oath he had sworn at his coronation at Aachen, and the one he was to swear on being crowned by the Pope. Finally, it was clear that the holding of a council and whatever negotiations took place on that occasion would necessarily end in war. And so it was better to try to settle these disorders by virtue of his imperial and absolute command, something which would probably succeed easily, and if it did not, to proceed immediately to force and arms, rather than to give the rein to the license of the people, the ambition of the nobles, and the perversity of the heretics.

These arguments, although unseemly in the mouth of Brother Giulio de'Medici, knight of Malta (as the Pope was called before he was made a cardinal), let alone that of Pope Clement VII, persuaded Charles all the same. They were assisted by Mercurio da Gattinara, imperial chancellor and cardinal, to whom the Pope made many promises, promising in particular to consider his relations and dependents for the first creation of cardinals, which was imminent. They were also assisted by Charles's wish to have more absolute power in Germany than his grandfather or his great-grandfather had had.

[Sarpi describes the death of Zwingli, Henry VIII's breach with Rome, and further negotiations for a council, cut off by the death of Clement VII in 1534.]

## Chapters Four and Five

It was necessary to cease negotiating with the Pope about the council because he fell into a long and fatal illness, and at the end of September passed to another life, to the great joy of the Curia, which, although it admired his abilities, his natural gravity, exemplary parsimony, and dissimulation, greatly hated his avarice, harshness, and cruelty, which were all the greater or all the more apparent during his last illness.

When the Holy See is vacant, it is the custom of the cardinals to compose a draft of important articles for the reform of the papacy, and each of them swears to abide by this if he becomes pope. However, it may be seen from all past cases that everyone swears with the intention of breaking his oath if he becomes pope. As soon as he is elected, he says that he had not had the power to make such a promise, and that now he is pope he is not bound by it. On the death of Clement the articles were drafted as usual, and one of them was that the next pope would be obliged to call the Council within a year. But the articles could not be finally agreed upon and the oath taken because on the same day, October 12, on which the conclave was locked in, Cardinal Farnese was unexpectedly elected pope, before his coronation with the name of Honorius V, and afterwards with that of Paul III. He was a prelate of many good qualities, and of all his abilities, he valued most highly his skill in dissembling. He had been a cardinal for six papal reigns, had been dean of the college, and was much experienced in negotiations. He did not give the impression of fearing the Council as Clement had done. On the contrary, he believed that it was to the advantage of the papacy to give the impression of desiring it very much, being confident that no one could compel him to hold it in a manner and in a place where it was not to his advantage, and that when he needed to place obstacles in its way, he could make use of the conflict between the Curia and the rest of the clergy. It was his judgment that the Council would also be useful for keeping the peace in Italy, which he thought was extremely necessary if he was to govern undisturbed. He saw very well that the Council would serve him as a cloak to cover many deeds with the excuse that he would not have done them of his own accord. As soon as he was elected, then, he gave it to be understood that although the articles had not been sworn, he had decided nevertheless to observe the one concerning the calling of the Council, since he knew it to be necessary for the glory of God and the benefit of the Church. On October 16, he held a general congregation of the cardinals (it was not called a consistory because the pope was not yet crowned), and this subject was raised. He put forward convincing reasons for thinking that the summons could be delayed no longer, since it was impossible otherwise to retain the friendship of the Christian princes and to stamp out heresy. He asked all the cardinals to think carefully about the maner of holding it. He deputed three cardinals to consider the time, place, and other details, with instructions to give their advice at the first consistory after his coronation. In order to encourage conflicts which might be useful to him on occasion, he added that the Council would undertake the reform of the clergy. It would not be seemly for the Council to have to reform the cardinals, so it was necessary for them to begin by reforming themselves, since it was his will that the Council be fruitful, and its principles would not seem efficacious if their effects could not be seen in the cardinals.

## Chapter Six

[*Sarpi goes on to describe the summons of the Council to Mantua; the unsuccessful attempts of Charles V to have the Protestants participate in the Council; the objections of the Duke of Mantua to the Council's meeting there, and its consequent suspensions.*]

So finished the year 1541, and in the next, the Pope sent Giovanni Morone, Bishop of Modena, to Speyer (where the Diet was being held in the presence of Ferdinand). The Bishop followed his instructions concerning the Council, and spoke as follows. The Pope had not changed his mind, but still wanted the Council to be held one day; he had suspended it for the sake of the emperor so as to open a way to peace in Germany, but seeing that this was a vain attempt, now returned to his first decision not to put it off any longer. As for holding it in Germany, the Pope could not agree to this because he wanted to take part in it himself, and his age, and the length of the journey, and the change of climate were obstacles to his going there. Besides, Germany was no more convenient for the other nations than Italy. There was also great danger that these matters could not be discussed in Germany without disturbances. Ferrara or Bologna or Piacenza seemed more appropriate to him, all large cities and most suitable. If these choices did not please them, he was prepared to hold the Council in Trent, a city on the borders of Germany. He would have liked the Council to have begun at Pentecost, but since that was so near he had postponed it to

August 13. He asked everyone to agree on this, to lay aside hate, and to deal with God's business sincerely.

Ferdinand and the Catholic princes thanked the Pope, saying that if a convenient place could not be found in Germany, like Regensburg or Cologne, they would content themselves with Trent. But the Protestants were not prepared either to agree that the Council should be summoned by the Pope, or that the place should be Trent, and so there was no further decision about the Council at the Diet.

Nevertheless, the Pope issued the bull summoning the Council on May 22, 1542. In the bull, referring to his desire to attend to the ills of Christendom, he said that he had continually thought about remedies, and since he found none more appropriate than the holding of the Council, he had firmly resolved to summon it. He referred to the summons of the Council to Mantua, and its suspension, to its summons to Vicenza, and the second suspension made in Genoa, and finally, to the indefinite suspension. He passed on to give the reasons which had persuaded him to continue that suspension until then. These were: Ferdinand's war in Hungary, the rebellion of the Netherlands against the emperor, and the events at the Diet of Regensburg, which made him wait for the time destined by God for his work. Finally, considering that every time is pleasing to God when holy things are concerned, he was resolved not to wait any longer for the agreement of the princes. Being unable to have Vicenza and wishing to satisfy the Germans as regards the place, and understanding that they would like it to be at Trent, although somewhere nearer the center of Italy seemed to him more convenient, nevertheless out of fatherly charity he inclined his own will to their demands and chose Trent for the holding of the Ecumenical Council on November 1. He allowed that space of time for the publication of his decree and the arrival of the prelates. And so in the name of the Father, the Son, and the Holy Ghost, and of the apostles Peter and Paul, whose authority he exercised on earth, with the advice and consent of the cardinals, he raised the suspension and summoned the holy Ecumenical and

General Council to that city, a free and suitable place and one convenient for all nations, to begin on the first of that month, and to continue and end there. He summoned all the patriarchs, archbishops, bishops, abbots, and all who by law or privilege had places in general councils, commanding them to present themselves in virtue of their oath to him and to the Apostolic See, and in virtue of their obedience, and on pain of the legal and customary sanctions against those who did not come. If they were unable, they were to give evidence of the hindrance or to send deputies. He asked the emperor, the most Christian king and other kings, dukes, and princes to take part or, if they were unable, to send ambassadors, men of gravity and authority, and to order the bishops and prelates of their kingdoms and provinces to come, desiring in particular the presence of the prelates and princes of Germany, for which reason the council was summoned in the city they had desired in order that there might be discussion of matters pertaining to the truth of the Christian religion, the correction of morals, the peace and concord of Christian princes and peoples, and the destruction of barbarians and infidels.

The bull was immediately sent out from Rome to all the princes, but it came at a bad moment because in July, Francis, King of France, declared war on the emperor, insulted him, published his declaration of war, and began his campaign in Brabant, Luxembourg, Roussillon, Piedmont, and Artois.

The emperor replied to the Pope that he was dissatisfied with the tone of the bull summoning the Council. He had never spared any trouble, danger, or expense in order that the Council might be held, whereas the king of France, on the contrary, had always tried to hinder it; so it seemed odd to him that the bull compared them on equal terms. He gave an account of all the injuries which he claimed the king had done him, and added that at the last Diet of Speyer the king had promoted religious discord by sending his ambassadors to promise his friendship and favor to each side separately. Finally, he asked His Holiness to consider whether that king's actions served to remedy the ills of Christendom and initiate the Council, for the king had always hindered it for his own ends and forced the emperor, who had noticed this, to find some other means to reconcile religious disputes. His Holiness should blame the king of France and not him if the Council was not held. And if he wished the common good, he should declare himself the enemy of that king; for this was the only means of bringing the Council to a successful conclusion, for settling religious affairs, and for a return to peace.

The king, as if he could foretell the accusations which the Council would make against him—of beginning a war to the detriment of religion and the service of God —anticipated them by publishing an edict against the Lutherans, commanding the Parlements to execute it rigorously. This edict ordered the denunciation of those who possessed heretical books, met in secret conventicles, or broke the commandments of the Church, especially those who did not keep the laws about fasting and abstinence, or prayed in a language other than Latin—and he ordered the Sorbonne to be diligent in seeking out such people. He then discovered the cunning of the emperor who was setting the Pope against him, and to remedy this he ordered that effective means be taken against the Lutherans, and that an organization should be set up in Paris to discover and accuse them, with penalties for those who did not give them up and rewards for those who informed against them. When he was fully informed of what the emperor had written to the Pope, he wrote the Pope a long letter defending himself and attacking the emperor, reproaching him with the capture and sack of Rome and the adding of insult to injury by holding processions in Spain for the liberation of the Pope whom he was himself keeping prisoner. He went on to mention all the causes of offense between himself and the emperor, blaming him for everything, and he concluded that it was not possible to hold him responsible for the hindering or delaying of the Council of Trent; for he gained no benefit from it, and it was contrary to the example of his ancestors. He followed their example and did all he could to preserve true religion, as the edicts lately made in France well showed, and so he begged His Holiness not to believe the calumnies, but to count on him always in all his needs and those of the Church of Rome.

[Sarpi concludes Book One by describing how at the Diet of Speyer, in 1544, Charles V proclaimed a religious truce, against which the Pope protested vehemently.]

# BOOK TWO

## Chapter One

The war between the emperor and the king of France
did not last long, because the emperor realized that while
he was involved in this, and his brother in the war
against the Turks, Germany was increasing its liberty to
such an extent that soon the imperial authority would
not even be recognized nominally there. In making war
on France, he was like Æsop's dog which followed the
shadow and lost the substance. And so, he listened to the
French peace proposals, with the aim not only of freeing
himself of that burden, but also of coming to an understanding with the Turks through the offices of the French
king and of attending to German affairs. Peace was
concluded between them at Crespy on September 24,
[1544], and among other things both rulers agreed to
defend the old religion and to work for the union of
the Church and the reform of the Curia, the cause of all
the disputes. To this effect they would jointly ask the
Pope to summon the Council, and the king of France
would send to the German Diet to persuade the Protestants to agree to it. The Pope was not dismayed by their
agreement about the Council and the reformation of the
Curia, since he was certain that once they had set hand
to the work, it would be impossible for them to reconcile their conflicts of interest for long. And he did not
doubt that, since their design was to be executed by
means of the Council, he could so manage matters that
his authority would be increased. However, it was his
opinion that if he were to call the Council at their request, men would believe that he had been forced to do
it, which would greatly diminish his prestige and encourage those who wished to limit the authority of the
pope. For this reason, he did not wait to be anticipated
by either monarch, hiding his suspicion of the emperor

for making peace without his intervention and on terms prejudicial to his authority. He issued a bull inviting the whole Church to rejoice at the peace, which removed the only impediment to the Council, and summoning the Council to Trent, once more, to begin on March 15.

He realized that this notice was too short to inform everyone, let alone to give the prelates time to make their arrangements and to travel, but he thought that it would be to his advantage, if the Council had to be held, to begin with only a few prelates present, and those Italians—courtiers and his dependents—whom he asked to arrive first. For at the beginning it was necessary to discuss the manner of procedure, which was the most important matter—virtually the only important matter—for preserving the authority of the pope, and those who came later would be forced to accept the decision of those who were there before them. It was no extraordinary thing that a general council should begin with only a few prelates, for this had happened at the Councils of Pisa and Constance, and these had been successful in the outcome. And, having penetrated to the true cause of the peace, he wrote to the emperor that in order to serve him he had anticipated him and summoned the Council speedily. He knew how His Majesty had been forced by the necessities of the French war to allow and promise many things to the Protestants, and the summoning of the Council would give him a means of making excuses to the Diet in September if he did not grant the truce which he had promised would last until the Council met.

The Pope's speed of action did not please the emperor, nor did he believe in the reason given for it. He would have liked to have been the main force behind the Council, for the sake of his own prestige, to make the Germans accept the Council more easily, and for many other reasons. Unable to do this, he acted as if he was the initiator and the Pope the follower. He sent embassies to all the princes to let them know of the summons and to ask them to send ambassadors to honor the proceedings and confirm the decrees that were made there. He made serious preparations, as if the enterprise had been his own. He gave various instructions to the prelates of Spain and the Low Countries, among other things to the effect that the theologians of Louvain should meet to consider the dogmas that ought to be put forward. They produced thirty-two points, which they did not confirm from any place in Holy Scripture; they only explained the conclusion. These were then confirmed by imperial edict and published with orders that everyone should hold and follow them. The emperor did not hide the fact that he was furious with the Pope in his remarks to the nuncio on this occasion and on others, and when in December the Pope created thirteen cardinals, including three Spaniards, he refused to allow them to accept the insignia, or to use the title or the costume.

The king of France, for his part, had the theologians of Paris assemble at Melun to confer about the dogmas necessary to the Christian faith which should be put forward at the Council. There was much controversy. Some wanted the confirmation of the conclusions of Constance and Basel and the reestablishment of the Pragmatic Sanction; others, thinking that the king would be offended with this because it entailed the destruction of the concordat between him and Leo, advised that this question be not raised. Afterwards, since the theology faculty disagreed about the sacraments, some making them efficient instrumental causes of grace and others not, and since everyone wanted his own opinion to be a matter of faith, all they could agree on was to remain within the limits of the twenty-five points published two years before.

The Pope told the king of France about the emperor's anger with him and asked him to support the Apostolic See by sending his ambassadors to the Council as soon as possible. He told the imperial nuncio to take every opportunity offered by the Protestants (when they offended the emperor) and to offer the emperor every assistance, spiritual and temporal, to recover his authority. The nuncio was not short of opportunities, and he acted to such effect that the emperor (realizing that he might need either the spiritual or temporal help of the Pope) ceased his hostility, showing this by allowing the new cardinals to use their titles and insignia, and by giving more friendly audiences to the nuncio, in which he talked more than usual about Germany.

## Chapter Two

*[After the emperor had made unsuccessful attempts to persuade the Protestants to attend, the Council finally opened on December 13, 1545.]*

December 13 came at last, and the Pope published a Jubilee Bull in Rome, in which he explained that he had summoned the council to heal the wounds which wicked heretics had inflicted on the Church. He exhorted everyone to pray to God for the Fathers assembled there, and to do this most efficaciously and fruitfully, they must go to confession, fast for three days, take part in processions, and then receive the most holy sacrament. He granted pardon for all their sins to whoever did this. The same day, in Trent, the Cardinals Del Monte,[1] Pole,[2] and Cervino[3] were appointed papal legates to the Council, and all the prelates, twenty-five in number, dressed in their robes, accompanied by the theologians, the clergy and the people of Trent and elsewhere, went in solemn procession from the Church of the Trinity to the cathedral. When they arrived, Del Monte, the chief legate, sang the Mass of the Holy Ghost, and the Bishop of Bitonto preached a long and eloquent sermon. When it was over, the legates asked that a very long admonition *de scripto* [in writing] be read, which may be summarized as follows. It was their duty to give advice to the prelates throughout the Council, and they ought to make a start right away, on the understanding that this admonition and all the rest were addressed to themselves as well as the others, since they were all equal. The

---

[1] Giovanni Maria Del Monte, Cardinal Bishop of Palestrina, later Pope Julius III (1550–55).

[2] Reginald Pole.

[3] Marcello Cervino or Cervini, Cardinal of Santacroce, later Pope Marcellus II.

156

Council had met for three reasons: to extirpate heresy, to reform ecclesiastical discipline, and to restore peace. Before doing this, it was necessary to have a true and deep sense of their responsibility for those three disasters. They had not provoked heresy, but they had not done their duty in sowing the seed of good doctrine and weeding out the tares. There was no need to mention the corruption of morals, since it was clear that the clergy and the pastors were both corrupted and corrupting. For these reasons, God had sent the third plague, that of war, both the civil war between Christians and the war with the Turks. If they did not recognize this sincerely and deeply, it would be useless holding a council or invoking the Holy Ghost. God's judgment in punishing them in this way was a just one; in fact, they had been punished less than they deserved. So they exhorted everyone to recognize their faults in order to mitigate the wrath of God, repeating that the Holy Ghost on whom they had called would not come if they refused to admit their sins like Esdras, Nehemias, and Daniel. They added that it was a great gift of God to have a chance of opening a council to restore everything. They did not lack opponents, but it was their duty to persevere and, like judges, to beware of being swayed by passion, and also to fix their minds on the glory of God alone—this being their duty to God, the angels, and the whole Church. In conclusion, they admonished the bishops sent by the princes to do them service honestly and diligently, but to put their duty to God above everything else. After this, the bull of 1542 summoning the council was read, also a brief appointing the legates and the bull opening the council which had been read in congregation. At this point, Alfonso Zorilla, secretary to Don Diego,[4] got up and produced the emperor's orders, which had already been presented to the legates, and also a letter from Don Diego, in which he apologized for his absence on the grounds that he was indisposed. The legates replied that they accepted the apology, and that as for the orders, although they could repeat their

---

[4] Don Diego Mendoza, imperial ambassador to Venice.

previous answer, they thought it more polite to read the orders again and then reply to them.

After these ceremonies had been performed in the customary Roman manner, everyone knelt down to pray quietly (in the manner which was to be customary at all sessions) and then aloud, "*Adsumus Domine*," and so on, "*Sancti Spiritus*," and so on, which the president said in a loud voice in the name of all. The litanies were sung, and the deacon read the Gospel, "*Si peccaverit in te frater tuus*" ["If thy brother does thee wrong"—Matthew 18:15], and finally, the hymn "*Veni creator spiritus*" ["Come, Holy Ghost"] was sung, and everyone sat down in his place. Then the Cardinal Del Monte put the question: Whether it pleased the Fathers, to the glory of God, the extirpation of heresy, the reformation of the clergy and people, and the destruction of the enemies of Christians, to decide and declare that the holy and General Council of Trent should begin. All replied with the word *placet* [yes], first the legates, then the bishops and the other Fathers. He then asked whether, given the impediments caused by the feasts of Christmas and New Year, they were pleased that the next session should begin on January 7, and again they replied in the affirmative. After this, Ercole Severoli, the *promoter* [organizing secretary] of the Council, told the notaries to write everything down. The "*Te Deum*" was sung, the Fathers took off their robes and put on their ordinary ones, and they accompanied the legates in procession behind the cross. These ceremonies took place in every session in the same way, so I shall not repeat them. . . .

In Trent, after the solemn opening, the prelates and the legates themselves still did not know what subjects should be discussed and what procedure should be followed. So the legates wrote a letter to Rome, explaining what had been done so far—a letter which deserves a full summary. They said first that they had determined that the next session would take place on the day after the Epiphany, which would prevent their being criticized because the interval was either too long or too short, and which would enable them to be advised on how to act in the other sessions, a matter on which they wished for guidance. They might be called upon at any time on a number of subjects, without having time to ask for guidance and receive a reply, so they asked to be sent instructions which were as detailed as possible. Above all they wanted guidance about the method of procedure and of proposing and making decisions, and about the agenda. They asked in particular whether the causes of heresy should be the first subject, and whether they should be treated in general or in detail; whether they should condemn heresy, or the most famous heretics, or both; whether, when they proposed to the prelates some article of reform which they thought everyone wanted, it should be discussed at the same time as the article on religion, or before, or after; whether the Council ought to announce that it had begun, inviting prelates and princes and exhorting the faithful to pray to God for its successful progress, or whether His Holiness wished to do that himself. If a letter or a reply had to be written, in what form and with what seal; similarly, they asked what form was to be used in the promulgation of decrees; whether they were to show that they knew about the colloquy and Diet in Germany, or to pretend not to know; whether the proceedings should move slowly or quickly, both in the case of ending sessions and in putting forward subjects for discussion. They said that some prelates thought that one should proceed by nations, but that they themselves thought that this method would lead to sedition, making all the prelates of one nation rebel together, and that the Italian majority, which was the most faithful to the Apostolic See, would be of no use if all its votes together were counted as the same as those of a few Frenchmen or Spaniards or Germans. They advised him, too, that it had been discovered that others had the intention of raising the question of the power of the Council and of the Pope, a dangerous matter which might give rise to a schism among the Catholics themselves, and that in the congregation of December 12, all the prelates together had insisted that they wanted to see their [the legates'] faculties. They had had to use great skill to avoid this since they did not yet know in what way they were to preside, and what His Holiness intended in this matter. They also asked that relays of horses be organized all along the way so that they could send and receive news every day and every hour, according to what was happening, and that there should be some instructions about the precedence of the ambassadors of princes and some provision of money, because the two thousand scudi sent them some days before had been spent on providing for the poorer bishops.

The prelates were pressing for the work to begin. The legates, to give them some satisfaction and to show they were not standing idle, held a congregation on the eighteenth. There, however, nothing was discussed except how they should live and bear themselves and govern their households. Many things were said against the new custom (especially prevalent in Rome) of wearing the costume of a prelate at ceremonies only and dressing the rest of the time as secular priests. Rich robes were criticized as well as vile and filthy ones. Much was also said about the age of their servants, but all decisions were postponed to the next congregation. This was held on the twenty-second, and it was spent entirely in discussing similar ceremonies, concluding that what was most necessary was an inward reformation: everyone see what should be remedied in himself and in his household, his criteria being what was appropriate to his rank and what would edify the people.

When the Pope received word that the Council had opened, he set up a congregation of cardinals and other members of the Curia to supervise and give advice on the affairs of Trent. He consulted with them and decided that things had not yet come to the point where it could be clearly seen what matters should be dealt with and in what order. He replied to the legates that it was not for the Council to invite princes or prelates, still less for them to ask anyone to pray for it, because he had done this in his Jubilee Bull and in the letter of summons. Similarly, the Council was not to think of writing to anyone, because the legates could do this with their own letters written in the name of all. When promulgating decrees, the Council should be entitled as follows, "the sacrosanct Ecumenical and General Council [*sinodo*] of Trent, with the apostolic legates presiding." As for the method of voting, the arguments against voting by nations were very good ones, and another reason for not doing so was the fact that this method was never used in ancient times, but introduced at the Council of Constance, and followed at the Council of Basel. The method followed in the last Lateran Council was a very good one, and they should follow that and use this recent precedent to shut the mouth of anyone who thinks differently. As for the condemnation of heretics and the subjects to discuss and their other requests, they would be answered when it was expedient; meanwhile, they should spend their time on preliminaries, as was the custom at the other councils. They should carry out their duty of presiding in such state as suited the legates of the Apostolic See, yet in such a way as to give satisfaction to all. And above all they should be careful to ensure that the prelates did not exceed the bounds of honorable liberty and reverence for the Apostolic See.

It was more urgent to help the prelates so that they might be able to pay their expenses, so he sent a brief in which he exempted from tithes all the prelates at the Council, and he granted them a share in all emoluments in their absence, just as if they were present. He also sent two thousand scudi to help the poorer bishops, ordering that this must be kept from becoming known, because it could only be interpreted as a loving gesture by the head of the Council.

At this point it is necessary, because of what has been said and what will be said on various occasions about the method of giving opinions at the Council, called "voting" [*dir li voti*], to say something about how it was done in ancient times and how the modern usage had come to be established. It is a very old custom that the whole Church should unite to discuss in God's name matters of doctrine and discipline. This method was used by the holy apostles in the election of Matthew and of the seven deacons. Diocesan councils are much like this. As for calling together Christians from a number of places, including distant ones, to confer together, the classic example comes from the Acts of the Apostles, when Paul and Barnabas and others from Syria met in Jerusalem with the apostles and other disciples who were there in order to discuss the question of the observance of the laws. This could be described as a return of the new church of the Gentiles to the old mother church, from which their faith was derived (a frequent custom in those first centuries, as Ireneus and Tertullian testify), and the letter was written by the Apostles, "elders" and brothers of Jerusalem alone. Nevertheless, it was not they alone but Paul and Barnabas, too, who spoke, so it may be correctly called a council. Following this precedent, the bishops who came after believed that all the Christian churches would unite, and that all the bishoprics would unite, too, so that each would not have a jurisdiction of his own, but that all of them would rule the whole (although each might pay particular attention to the area which was personally entrusted to him, as St. Cyprian clearly shows in his golden book on the *Unity of the Church*). If any particular church had a special need, although persecution sometimes made it dangerous, all who could met together to provide for this need in common. In these meetings Christ and the Holy Ghost presided, the passions of man had no place but only charity, and advice was given and solutions were reached without ceremonies or prescribed formulas. After some time, however, the passions of man did become mixed with the charity, and it became necessary to draw up regulations. And so, the most outstanding man present, whether for his learning or for the importance of the city or church he represented, or for some other kind of eminence, assumed the task of putting matters before the meeting and guiding the proceedings and gathering the opinions. After it pleased God to give peace to the faithful and after the conversion of the emperors, problems of doctrine and discipline arose more often and created disturbances, partly because of the ambition and other wicked passions of those who had a reputation and a following. The result was the appearance of another sort of meeting of bishops, one called by the emperors or their subordinates to find a means to calm down the disturbances. In these meetings the initiative was taken by the emperor or magistrates who summoned them, and they intervened in the proceedings, put propositions before the meeting, guided the discussion, and interrupted to settle differences of opinion, although they left the final decision to the sense of the meeting. This form of organization may be seen in those councils whose proceedings have survived. The colloquy of Catholics and Donatists in the presence of Marcellinus may be cited as an example, and there are many others. But to speak only of general councils, this may be seen in the first council of Ephesus, before Count Candidianus, appointed by the emperor to preside, and more clearly in the Council of Chalcedon, before Marcian and judges appointed by him; and in the Trullan Council at Constantinople, before Constantine IV, where the prince or the presiding magistrate decided what subjects should be discussed, what the procedure should be, who should speak, who should be silent, and when there were disputes on these matters, he decided them himself. In the case of other general councils whose proceedings have not been preserved, like the first Council of Nicæa or the second Council of Constantinople, the historians of the period bear witness that Constantine and Theodosius did the same. In these same times, when the bishops met on their own initiative, laymen did not intervene; the proceedings were guided, as has been said, by one of the bishops, and the decision was taken according to the sense of the meeting. Sometimes the problems dealt with could be dispatched easily, in one session; at other times, they were so difficult or complex that it was necessary to hold many sessions of the same council. The councils were never purely formal meetings, nor meetings held simply to make known decisions already taken elsewhere, but they were summoned in order to find out the opinion of each member. The discussions and arguments and whatever was said and done were called the proceedings of the council. It is a new idea and one rarely put into practice, even if it was confirmed at Trent, that the decrees alone should be called the proceedings of the council, and that these only should be made public; in ancient times everything was made known to everyone. Notaries were present to record the opinions, and when a bishop spoke and no one contradicted him, they would not write down his name, but "the holy synod said." And when many said the same thing, they would write "the bishops exclaimed" or "affirmed," and the things they said were taken as decisions. If they did disagree, the different opinions and the names of those who put them forward were noted, and the judges or presidents decided. Doubtless, insults were offered sometimes as a result of human imperfection, but charity, which excuses the defects of our brethren, covered them. The majority who took part would come from the province where the council was held and from neighboring districts, but there would not be any spirit of competition, each man desiring to obey rather than make laws for others.

When the Eastern and Western Empires separated, there were still some remains in the west, too, of those councils which princes used to summon. And there were many summoned by the Carolingians in France and Germany, and not a few by the kings of the Goths in Spain. In the end, as princes gave up intervening in ecclesiastical affairs, this kind of council disappeared, and there remained only the other which churchmen summoned themselves. The convocation of these was virtually taken over by the pope, who sent his legates to preside, whenever he heard that there were discussions about holding a council. After a time, he also claimed the power which the Roman emperors had had, that of calling councils of the whole empire and of presiding if he were present, or if he were not, of sending someone to preside and guide the proceedings in his name. The prelates assembled in the synod no longer had the fear of a secular ruler to keep them in order, and worldly considerations were becoming immensely more important. This increased the number of embarrassing situations, so the prelates began to go through the agenda in private in order to preserve decency in the public sessions. Then this became formalized, and committees were created to draw up agenda. And when this was complicated it was divided, and each part was referred to a different committee. Even this did not suffice to remove all embarrassments (because those who were not on the committees had different interests and raised difficulties in public), and so besides special committees a general one was introduced which took place before the session and in which everyone took part. This one, which is concerned with ancient customs, is the real council, and the session itself, now that everything is decided beforehand, is nothing but ritual. After a little more than a century, differences of interests caused some competition between the bishops of different nations; those from distant countries, who were few, were unwilling to accept the fact that they were always outvoted by the majority from the countries near Rome. To give them an equal chance it was necessary that each nation should meet separately to vote on its collective opinion, and that the decision of the council should be decided not by the votes of individuals, but by the votes of nations. This was the procedure at the Councils of Constance and Basel. It is an extremely appropriate method where men govern themselves freely, as in the days when there was no pope in the world, but inappropriate in Trent, where what was looked for was a council subject to the pope. And this was the reason why the legates in Trent and the Curia in Rome made so much of the methods of procedure and of who should preside and what authority he should have.

## Chapter Three

[*During the third session of the Council, in February 1546, the news of the death of Martin Luther was announced.*]

The Fathers in Trent and the Curia in Rome conceived great hopes when they saw that a man was dead who had powerfully opposed the doctrine and ceremonies of the Church of Rome, and who had been the principal, almost the sole cause of the divisions and innovations that had been introduced. They took this as an omen for the good success of the Council, especially because Luther's death became legend and was described in Italy as having been attended by many portents which were considered miracles and were ascribed to divine vengeance; not that anything happened which does not usually happen at the death of men of sixty-three, which was Martin's age when he died. However, what has happened between 1546 and our time has made it clear that Martin was simply one of the instruments of the Reformation, and that the causes were both more powerful and more remote.

In the first and second sessions, the Council had simply discussed its own title and the order of business, agreeing to discuss matters of dogma and the reform of the Church simultaneously. The third session opened with a reading of the Creed—one prelate commented, "They will say that after twenty years' negotiations, it was decided to meet to listen to the Creed being read." The legates wrote to the Pope that it was difficult to carry on with unimportant matters any longer.

The Pope thought a great deal about the letter from Trent, weighing the possible disadvantages if he continued to keep the Council, as he put it, "at anchor," and the dissatisfaction of the bishops who were present, against the dangers that might arise when reform began. In the end, realizing that it was necessary to take some chances, and that the counsel of prudence was simply to avoid the greater evil, he decided to write back to Trent, saying that they should begin the Council actively as they had suggested, but not raise new difficulties in matters of faith, nor decide any of the controversies between Catholics, and that they should proceed very slowly in the reform. The legates, who had till then only raised general matters in the congregations, now that they had received the power to go ahead, proposed in the congregation of February 22 that now that the foundation of the faith had been laid, they could deal with a wider issue—that of Holy Scripture. This matter was relevant to the controversies with the Lutherans over dogma and also to the reform of abuses, including the most important ones, of which there were so many that there might not be time to remedy them all before the next session. There was a discussion both of the controversies with the Lutherans on this point and of the abuses, and much was said by various prelates.

Up to this time the theologians, of whom there were thirty, mostly friars, had done nothing at the Council except to preach some sermons on feast days honoring the Council or the Pope, or skirmishing with the Lutherans. However, now that it was a question of deciding on some controversial dogma and reforming the errors of intellectuals rather than of others, their value began to be apparent. On the matter of procedure, it was decided that propositions should be extracted from Lutheran books attacking the orthodox faith and given to the theologians to study and judge; each of them would declare his opinion, and thus the raw material for the decrees would be prepared. These would be proposed in congregation and examined by the Fathers, and each of them would declare his opinion, and then they would decide what would be promulgated. As for abuses, everyone would mention what he thought needed to be reformed, together with the appropriate remedy.

The articles on the ideas taken from Luther's books were as follows.

I. That the doctrine necessary to Christian faith was entirely contained in the Holy Scriptures; that it is an invention of man to add to them unwritten traditions, as if they had been left by Christ and the apostles of the Holy Church, and had come down to us by means of the unbroken succession of bishops; and that it was sacrilegious to consider them of equal authority with the Old and New Testament.

II. That among the books of the Old Testament, only those received from the Jews should be included; and in the New Testament, the six Epistles (that is, those going by the names of St. Paul to the Hebrews, St. James, the second of St. Peter, the second and third of St. John, and St. Jude) and the Apocalypse.

III. That to have a true understanding of Holy Scripture or to quote it, it is necessary to go to texts in the original language in which it was written, and the Latin translation should be condemned as full of errors.

IV. That Holy Scripture is simple and clear and needs no gloss or comment to be understood, but only the spirit of one of Christ's flock.

V. Whether canons with anathemas should be drawn up against all these articles.

The theologians spoke on the first two articles in four congregations; and on the first, they all agreed that the Christian faith derives partly from Holy Scripture and partly from traditions; and they spent much time in quoting Tertullian (who often discusses the subject and enumerates many traditions), Ireneus, Cyprian, Basil, Augustine, and others. In fact, some said that the whole of Catholic faith was based only on tradition, because the reason for believing in Scripture is that it has been handed down by tradition. . . .

In the third congregation there was much controversy about the Latin translation of the Bible between some few who had a good knowledge of Latin and some taste of Greek and others innocent of languages.

Brother Aloisio de Catanea said that on this question nothing was more relevant than the judgment of Cardinal Cajetan, a man very well versed in theology, who had studied since he was a boy and had become the first theologian of this and many other ages as a result of his great intelligence and hard work. There was no prelate or anyone else at the Council who was his equal in learning, or who could not learn from him. When he went to Germany as legate, in 1523, to find out most carefully how those who had strayed could be brought back to the Church and how the heresiarchs could be convinced, he found the real answer: the literal understanding of the text of Holy Scripture in its original language. For the eleven years which remained to him, he gave himself completely to the study of Scripture, making use not only of the Latin translation, but of the sources—Hebrew for the Old Testament and Greek for the New. He had no knowledge of these languages, but made use of people who did, who translated the text word by word for him, as his books written on the Scriptures show. The good cardinal used to say that to understand the Latin text was not to understand the infallible word of God, but the word of the translator, which was subject to errors; and that Jerome had said well that "prophesying and writing inspired books came from the Holy Ghost, but translating them into another language was the work of human skill"; and he used to sigh and say, "Oh, that it had pleased God that the Doctors of previous centuries had done their work so that the Lutheran heresies had had no opportunity!" He added that no translation can be approved without contradicting the canon *Ut veterum d.9.*, which commands the Old Testament to be examined with reference to the Hebrew text, and the New Testament with reference to the Greek. To approve a translation as the correct one was to condemn St. Jerome and all other translators; if one is correct, what is the use of the others? It would be useless to produce uncertain versions when there were correct ones in existence. They ought to believe with St. Jerome and Cajetan that every translator can make mistakes, however hard he tries to follow the original text. It was certain that if the holy Council were to examine and amend the text, the Holy Ghost, who assists at synods in matters of faith, would prevent their falling into error; and a translation examined and approved in this way could be called correct. But he dared not say (unless the holy synod so decided) that a translation could be approved without such an examination, yet with assurance of the help of the Holy Ghost. Even in the council of the holy apostles a careful examination had come first. However, such a task would take decades, and since it could not be undertaken, it seemed better to leave things as they had been for one thousand five hundred years, checking the Latin translations against the original texts.

In opposition to this the majority of the theologians said that it was necessary to declare that the translation which had been read in churches and used in schools in past times was inspired and completely correct; otherwise, they would be giving in to the Lutherans and opening a door to innumerable future heresies and continually disturbing the peace of Christendom. The doctrine of our holy mother the Church of Rome, the mother and the leader of all the others, was largely based by the popes and by the scholastic theologians on certain passages in Scripture. If they gave liberty to everyone to examine whether these passages were correctly translated, checking them against other translations or against the Greek and Hebrew originals, these new grammarians would upset everything and make themselves judges and arbiters of the faith; and when bishops and cardinals were appointed, pedants would be preferred before theologians and canonists. The inquisitors would not be able to proceed against the Lutherans unless they knew Latin and Greek—for the accused would reply to them that the text did not say this, that the translation was not faithful. Every new or capricious interpretation that some grammarian might see in the text, out of malice or out of ignorance of theological matters, as long as he could back it up with some tiny piece of linguistic knowledge, would have a basis, so that one would never reach the end of all this. It was evident now that, after Luther had begun to translate Scripture, many different and contradictory versions had come to light, which rather deserved to be hidden in eternal darkness, and that Martin himself had often altered his own translation, so that it was never reprinted without some serious alterations, not of one or two passages, but of hundreds. If this liberty were given to everyone, Christians would soon have no idea what to believe.

The majority applauded these arguments. Others added that if Divine Providence had given a correct Scripture to the synagogue and a correct New Testament to the Greeks, it was rather derogatory to say that the Church of Rome, most beloved of all, had been left without so great a benefit, and that the Holy Ghost, who had dictated the books of the Bible, had not also dictated this translation which ought to be accepted by the Roman Church. Some thought it a hard thing to make a man a prophet or an apostle simply for the sake of translating a book; and so they put in a qualification, saying that the translator did not have the prophetic or apostolic spirit, but something quite close to it. But if it was difficult to give the assistance of the Holy Ghost to the translator, it could not be denied to the Council; and when the Vulgate had been approved and those who would not accept it cursed, then it would be the correct version, not because of the inspiration of the translator, but of that of the synod which had accepted it as correct.

Don Isidoro Clario of Brescia, a Benedictine abbot, well versed in these studies, opposed this opinion on historical grounds, saying in substance that in the primitive Church there were many Greek translations of the Old Testament, which Origen had collected into one volume facing one another in six columns. Of these, the principal one was called that of the Seventy (Septuagint], from which various Latin versions were made. Similarly, there were different Latin versions of the New Testament, one of which, the most popular among the churches, was called the Itala version and was considered by St. Augustine to be the best, though he certainly thought the Greek text should be held more reliable still. But St. Jerome, skilled in languages, as everyone knows, seeing that the Latin version of the Old Testament deviated from the truth of the Hebrew one, partly because of the mistakes of both the Greek translator and the Latin one, made another directly from the Hebrew; he emended the Latin version of the New Testament in the light of the Greek text. As a result of Jerome's reputation, his translation was accepted by many and rejected by others, whether out of rivalry (as he lamented) or out of their love of old errors and their hatred of novelties. But after some years the envy disappeared, and St. Jerome's version was accepted by all the Latins. And both versions were used, called the old and the new. St. Gregory, writing to St. Leander about Job, bears witness to the fact that the Apostolic See used both, and that he in expounding that book chose to follow the new, as closer to the Hebrew; but in the notes, he would sometimes use one and sometimes the other, according to which suited him best.

In the next period these two versions were combined into one, taking part from the old, part from the new, as chance would have it, and this composite version was given the name of the Vulgate. The psalms were all from the old version, because they were sung daily in the churches and so could not be changed. The minor prophets were all from the new version; the major prophets came some from one version, some from the other. It was certain that all this had come about by the will of God, without which nothing happens at all; but all the same, it could not be said that more than human abilities had been at work. St. Jerome openly admits that no translator has been inspired by the Holy Ghost. The version which we have is mostly his. It would be an extraordinary thing to attribute divine assistance to someone who admitted, in fact asserted, that he did not have any; and so, no translation of the Bible could ever equal the text in its original language. All the same, he was of opinion that the Vulgate should be the approved version, if it were corrected with reference to the original text, and that it should be forbidden to make another translation; this one should be emended, the others destroyed. Thus all the troubles caused by new interpretations would cease, which had already been judiciously noticed and criticized in the congregation.

Brother Andres de Vega, a Franciscan, following a middle course between these opinions, approved the opinion of St. Jerome that the translator was given no prophetic spirit or other divine gift which would ensure him infallibility, and he agreed with the views of the same saint and of St. Augustine that translations should be corrected with reference to the texts in the original language; but added that it was not inconsistent to say that the Latin Church should treat the Vulgate as correct, because that meant that there was no error in it concerning faith or morals, not that it was correct in every tiny respect, since it was impossible for every word of one language to be translated into another without there being a restriction or an amplification of the sense or of metaphors and other figures of speech. The Vulgate had already been scrutinized by the whole Church for more than a thousand years, and it had been recognized that there was no error in it concerning faith or morals. It had been esteemed and used as such in the ancient councils, and so it ought to be esteemed and approved. And so it could be declared correct, that is, it could be read without danger, which should not hinder the more diligent from going back to the Hebrew and Greek sources, but forbade so many complete translations as would cause confusion.

The doctrine of the late Cardinal Cajetan gave rise to controversy about the article on the meaning of Holy Scripture. He taught (and practiced what he preached) that new interpretations should not be rejected when they fitted the text and did not contradict other passages of Scripture and the doctrines of the faith, even if this meant swimming against the stream of the opinions of the learned. His Divine Majesty had not bequeathed the meaning of Scripture to the Doctors of old, otherwise there would be nothing for the present and future to do except copy them out. Some of the theologians and Fathers supported this view, others attacked it.

The supporters thought it a spiritual tyranny to forbid the faithful to use the brains God had given them; this would be to forbid the spiritual employment of God-given talents. Men should be given every encouragement to read the Bible, and if they were to lose the pleasure of novelty, they would hate it; such a strictness would make the learned desert biblical studies for other sorts of literature, and so abandon piety as well. This variety of spiritual gifts belonged to the perfection of the Church, as could be seen from reading the Fathers, in whose writings there was great diversity and often contradiction (although great charity, too). And why should this age not enjoy the same liberty as the others had enjoyed with spiritual fruitfulness? Although the scholastics did not dispute about the meaning of the Bible, they had serious disputes over points of religion, and these were no less dangerous. It was better to imitate the ancients who did not restrict the expounding of Scripture, but who left it free.

The contrary view was that popular license was worse than tyranny, and that in these times it was fitting to curb unbridled wits, for otherwise they could not hope to see the end of the present contentions. In ancient times, it was permitted to write about the Bible because there were few interpretations, and so more were needed; the men of those times were men of holy life and calm judgment, so that no disturbances were to be feared from them as they were at present. And so the scholastic theologians, seeing that there was no need in the Church for other interpretations and that the Bible was not only self-sufficient, but also thoroughly commented on, approached religion in another way. They saw that men were inclined to argument, and they judged that men would do better to examine the arguments of Aristotle and continue to treat Holy Scripture with reverence, which would be difficult if it was frequently argued over and treated as material for the curious to study and dispute about. This opinion went so far that Brother Richard de Mans, a Franciscan, said that the dogmas of the faith had been so clarified by the scholastics that one should no longer learn them from Scripture. It used to be read in church to teach the people, and it was studied for the same reason, whereas at present it was read in church only as a form of prayer. This is how everyone should treat it and not study it, and this would express the reverence and veneration which everyone owes to the word of God. At least no one should be allowed to read it for reasons of study who was not first qualified in scholastic theology. It was just those who studied Scripture who were attracted to the Lutherans. This opinion was not without followers.

Two opinions took the middle way between these others. One was that it was not good to restrict the understanding of Scripture to the Fathers of the Church alone, because most of their interpretations were allegorical, and few were literal. And those that were literal were adapted to their own time, so that the interpretation was not appropriate for ours. Cardinal Nicholas of Cusa, a man of excellent doctrine and life, had said authoritatively that the interpretation of Scripture must be adapted to the age and its customs, and it was not to be wondered at if the Church adopted one interpretation in one age, and another in another. The last Lateran Council shared his view in resolving that Scripture should be interpreted according to the Doctors of the Church and ancient usage. The conclusion was that new interpretations should only be forbidden when they were inconsistent with the general consensus of the time.

Brother Domingo Soto, a Dominican, distinguished matters of faith and morals from the rest, saying that in such matters it was right to keep every mind within bounds already set, but that in other matters it would not be inconvenient to let everyone choose his own interpretation, saving piety and charity. The Fathers had not intended that everyone should be forced to follow them, except in necessary matters for faith and works. Nor did the popes, when in their decretals they interpreted some passage of Scripture in a certain way, intend to canonize it so that no one was allowed to give the passage any other meaning, when he had reasons for so doing. This is what St. Paul meant when he said that prophecy (that is, the interpretation of Scripture) should be used according to faith, that is, with reference to the articles of faith. If this distinction were not made, serious difficulties would arise because of the inconsistencies between different interpretations given by the Fathers.

The difficulties that had been raised were not so effective as to prevent the congregation of Fathers from approving the Vulgate almost unanimously. The argument that the grammarians would take it on themselves to teach the bishops and theologians had made a powerful impression on the prelates.

## Chapter Four

[*The fourth session began in April, 1546. The Council discussed original sin.*]

When the decision was announced to condemn in the same session the Lutheran doctrines of original sin, it was alleged that, in order to preserve the system of dealing with both subjects [dogma and reform] together, it was necessary to deal with something *de fide* [concerning faith], for there was nowhere else to begin; and articles were proposed extracted from the doctrine of the Protestants on this matter, to be examined by the theologians in the congregation and discussed to see if they should be condemned as heretical. Cardinal Pacheco[1] said that the Council was only supposed to be dealing with articles *de fide* in order to win back Germany, and whoever wished to do this at the wrong moment would not only be unsuccessful, but would make matters worse. When the time was ripe this would not be known at Trent, but by the man who was at the helm of Germany and, seeing all the details, would know when it was time to administer this medicine. And so, he advised writing to the chief prelates of that nation for their views before going any further, or the nuncio could talk to the emperor about it. The prelates of the Empire agreed with this, persuaded by the Ambassador.[2] But the legates, having praised the judgment of the prelates and promised to write to the nuncio, added that it would save time if the theologians could discuss these articles all the same. The Cardinal and the others agreed, hoping that many difficulties would arise to cause delays, and the Ambassador Toledo was content because the summer would pass before a definition was arrived at. . . .

After the theologians had given their opinions, the

[1] Pedro Pacheco, Bishop of Jaen, leader of the Spanish prelates before Granada.

[2] Francisco de Toledo, Charles V's ambassador to the Council.

Fathers discussed the matter to decide on the form of the decree. The bishops, few of whom had any knowledge of theology (they were either lawyers or humanist-courtiers), were confused by the scholastic method of treating the subject, full of thorns, and the differences of opinion among the theologians were so great that they could not decide what the essence of original sin was. The opinion they found most easy to understand was that of Caterino, because it was expressed in political terms as a treaty which a certain man had on behalf of his descendants—a treaty which had been broken, but which was without any doubt binding on them all. Many of the Fathers favored this opinion, but they did not dare to make it official when they saw how the other theologians contradicted it. As for the remission of sins, all that was clear to them was that before baptism everyone is guilty of original sin, but that they are completely cleansed afterwards; and so they decided that this should be laid down as matter of faith and the contrary condemned as heresy, together with all opinions that deny original sin, in whatever manner. But as for what original sin was, since the theologians disagreed so much among themselves, it was impossible to define it so as to satisfy all of them, and it was impossible to condemn the opinion of one of them without danger of causing a schism.

## Chapter Five

[*In January, 1546, a colloquy or conference was held at Regensburg, which the Protestants attended. In March, the demands of the Protestants were rejected, and they broke off negotiations. In June, the Diet assembled at Regensburg. Sarpi describes the proceedings.*]

The emperor showed great displeasure that the colloquy had been fruitless, and he asked everyone to suggest what should be done to pacify Germany. The Protestants suggested that the differences in religion should be composed by a national council as laid down by the recess of Speyer, saying that this was more to the point than a general one, because the difference of opinion between Germany and the other nations was so great that it was impossible to avoid even great contention in a general council.

Anyone who wanted to force Germany to change her opinion would have to kill endless thousands of men, to the loss of the emperor and to the delight of the Turks. The imperial ministers replied that the non-execution of the decree of Speyer was not the fault of His Majesty, and that it was well known to all that to make peace with the king of France (as he had needed to), he had been forced to do what the Pope wanted in religious matters; that the decree was framed to meet the necessities of that time, and as circumstances had changed it was necessary for policy to change, too; that morals had sometimes been corrected in national councils, but matters of faith had never been dealt with there; that in colloquies one has to deal with theologians, who for the most part are difficult and obstinate, so that they make it impossible to arrive at counsels of moderation, such as are necessary; that no one loved religion more than the emperor, and he would not depart one jot from what was just and honorable to please the Pope, but he knew well that in a national council he would not be able either to make the two sides agree, or to find an arbitrator. The Ambassadors of Mainz and Trier separated themselves from the other four and, united with all the Catholics, approved the Council of Trent, and they begged the emperor to protect it and to persuade the Protestants to join it and submit to it. The Protestants said that the Council of Trent was not a free council, as had been requested and promised in the imperial Diet, and they reiterated that the emperor should keep the peace and command that religious matters should be settled either in a legitimate German council, or in an imperial diet, or in a colloquy of the learned men of both sides.

Meanwhile, the emperor had secretly made preparations for war which could not remain secret, but came to the notice of the Protestants assembled in the Diet. Peace had been made with the king of France, and a truce had been made for that year with the Turks, so that everyone could easily see his aim all the more because of the rumor that the Pope and Ferdinand were arming, too; and so everything was in confusion. The emperor saw that he was discovered, and on June 9, he sent the Cardinal of Trent[1] posthaste to Rome to ask the Pope for the help he had promised. He sent captains to Flanders and to Italy with money to raise troops, and he asked the German Protestant princes and captains who were not members of the Schmalkaldic league to follow him, claiming and promising that he did not want to make war for religious ends, but to put down the rebellion of some who were using religion as a pretext to disobey his laws and his authority. This promise also pacified many cities which had already reformed their religious ceremonies; the emperor promised to show favor to the obedient and gave them assurances about their religion. . . .

In Rome, on June 26, the Cardinal of Trent concluded the league between the Pope and the emperor against the Protestants of Germany, negotiations for which had been begun by Cardinal Farnese in Worms the year before, as has been said, and afterwards reopened many times by other intermediaries. The alleged causes and the conditions of the league were as follows. Germany had been obstinate in heresy for a long time, for which reason the Council of Trent had been summoned and had begun. The Protestants, however, refused to submit to it, and so the Pope and emperor, for the glory of God and the salvation of Germany, had decided that the emperor should take arms against them and bring them back to the obedience to the Holy See. To this end the Pope had deposited a hundred thousand scudi in Venice, besides the hundred thousand already deposited there, to be spent for this purpose only. And besides this, he would send to war at his own expense twelve thousand Italian infantry and five hundred light horse for six

[1] Cardinal Cristoforo Madruzzo, Prince Bishop of Trent.

months; he gave the emperor half the revenues of the churches of Spain for that year and power to alienate five hundred thousand scudi's worth of monastic income in that kingdom. During those six months the emperor could not come to terms with the Protestants without the Pope, and the Pope was to share in any of his gains. And if the war continued after that time, they would make new terms according to what both parties thought best; it would be possible for others to join the league, sharing in the expenses and in the gains. There was also a secret clause which referred to the king of France: if any Christian prince attacked the emperor during this war, the Pope would be obliged to use his spiritual and temporal weapons against him.

A few days later, the Pope wrote to the Swiss, inviting them to help him and declaring elaborately that he was well disposed toward them, and that he was pained because some of them had alienated themselves from him. He thanked God for those who continued to obey him and praised them all because although differing in religion they were at peace, whereas elsewhere there were disorders for the same cause. He added that to remedy these he had summoned the Council of Trent and hoped that no one would refuse to submit to it; he was sure that those of them who had remained obedient up till now would obey the Council, and that the others would not despise it. He invited them also to come to it, complaining that in Germany many so-called princes arrogantly despised and insulted the Council, whose authority was more divine than human, and so he had had to think in terms of force and arms. And since the emperor had taken the same decision, he had had to ally with him and help him, with his own power and that of the Church of Rome, to restore religion by force. He had wished to explain his intentions to them so that they would join their prayers to his, give back its former honor to the Church of Rome, and help him in a pious cause.

The emperor, however, made a show of undertaking the war not for religious but for political reasons, because some people refused to obey him; they plotted with foreigners against him and illegally usurped the possessions of others, principally those of the Church, making bishoprics and abbacies hereditary. He had tried various ways of persuading them to obey, but they had become more and more insolent.

The Protestants, on the other hand, tried to show the world that everything arose from the instigation of the Pope and the Council of Trent; they reminded the emperor of the articles to which he had sworn in Frankfort when he became emperor, and they claimed that he was breaking them. But many of those same Protestants supported the emperor, being unable to believe that other than political considerations were involved. The Archbishop of Cologne, too, of whom it has been said above that, although he had been sentenced and deprived by the Pope, he continued to rule none the less and to be obeyed by his subjects, supported tthe emperor, who continued to recognize him as elector and archbishop. The emperor wrote asking him not to allow any of his subjects to fight against him, and the Archbishop tried sincerely to do this. When the elector of Saxony and the landgrave [of Hesse] saw this, on July 15, they published a manifesto, to show that this war had been undertaken for religious reasons, and that the emperor was hiding his true intentions behind the pretext of punishing the rebellion of a few people in order to divide the allies and destroy them all little by little. They claimed that Ferdinand and Granvelle and other imperial ministers had attributed this war to the fact that the Council had been despised. They reminded their readers of the papal sentence against the elector of Cologne and added that the Spanish prelates would not have contributed so much of their revenue for any other cause. They showed that the emperor had no grounds for displeasure against them anyway. . . .

## Chapter Six

The Pope in Rome published a Jubilee Bull on July 15, which saved the German princes the trouble of investigating the true cause of the war or of persuading others of it. In this bull he explained elaborately his pastoral solicitude for the salvation of mankind; mentioned the continual loss of souls as a result of the increase of heresy, saying that the Council had already started in order to extirpate it; and complained of the obstinacy of the heretics who despised it and refused to obey it or submit to its decisions. To remedy this he had made an alliance with the emperor to force the heretics to obey the Church by military means. Everyone should ask God, by praying and fasting, confession and Communion, to grant a happy issue to this war undertaken for His glory, the exaltation of the Church, and the extirpation of heresy.

The emperor, having decided to conceal the religious issue, published on the twentieth of the same month a ban against the elector and the landgrave, in which he accused them of having always hindered his plans, of never having obeyed him, of having conspired against him, of having made war on other German princes, of having seized bishoprics and other territories, depriving many of their property, and of having covered all these things with the sweet and specious names of religion, peace, and liberty, while their true aims were quite different. He outlawed them as being treacherous, rebellious, and seditious, and guilty of high treason and disturbing the peace. He forbade anyone to help them or join them. He absolved the nobles and the people of their dominions from their oath of fealty, and he included in the ban all those who continued to obey them.

The reasons which the emperor advanced for the war greatly grieved the Pope, and the reasons which the Pope advanced greatly grieved the emperor, each of them hindering the other. For although the Pope claimed to have issued the bull in order that all Christians should beg God to help the emperor's forces, every man of judgment understood very well that it was to tell Germany and all the world that the war was a religious one. Even the men of less judgment realized this soon after, because the Pope's letter to the Swiss was published (mentioned above) and also a copy of the articles of the treaty with Madruzzo. The Pope's motive in contradicting the emperor in public was that although he wanted the Protestants to be weakened, he did not want the emperor to be strengthened. For them to be well balanced, he thought it necessary to force all those professing the new religion to unite against the emperor. It is certain that the Pope's action hindered the emperor's plans; for, having asked the Swiss to continue their alliance with the house of Austria and Burgundy and not to help his rebels, they replied that they wished first to be certain that the war was not a religious one. And so it happened that even before the war began there was discord between these two princes who had only just made an alliance.

[*Fifth session: doctrine, the prelates discuss articles taken from the writings of the Zwinglians, the first one being, "concerning predestination and reprobation the will of God is the only cause, and man does nothing on his side."*]

The most esteemed theologians held the article to be a Catholic one, and the contrary to be heretical, because the good scholastic writers, St. Thomas, Scotus, and the rest, thought so; that is, that God has from the creation of the world chosen a few out of the whole mass of the human race to be saved, out of pure mercy, and He has given them the means to obtain salvation, which is called "predestination"; that the number of these chosen is definite and limited, and no one can be added to it. Those who are not predestined cannot complain, because God has given them enough help for them to be saved, even if it is only the elect who will in fact be saved. Their most important argument was that St. Paul in his Epistle to the Romans pointed to Jacob as a type of the elect and to Esau as a type of the reprobate, and he produced God's decree pronounced before they were born, pronounced not as a result of any of their works, but simply because He so wished. To this they added the illustration given by the same apostle, that just as a potter makes out of the same lump of clay one vessel for an honorable use and another for a base use, so God out of the same mass of men chooses those who please Him and leaves the others. They pointed out that St. Paul proved this from the passage where God said to Moses: "I will show pity on those whom I pity; I will show mercy where I am merciful." He concluded that "the effect comes, then, from God's mercy, not from man's will, or man's alacrity," adding that "He shows mercy where it is His will, and where it is His will He hardens men's hearts." They also said that for this reason predestination and reprobation are called by the same apostle the height and depth of wisdom, unsearchable and incomprehensible. They added passages from the other epistles, where it is said that we have nothing that we have not received from God, and that we are not sufficient in ourselves even to think well, and where, explaining why some had rebelled against the faith, while others had stood firm, he said it was because the foundation of God stands firm, which has this seal, "The Lord knows His own." They added various passages from St. John's Gospel and innumerable ones from St. Augustine, because that saint in his old age always wrote in favor of this doctrine.

But some others, although of less reputation, opposed this opinion, calling it hard, cruel, inhuman, horrible, and wicked, as if it showed God to have favorites, choosing some and casting out others without any motive, and to be unjust, since He destined men to damnation because it was His will, not because they had sinned, and because He had created such a multitude of men only to damn them. They said that this doctrine was fatal to free will, because the elect could not, in the last analysis, do evil, nor the reprobate, good; that it forced men into the abyss of despair, with the suspicion that they might be reprobate; that it gave the perverse an opportunity to do nothing but evil, without worrying about repentance, thinking that if they were of the elect, they would not be damned, and if they were reprobate, it would be useless to do good because this would not save them. They admitted that works are not the cause of election, because election is from eternity and therefore precedes them. They admitted that not even good works foreseen by God could move Him to predestine, but they argued that by His infinite mercy He wished everyone to be saved and gave everyone grace sufficient to this end, which every man (having free will) accepted or rejected as he pleased. God from all eternity foresaw which men would accept His grace and which would reject it; He elected the first and damned the others. They added that otherwise it was impossible to see why in Scripture God lamented about the sinners and exhorted everyone to repentance and conversion if He did not give them the means to obtain it. They said that the "sufficient grace" which the others had invented was insufficient, because, according to them, it had never had and never would have any effect.

The first opinion was difficult and mysterious; it kept the mind humble and resigned to God's will, without any confidence in itself, knowing the deformity of sin and the excellence of God's grace. The second was plausible, popular, encouraged human presumption, and was, superficially, most attractive. It appealed rather to the friars, professional preachers, than to the theologians, and it seemed probable to the courtiers for political reasons. It was supported by the Bishop of Bitonto and most strongly by the Bishop of Salpi. The defenders of the second opinion had the better of the argument from reason, but were clearly worsted in the argument from Scripture.

[*Fifth session: reform, the Council discusses whether the residence of bishops is* de iure divino (*by the law of God*). *The significance of the discussion, as Sarpi points out in Book Seven, when the question came up again in 1562, is that if the duty of bishops to reside was based on the law of God, then bishops were instituted by God. If this was so, then the keys were not given to Peter alone, and the Council was above the Pope. See below.*]

The Spaniards not only supported but also egged on the theologians *de iure divino*, having a secret plan which was known only among themselves, to increase the authority of bishops, because if it were once decided that Christ had given them the duty of ruling their Church directly, it would follow that He had given them the necessary authority, and that the pope could not limit it. These designs were smelled out by the supporters of the Curia, and seeing the importance of the matter, they encouraged the defenders of the contrary view. The legates thought the best way to avoid the danger was to seem to be unaware of it; and so, they said that the matter was difficult and needed more careful consideration. Where there are controversies among Catholics themselves, one should not come to a decision which condemns one side, in order not to create a schism, and in order not to sow contentions, which would hinder a united front against the Lutherans. Therefore it was better to postpone the declaration about which law enjoined residence to another session.

## Chapter Seven

[*January, 1547: the sixth session, publication of decrees on dogma and on reform.*]

The first contained sixteen articles with a preamble and thirty-three anathemas. In substance, after having forbidden belief, preaching, and teaching other than such as was allowed and explained in the decree, it declared:

I. Neither the pagans by the light of nature, nor the Jews by the letter of the law of Moses were able to free themselves from sin.

II. And so God sent His son to redeem both.

III. Although He died for all men, only those to whom His merits are communicated enjoy the benefit.

IV. The justification of the wicked is simply a change from the status of son of Adam to the status of adopted son of God through Jesus Christ, a change which after the spreading of the Gospel cannot be made without baptism or the desire for it.

186

V. The beginning of justification in adults comes from grace, which invites them to accept it freely and to co-operate with it, which they do of their free will and are able to refuse.

VI. The method of preparation is first to believe freely in God's revelations and promises; to know oneself to be a sinner and to move from fearing that one has not the grace of God to hoping in His mercy and pardon, and so to begin to hate sin; and finally to decide to receive baptism, to begin a new life, and to keep God's commandments.

VII. Justification follows this preparation, and it is not only remission of sins, but sanctification as well. And it has five causes: the final cause, the glory of God and eternal life; the efficient cause, God; the deserving cause, Christ; the instrumental cause, the sacrament; the formal cause, the justice granted by God according to the pleasure of the Holy Ghost and the disposition of the recipient who receives (together wtih the remission of sins) faith, hope, and charity.

VIII. When St. Paul said that man was justified through faith and as a free gift, this is to be understood as meaning that faith is the beginning, and that the acts which precede justification are not deserving of grace.

IX. If a man presumes on his faith and the certainty of remission, his sins are not pardoned. Nor may it be said that faith alone justifies. The mercy of God, the merits of Christ, and the efficacy of the sacraments may not be doubted, but everyone may have doubts about his own indisposition, being unable to know that he has obtained grace with the certainty of infallible faith.

X. The just are still more justified by observing the commandments of God and of the Church.

XI. It cannot be said that God's commandments are impossible to the just man, who may fall into venial sin, but who does not cease to be justified. No one must rely on faith alone, or say that the just man sins in every good work, or sins if he does anything for reward.

XII. No one should presume that he is one of the

elect and believe that the justified man can sin no more, or that if he sins he can promise himself repentance.

XIII. Similarly, no one can promise himself absolute certainty of persevering to the end, but must hope in God's aid, which will continue if man does not fail.

XIV. Whoever falls into sin may obtain grace again, recovering it with God's encouragement and by means of repentance. This grace is different from the grace of baptism, since it contains not only contrition, but the sacrament of confession and absolution by the priest, at least in intention, and besides that, satisfaction for temporal punishment. These are never remitted all together except in baptism.

XV. The grace of God is not only lost through loss of faith, but through any mortal sin, even if that does not lead to loss of faith.

XVI. It proposes to the just the exercise of good works, through which eternal life is gained, as a grace promised by the mercy of God and as a reward which God has promised to good works. And it concludes that this doctrine does not establish a justice of our own, repudiating God's justice, but may be called ours because it is in us, and God's, because He has poured it into us through the merits of Christ.

. . . After I had written this summary of the decree, it occurred to me that it was superfluous, because all the decrees of this Council are in a printed volume in the hands of everyone, and I could also refer to this book for the wording of the acts which follow, and I was going to cross out this page. Then I considered that it might perhaps please someone to read the whole story in one book, and that whoever was more interested in the original could leave out my summary. So I decided not to change anything and to use the same method for the matters that will follow. And then I considered the annoyance I feel when I see that Xenophon or Tacitus have left out something well known in their own time, which is unknown to me, because there is no way of knowing it now. So I decided to hold to the maxim, that one book should never refer the reader to another. I come now to the summary of the decree about reform, which was in substance as follows.

I. The Council, wishing to reform the corrupt manners of the clergy and the people, believed that it should begin with those in charge of the greater churches. Trusting in God and in His vicar on earth that men would be appointed who were worthy and who had been trained in ecclesiastical discipline from their youth, it admonished them to do their duty, which could not be done if they did not reside in their Sees. Nevertheless, many leave their flocks and the care of their lambs and wander about courts and take part in secular affairs. And so, the Council renews all the ancient canons against nonresidence, and besides this, orders that whoever is set over a cathedral church, whatever his title and status, who without just and reasonable cause remains out of his diocese for six months at a time, should lose a quarter of the income; and if he continues to be absent for another six months, he is to lose another quarter; and if this continues, the metropolitan (under pain of being unable to enter his church) must inform the pope within three months, who can by his supreme authority inflict a greater punishment and provide the church with a more useful shepherd. And if the metropolitan commits the same offense, the senior suffragan should inform the pope about him.

II. The clergy who are of lower rank than the bishops and whose duty it is by law or custom to reside should be forced to do so by the bishops, who should annul every permanent exemption from residence. Temporary exemptions shall remain in force if there is a good reason for them, and the bishop should examine this. He should also make sure (as the representative of the Apostolic See) that the cure of souls is confided to a suitable vicar with a fair share of the income, notwithstanding privileges and exemptions.

III. There should be no exemptions—neither personal exemptions for the secular clergy, nor exemptions of whole orders for members of the regular clergy living outside their monastery—which may hinder visitation by the bishop, and punishment if necessary.

IV. Similarly, the chapters of cathedrals and other colleges should not be free from visitations by their bishops and other important prelates whenever there is need of them, whatever exemptions or customs or oaths or agreements there may be.

V. Finally, it was ordained that no bishop should, under pretext of privilege, exercise official powers in the diocese of another without his permission, and then only over his own subjects.

It was decided that the next session would begin on March 3.

In Rome, the decree on faith did not cause any stir, as it was not new and had been examined in public, as has been said, and because everyone knew that all the German ideas had to be condemned. The bishops who resided at the Curia, who had been in suspense for a long time by reason of the discussion of the article concerning residence, were now at ease, being sure that the decree of the Council could have no more effect than the papal decretals had had before. But the lesser courtiers were full of discontent when they saw that the bishop had the power to force them to reside. They complained of their ill fortune, that they had to work all their lives to obtain enough to live on, and that after so much effort their reward was to be confined to some country area, or by means of a vile canonry to be subjected once more to the tyranny of bishops, worse than before, who would keep them as it were tied to a stake, and who with visitations and with the pretext of reforming them would keep them in miserable subjection, or fill their lives with troubles and expenses.

Elsewhere, especially in Germany, when the decrees were made public, it was those concerning faith which gave rise to the most discussion. It was necessary to read and reread them most carefully and to think about them, since they could not be understood without a perfect knowledge of the inner movements of the soul, and without knowing in which ways it was active and in which passive. These were most subtle matters, and because of the various apparent possibilities they were believed to be endlessly controversial, so that the whole doctrine of the Council turned upon this hinge: "Whether the first object of the will works upon the will, or the will upon it, or whether both of them are both active and passive." Some wits said that if the astronomers who did not know the true causes of the motions of the heavens had introduced eccentrics and epicycles to save the appearances, it was no wonder if, wishing to save the appearances of still higher motions, the theologians had introduced eccentric opinions. The grammarians could not leave off marvelling and smiling at the construction of the proposition in the fifth article, *"neque homo ipse nihil omnino agat"* [and man himself does not act entirely in vain], which they said was unprecedented and unintelligible. If the Council had meant *"etiam homo ipse aliquid agat"* [besides, man himself acts to some purpose], it should have said so clearly, as is appropriate in matters of faith, where the most simple expression is the best. And if they wanted an elegant turn of phrase, nevertheless, they could say, *"etiam homo ipse nihil non agat"*[1] [besides, man himself does not act to no purpose]. But, once the word *omnino* [entirely] was put in, the proposition became self-contradictory and meaningless, like all propositions containing two negatives which cannot be turned into an affirmative. And so, treating this proposition in this way, it would be better to say, *"etiam homo ipse aliquid omnino agat"* [besides, man himself acts entirely to some purpose], but this is still inconsistent, for in this proposition it is impossible to work out what *aliquid omnino* means, because this would be to say that man acts in a certain way, which in other ways does not count as action.

In the defense of the Fathers, it was said that one should not examine the manner of speech so strictly, because it was only quibbling. To this it was replied that ordinary forms of speech deserve a charitable interpretation, but if someone abandons what was clear and customary and invents some self-contradictory formula in order to quibble and support both sides at once, then it is a public service to unmask his design.

---

1 Reading *nihil non* for *nihil*.

Those who understood theology said that the doctrine that man could always refuse God's grace was much contrary to the ancient and official opinion of the Church, *"et ad te nostras etiam rebelles compelle propitius voluntates"* [and graciously compel us to come to Thee, even if we are rebellious]. This did not mean that it was a vain and deceptive desire, but that it was made *ex fide* [out of faith], as St. James says, and that God would grant the desires of His elect. They added that one would no longer be able to say with St. Paul that what separates the vessels of wrath from those of divine mercy does not come from man—that which separates being that human *non nihil omnino*. Many people wondered about that place in the seventh article where it is said that justice is measured out according to God's pleasure and the disposition of the recipient, since both these things could not be true. Because if it pleased God to give more to a man who was less disposed, it would not be measured out according to disposition, and if it was measured out according to disposition, that would always be the way in which God worked, and He would never use His prerogative. People marvelled how the Fathers had condemned those who said that it was not possible to keep God's commands, because the same Council, in the decree of the second session, exhorted the faithful in Trent to repent, to go to confession and Communion, and to keep God's commands *quantum quisque poterit* [as much as they were able]. This qualification would be insulting to God, if the righteous could keep His commands absolutely. They noticed that the same word *præcepta* [commands] was used, so that quibbling was impossible.

Those who understood the history of the Church said that in all the councils held in the Church from the time of the apostles to the present, taken all together, so many articles had never been agreed on in one session. Aristotle had played an important part, with his distinction between all the kinds of cause. If he had not done this, we would lack many articles of faith.

The politicians, too, although they ought not to examine religious matters, but just follow them, found something to say about this decree. They saw that the duty of obeying the commands of God and the Church was mentioned in the tenth article and repeated in the twentieth canon, and they were scandalized because the duty to obey the commands of princes and magistrates was not mentioned as well. The obedience due to them was clear enough in Holy Scripture. The Old Law was full of it, and in the New Testament the doctrine was clearly expressed by Christ Himself and treated at length by Saints Peter and Paul. As for the Church, it was our duty to listen to her, but whether we should obey her was not so clear. He who commands by virtue of his own power is obeyed; he who proclaims the words of another has our attention. These men were not satisfied with the excuse that the commands of princes were included in those of God; that they should be obeyed because God had commanded that they should be obeyed. They replied that on that argument, there was all the more reason to omit the Church. The Church had been mentioned, and the State was omitted because of the old design of the clergy to make the people believe the pernicious opinion that they should obey them for conscience sake, but obey the princes and magistrates only to avoid temporal punishment—otherwise they could freely disobey their orders. In this way the clergy made out that every form of government was tyrannical; they caused it to be hated and subverted it. They argued that subjection to priests was the only way of attaining salvation; they would begin by acquiring all jurisdiction, and end by acquiring all power.

The decree about reform was said to be nothing but an illusion. To leave the selection of men fit to govern churches to God and to the pope was a pious hope rather than a reformation. To alter the ancient canons with nothing but a word (and a vague one at that) would simply confirm them in their neglect. For a genuine revival it was necessary to attack the causes which had led to the neglect and to give the remedies efficacy with penalties and men to enforce them, and with the other means by which laws are introduced and enforced. In the last analysis, all that they had done was to establish that, if one were to lose half one's income, one could remain absent the whole year; they had encouraged people to absent themselves for eleven months or more without penalty (providing those thirty days or less were spread out through the rest of the year). And anyway, they had spoiled the decree by allowing as an exception "just and reasonable causes." Who would be so simple that he could not find such cause—having as his judges men in whose interest it was that the residence not be enforced.

## Chapter Nine

[*After a congregation in which the reform of matters concerning benefices was discussed, the Spanish prelates, led by Cardinal Pacheco, drew up a "censure" of eleven articles of reform, which they presented to the legates on February 3. Here is the Pope's reaction to the censure and to the sixth session in general.*]

The Pope thought about the news he had had from Trent and from his nuncio in Germany, and he discussed it with his intimates. He feared that the Council would bring forth some monstrosity to the prejudice of himself and the power of the papacy in general. He considered the theologians' factions, especially those of the Dominicans and Franciscans, ancient rivals and doctrinal opponents, who had been carried away at the Council and overstepped the limits which the prudent had laboriously set. The differences between them were no less than those with the Lutherans, and the controversy was as sharp, so that if they did not come to some understanding, there was a danger that something serious might happen. He thought particularly about the dispute whether residence was *de iure divino*, and about the daring of Brother Bartolomeo Carranza, who, egged on by many people, had gone so far as to call the contrary opinion a doctrine of the devil. He saw how easily another disease might arise, like that of Luther, and if residence were made a matter of faith, the papacy would be reduced to nothing. He considered that all the reforms had as their aim the limitation of the authority of the pope and the increase of that of the bishops. He had realized how little his authority was respected when the Council had given him hope of entrusting the task of reform to him (and he had even drawn up the bull, taking it all upon himself) and had then gone on discussing still more sharply without thinking about him. He greatly distrusted the liveliness and boldness of the Spaniards, having noticed that in general the Spaniards do not act at random, that they show greater respect than they feel, that they are closely united, and that they do not take a step without looking a hundred paces ahead. It seemed to him a most serious matter that they had met together and drawn up a censure in common. He thought it plausible that the emperor had suggested this, since his ambassador met them every day. He also suspected the intentions of the emperor because of his good fortune, which makes men unable to set limits on their plans. He considered the emperor's policy of toleration and explained it in terms of his wishing to curry favor with the Lutherans. He considered the complaints not only of the emperor, but of his ministers as well, when the Italian troops departed, that they had been abandoned in their time of need. He knew that the emperor blamed the duke of Piacenza (the Pope's son) for the rebellion of Genoa; and above all, he reflected on the emperor's words to the nuncio, that he had no greater enemy than the Pope. He feared that if the emperor were to obtain absolute power over Germany, he would then come to think of doing the same in Italy and use the Council as a weapon against the Pope. He saw that the emperor would have no rivals, given the incurable illness of the king of France, who was bound to die soon, and the fact that the Dauphin could not be counted on, being young and without experience. He was sure that the prelates who had supported the Curia up till now would declare for the emperor as soon as he came out openly against the Pope, whether out of fear, because the emperor was more powerful, or out of the universal envy of the Pope's authority—an envy which they would no longer hide once they saw that his authority could be limited in safety.

These considerations made him decide to do something about the Council. It did not seem possible to put an end to it, because of all the business that had still to be discussed. To suspend it he needed some important reason, and in any case this was not effective enough, because he would immediately be asked to raise the suspension. The best plan seemed to be the translation of the Council to a place over which he had absolute power. If this had to be done, it must be done in such a way as to remedy all dangers; this meant holding the Council in his own territories. Thinking about it, he decided that it would not be a good idea to hold it in Rome, because this would cause such a stir in Germany. Bologna seemed the best place, because it was large, fertile, and convenient for those who came from the other side of the Alps. Thinking along these lines, he decided to keep out of the affair personally, but to make it appear that the legates had done everything on their own initiative, by virtue of the authority which he had given them in the bull of February 22, which had been sent to them in August, 1545. In this way, if there was any opposition to the translation, the legates would bear the brunt of it, and he, as one who was not involved, could support them all the more easily. And if for some reason he changed his mind, he could do so without loss of face. So he sent a gentleman belonging to Cardinal Del Monte's household, with a letter of credence and instructions not to arrive before the session began, to tell the legates to transfer the Council to Bologna, making this seem in some way necessary and to work so fast that the enterprise would be carried out before any impediment could be interposed.

## Chapter Ten

[*The seventh session, the arrival of the Pope's message March 3, 1547, and the translation of the Council.*]

Cardinal Santacroce was dumbfounded, but del Monte calmly said that he knew that the Pope was always a wise prince, and now they had seen his masterstroke. It was necessary to do this to preserve the authority of the Apostolic See; and so, they must serve His Holiness faithfully, secretly, and thoroughly. Many of the members of the prelates' households were conveniently ill at this time, whether because of the carnival or the recent humidity in the air. Del Monte had some of his household ask the doctors whether there was any danger of contagion. Doctors always make as pessimistic a diagnosis as they can. If they are right, they seem learned. And if they are wrong, still more learned, because they were able to cure the ill. So these doctors said something vague, which was carefully spread about and believed by those of little judgment, then believed by the lesser sort and by those who, wishing to leave, would have been glad if this were true. And a bishop conveniently died in these days after the session, and the whole Council went to his funeral, which made the whole thing very conspicuous. Trent and neighboring areas, too, were full of the rumors that the disease was contagious.

The legates held themselves obviously aloof from the rumors, and the day after the session was ended, they held a general congregation to decide what points should be raised about the sacrament of the Eucharist, and the following week the theologians' committees began. But the rumor was spreading, so Cardinal Del Monte ordered Ercole Severoli, the Promoter of the Council, to hold an enquiry into the illness. The doctors were examined, including Girolamo Fracastoro, who had the title of "Doctor of the Council." It was reported that the neighboring areas were making preparations to cease trade with the city. This made many prelates ask for permission to leave, whether because they were afraid or because they wanted to leave anyway. Del Monte gave permission to some so that he could include their leaving as one of the causes of the translation of the Council; others who were close to him he persuaded to stay. The real reason for this was not to deprive himself of support when he proposed the translation; the apparent reason was in order not to show that he was letting the Council be dissolved. He said that they should make a protest in the congregations, so that measures would be taken. And so, the enquiry went on until March 8, when news came (whether true or false) that Verona was about to cease trade with Trent, which troubled everyone because this was to make them all prisoners.

And so, on the ninth, a general congregation was held on this subject. The results of the enquiry were read out, and it was asked what should be done in order not to stay there cooped up with sickness raging and without food and other necessities. Many said that they wanted to leave, and that they could not be kept there. And after much had been said, Del Monte proposed to transfer the Council, saying that he had had apostolic authority to do this from the beginning. He had the papal bull read which was addressed to the three legates, Del Monte, Santacroce, and Pole. The bull explained that the Council had been established in Trent, and that they had been sent there as his legates and angels of peace, and it went on to say that in order that such a holy work should not be hindered by the inconvenience of the place, he gave authority to two of them, in the absence of the other, to transfer it to another more convenient and safer city; to command the prelates on pain of censure and punishments to proceed no further in Trent, but to continue the Council in the city to which it had been transferred; to summon there the prelates and other members of the Council of Trent, under pain of breaking their oaths and the penalties mentioned in the letter convoking the Council; and he would ratify everything that they did, whatever happened. The prel-

ates from the Empire immediately replied that the sickness and the danger were not so great; that they could
give the timid permission to leave until the rumor was
over (which, with God's help would be soon); that they
could postpone the session, which was not of great consequence, since the year before, many of them, fearing
that war might break out, had left in the same way, and
the session had been postponed six months and more;
they could do this again now, if there was need. Other
similar arguments were put forward. There was a long
argument about this. The imperialists left the congregation and conferred among themselves and began carefully to investigate what they had not bothered about
before, and they smelled out the fact that the sickness
was just a pretext.

The next day a congregation was held on the same
subject. It was found that eleven prelates had left, and
they began to discuss where to move. All hated the idea
of going to Germany, and they could not enter the
territory of any prince because they had not negotiated
this. That left only the states of the Church. The legates
suggested Bologna, which pleased all those who approved
of the translation. The imperialists again attacked this
idea, and some virtually made a protest; but the majority agreed to it. Some thought that the Pope might take
the move badly, since it was done without his knowledge; but Del Monte said that cases of emergency and
matters of life and death were exempt from protocol,
and that he would stake his career that the Pope would
be pleased. They also considered the emperor and the
other princes and decided that they could satisfy the
respect they owed them by mentioning them in the
decree. To satisfy those who did not approve of the
translation they would make some reference to return-
ing. The decree was drawn up in the form of a motion.

Does it please you to declare that this disease (for
the above-mentioned and other reasons) is so manifest that the prelates cannot remain in this city without danger to their lives? And that they cannot be
held there against their will? Given the departure of

many and the protests of others, departures which dissolve the Council, and other true and legitimate reasons adduced by the Fathers, does it please you to declare that (to preserve the lives of the prelates and carry on with the Council) it should be transferred to Bologna? And that it is so transferred from now on. And the session of April 21 should be celebrated there, and the proceedings thereafter, unless it should seem good to the Pope and the Council for it to return here or elsewhere, following the advice of the emperor, the most Christian king and the other Christian kings and princes.

The following day, a session was held. The decree was read and thirty-five bishops and three generals assented; the Cardinal Pacheco and another seventeen bishops voted against. Of all those in favor only one was a subject of the emperor, Michele Saraceni, a Neapolitan, Archbishop of Matera. But among the eighteen against there was Claude de la Guiche, Bishop of Mirepois; Martelli, Bishop of Fiesole; and Marco Viguerio, Bishop of Sinigaglia. Of the latter it is said that when the Cardinal Del Monte taxed him with ingratitude to the Apostolic See (which had made his uncle a cardinal out of most humble beginnings, whence came the greatness of his family and his own bishopric), he replied in Latin with the words of St. Paul, "God is not mocked." The legates departed with the cross carried before them, accompanied by the bishops with ceremonies and prayers.

The imperialists were commanded by the imperial ambassador not to leave until His Majesty told them. In Rome, the Curia was pleased to be free from suspicions, because there was great confusion there while the pluralists were trying to sell off their benefices and yet not show a loss on them. The Pope said he could not but approve what the legates had done, for he had given them authority to transfer the Council and had promised to ratify all their decisions and to execute them. And he believed the cause, the infection of the air, was a legitimate one, and most of the prelates had agreed to it.

However, no one was so naïve as not to believe that everything had been done by papal command, for it was certain that nothing was done at the Council, however small, without orders coming from Rome. Every week there were letters between Trent and Rome, sometimes two dispatches, and so it could not be believed that in a matter of such great importance the legates took the initiative. Simply to take so many people to a proud city like Bologna without knowledge of its prince seemed something that the legates would never have attempted themselves. Many even believed that the bull did not carry the true date, but had just been made and had been back-dated and given the name of Cardinal Pole so that it would the more easily be believed. Otherwise, the clause in which the authority to transfer the Council was given to two of the legates if the third was absent seemed like a prophecy that Pole would be absent; and the power to transfer the Council to whatever city they wanted seemed too wide and so implausible, given the universal fear of popes that a council might be held in a city that could not be trusted (a fear which Pope Paul had shown more than ever in calling it). And so, they could not believe that he could have confided such an important matter to the judgment of anyone else unless he had been forced to. However, I, following the papers which I have seen, which I have described in their place, am certain that the bull was drawn up two years before and sent eighteen months before this time. But what could not be hidden, and what scandalized everyone, was that this bull made plain the servitude of the Council. If two legates could command all the prelates together to leave Trent, and force them by penalties to do so, then let he who can say what kind of liberty they had.

[*The next three books of Sarpi's* History *are omitted. Book Three deals with events between April, 1547 and April, 1551. On April 21, 1547, the Council reopened in Bologna, with only thirty-six bishops present. Here, the eighth, ninth, and tenth sessions were held, and the doctrine of the sacraments discussed. A minority of bishops, mostly Spaniards, remained at Trent and demanded that the Council return there. The emperor supported this demand, and in January, 1548, solemnly protested against the translation. In June, the rump of the Council at Bologna adjourned, while at the Diet of Augsburg, Charles V (whose troops had defeated and captured the Elector of Saxony, the Protestant leader, at the battle of Mühlberg in 1547) imposed a compromise settlement on both Protestants and Catholics until the Council reassembled. This interim settlement, which did in fact become known as the Interim of Augsburg, was promulgated in June, 1548. In 1549, Pope Paul III died. He was succeeded by Cardinal Del Monte, the former legate, who took the name of Julius III, and worked for the resumption of the Council.*

*Book Four deals with events between May, 1551, when the Council returned to Trent for its eleventh session, and August, 1552. Cardinal Crescenzio was now legate. In the thirteenth session, the doctrine of the Eucharist was defined; in the fourteenth session, decrees on Penance and on Extreme Unction were passed. There was less agreement in the debates on reform; some bishops wanted to go much further in this direction than the legate would allow. Deputations from the German Protestants arrived, but no agreement could be reached with them. The Council was brought to an end by Elector Maurice of Saxony's surprise attack on the emperor in March, 1552. The emperor fled from Innsbruck, and in April, the Council, now in its sixteenth session, was suspended.*

*Book Five deals with the events between September, 1552 and December, 1561, a decade in which the Council did not meet at all. During this time there were three changes of pope. Marcellus II, who succeeded Julius III in 1555, reigned for only a few weeks, and was himself succeeded by Paul IV, Gian Pietro Caraffa, who had no intention of reassembling the Council. After a four-year reign of terror, Paul was succeeded by Pius IV, Gian Angelo de'Medici, in 1559. The Empire changed hands, too; in 1555, Charles V abdicated, one of the last acts of his reign being to make the religious peace of Augs-*

burg (the famous "cuius regio eius religio" settlement).
The bull convoking the Council was issued in 1560.
Whereas the Council had first met to combat the danger
of Lutheranism in Germany, it now met, above all, to
fight Calvinism in France.]

# BOOK SIX

## Chapter One

[*The third period and the seventeenth session of the Council began at Trent on January 18, 1562. Cardinal Seripando was legate. Among the subjects discussed at this session was the Index of Prohibited Books. Sarpi introduces this subject with a digression on the history of censorship.*]

At this point it is necessary to say something about the origin of prohibiting books, and how things had arrived at the state they were in at that time, and what new order was taken then. In the Church of the time of the martyrs there was no ecclesiastical prohibition, although some pious people would not read bad books as a matter of conscience, so as not to break one of the three articles of the law of God: to flee the contagion of evil, to refuse to expose oneself to temptation unless it is necessary and useful, and to refuse to spend one's time in frivolous pursuits. These laws are like laws of nature and are always in force, and they oblige us to keep ourselves from books which are not good, even when there is no ecclesiastical law about it. Then came the case of Dionysius, Bishop of Alexandria, who about the year 240, after being criticized by his priests about these matters, and hesitating for these reasons, had a vision in which he was instructed to read every book because he was fit to pass judgment on them. At that time, they believed that there was more danger from pagan books than heretical ones. They were all the more abhorred, and the reading of them was all the more criticized because many learned Christians studied them in order to learn eloquence. For this reason, St. Jerome was beaten by the devil, either in a vision, or in a dream. And so, at this time, about 400, a council at Carthage forbade bishops to read pagan books, but allowed them to read heretical books. This decree is included among the canons collected by Gratian. This was the first canonical prohibition, but there was also the advice of the Fathers to obey the laws of God quoted above. Heretical books, containing doctrines condemned by councils, were frequently prohibited by the emperors for the sake of keeping the peace. For example, Constantine prohibited the books of Arius; Arcadius, those of the Eunomians and Manichæans; Theodosius, those of Nestor; and Marcian, those of the Eutychians; and in Spain, King Recaredo prohibited those of the Arians. The councils and bishops considered it sufficient to show which books contained doctrines which had been condemned or were not orthodox, as Gelasius did in 494, and went no further, leaving it to everyone's conscience whether to avoid them or to read them as if they were good. After the year 800, the popes, assuming a great deal of political power, also prohibited and burned books whose authors they condemned; but all the same, until the present century, there were very few books prohibited in this way. A general prohibition on pain of excommunication and without further judgment, affecting books containing doctrines either heretical or suspected of heresy, was not then the custom. Martin V in his bull excommunicated all the sects of heretics—Wycliffites, and Hussites, especially—without making any other mention of those who might read their books, although many of these were in circulation. When Leo X condemned Luther, at the same time he forbade his books to be read, on pain of excommunication. The following popes, in the bull *In cœna Domini*, condemned and excommunicated all heretics, and at the same time excommunicated those who read their books, and in other bulls against heretics in general, excommunicated the readers of heretical books. This soon created confusion, because the heretics were not condemned by name, so that heretical books had to be recognized by their contents, not by their author. But the contents seemed different to different people, and there were innumerable scruples of conscience. The more conscientious inquisitors made lists of the heretical books which had come to their notice, but as these lists were not compared, they did not eliminate the problem. King Philip of Spain was the first to give them a more convenient form, by making a law, in 1558, that the catalog of books prohibited by the Spanish Inquisition should be printed.

Following this example, Paul IV, in Rome, ordered that the Holy Office should draw up and print an Index, which was done in 1559. This was to go much further than in the past and to lay foundations for maintaining and increasing the authority of the Curia to a much greater extent, by depriving men of that knowledge which is necessary to defend themselves from usurpations. Up to that time, it had only been a question of heretical books; books were not forbidden unless their authors had been condemned. This Index was divided into three parts. The first part contains the names of all those whose books (even if on secular subjects) are condemned, and these include not only those who have professed doctrines contrary to those of the Church of Rome, but also those who have lived and died in that Church. In the second part, there are the names of books which are condemned by authors whose other works are not condemned. In the third part are anonymous works, although there is a general rule prohibiting books which do not carry the author's name, written after 1519. Many authors and books are prohibited which for a hundred, two hundred, or three hundred years had been in the hands of all educated men in the Church of Rome—the popes knowing this and not objecting all this time. And among modern books, some are forbidden which had been printed in Italy, even some which had been printed in Rome with the approval of the Inquisition and also approved by the Pope himself with his briefs, as for example, the *Annotations* of Erasmus on the New Testament, which Leo X read and approved by a brief dated from Rome, September 10, 1518. It is a most serious matter that, under color of religion, the same severity is used to condemn the authors of books in which the authority of princes and magistrates is defended against ecclesiastical usurpations, and in which the authority of councils and bishops is defended against the Curia. Here the hypocrisy and tyranny by which the people are deceived and outraged under the pretext of religion is exposed. In fact, there was never a better scheme for using religion to make men crazy. The Inquisition went so far as to make a catalog of sixty-two printers and to prohibit all the books they printed, of whatever author, language, or subject. And, still more serious, it included books printed by other printers who have printed books by heretics, so that there were no books left to read. And the height of rigor was that the prohibitions of books on the list were on pain of excommunication *latæ sententiæ*, reserved to the pope, loss of offices and benefices and ineligibility for appointment, perpetual infamy and other arbitrary penalties. Complaints about this severity were made to Pope Pius when he succeeded, and he referred the Index and the whole affair to the Council, as has been said.

There were various opinions about the articles proposed. Ludovico Beccatelli, Archbishop of Ragusa, and Brother Agostino Salvago, Archbishop of Genoa, thought that there was no advantage in discussing the question of books at the Council, for it might hinder the ends for which the Council was principally assembled. Paul IV, with the advice of all the inquisitors and many important people who sent him information from all parts, had made a most complete list; there was nothing to add except perhaps some book which had appeared since, and this was not worth doing by the Council. To allow books which had been prohibited in that list would be to declare that Rome had acted imprudently and thus destroy the credit both of the Index already published and of the new decree, since it is a common proverb that new laws weaken their own force more than that of the old. Besides (said Beccatelli), there is no need of books; the world has too many already, especially since printing was invented. It is better that a thousand books should be prohibited which did not deserve it, than that one book should be allowed which deserved prohibition. It would not be useful for the Council to give itself the trouble of explaining prohibitions, making judgments, or approving those already made by Catholics in different places. This would be asking for contradiction. It is for the doctor to justify what he says; the legislator who does so diminishes his authority because the subject will attack the grounds alleged, and when he believes he has refuted them, he thinks that the law has no more force. Nor was it a good thing to correct or to expurgate any book, for the same reason; it would incite people to say that something was left out which deserved correction, or that something was corrected which should not have been. Then the Council would make itself unpopular with all those who liked the books which were prohibited; this would induce them not to accept other necessary decrees which it made. He concluded that Paul's Index was good enough, and that they should not waste time doing again what had been done already, or undoing something which had been done well. Many other arguments were put forward in support of this view by many bishops who were Paul IV's men and admirers of his ecclesiastical discipline, which they wanted to preserve or to make still more strict in order not to stain the purity of religion.

Giovanni Tommaso Sanfelicio was of a completely contrary opinion. He held that the Council should discuss the question of the books afresh, just as if no prohibition had already been made. This was because the prohibition made by the Roman Inquisition was odious to other Europeans because of its very name, and in any case, it was so strict that it could not be observed. Nothing makes a law lose its force so easily as the impossibility or the great difficulty of observing it, together with great strictness in punishing breaches of it. It was necessary to preserve the reputation of the Holy Office, but this could be done well enough by not mentioning it, and otherwise, by making only those provisions which were necessary, and by providing moderate penalties. It seemed to him that the important thing was the way in which this was done. He said that he thought the best thing would be for the books which had not yet been censored to be shared between the Fathers and theologians present at the Council and others who were absent, who would examine them and pass judgment. The Council would appoint a small committee which would arbitrate between the censor and the book, and the same would be done with the books already censored. When this had been done, the matter would be raised in the Council itself, which would make whatever general decree it considered was for the public benefit. As for whether or not to summon the authors, he said that there were two sorts, those who were members of the Church and those who had left it. No account need be taken of those who had left, because by so doing they had, as St. Paul says, condemned themselves and their works, so that there was no need to hear more. As for those who were members of the Church, there were those who were dead and those who were alive. The living it was necessary to summon and hear, because it was a matter concerning their honor and reputation, and so it was not possible to proceed against their works without listening to their arguments. As for the dead, since personal considerations were not involved, they could do whatever the public good required, without any danger of harming anyone. Another bishop added that Catholic authors who were dead should receive the same form of justice as the living because their families and disciples remained, who shared the reputation or infamy of the dead, and so had an interest in the matter. Even if there was no relative or disciple, the memory of the dead man could not be judged unless defense was made.

There were also some who thought it unjust to condemn the works of Protestants without hearing them, because, although they had condemned themselves, it was illegal to declare them condemned without summoning them, even if the matter was notorious; and no less could be done about the books, even if it was notorious that they contained heresy. Brother Cristoforo, the General of the Augustinians, said that it did not seem necessary to him to be as subtle as that: the prohibition of books was just like the prohibition of certain food for medical reasons, which was no judgment against the food nor against the cook, but advice to the patient by the man who is in charge of his health. It was not a matter of the cook's reputation, but of the patient's health. A food which was good in itself might be forbidden because it was not good for the patient. Similarly, the Council, which is the doctor, should keep what it is useful for the faithful to read and forbid what is not— what is harmful and dangerous. This would do no wrong to anyone, because a book might be good in itself, but not good for the sick minds of this age.

## Chapter Three

[*Eighteenth session, April, 1562: the discussion on residence. See p. 185-6 for the earlier discussion.*]

Of those who had taken part at the first Council, when this subject was discussed with some difference of opinion (not to say controversy), only five bishops were present at this. Nevertheless, as soon as this subject was proposed, the Council divided into parties, just as if the controversy had been an old one for them. This happened in no other question, either in the first Council, or in the one under Julius III, or in the present one. Some said that the cause of this was that the other subjects were theological, not understood very well, and dealt with by those who understood them in a theoretical manner, without emotional involvement—apart from their hatred of the Protestants, who had given them the trouble of raising these questions. This matter, however, affected the prelates themselves. Among the courtiers, the chief motive was ambition or the obligation of following the opinion useful to their patrons. Among the others, envy was important; not having the skill to raise themselves to the heights of the achievements or aspirations of the others, unable to equal them by raising themselves, they wanted to pull the others down to their own level, so that they would all be equal. On this article all made great efforts, on one side or the other, according to their own feelings, and all took careful note both of what they said themselves and of what others said which was in some way remarkable. Of all these, thirty-four speeches have come into my hands just as they were delivered; I only know the conclusions of the others. But here I shall set down only what is noteworthy.

The Patriarch of Jerusalem pointed out that this article had been dealt with in the first Council, and it was decided that there were two methods of dealing with the problem. The first was to punish those who did not reside; the second was to remove the impediments to residence. The first method was thoroughly considered in the sixth session, and there was nothing to add to it—it being understood that the loss of half the income was a most serious financial penalty and could not be increased without sending the bishops begging. A greater penalty could not be found, apart from deprivation. The only person who could enforce this was the pope, since the ancient custom of the Church was that bishops' cases should be judged by the Holy See. And so, in that session the question was referred to His Holiness to find a remedy, whether by means of a new provision or in another way; and the metropolitan was obliged to inform the pope about cases of nonresidence. That Council also began to make use of the second method, and decrees in that session and others removed many exemptions which prevented bishops from residing. All that now remained was to go on and remove the others, choosing a group of Fathers (as had been done then) who would collect information about the impediments, so that proposals and provisions could be made in the Council itself.

The Archbishop of Granada[1] added that in that Council there was proposed another remedy more powerful and efficacious, which was that the obligation of residing was the law of God, and this proposal was examined and discussed for ten months. If the Council had not been broken off, this would have become an essential article of the doctrine of the Church, in fact one of the most important ones. It was not only discussed at that time, but various people printed the arguments

[1] Pedro Guerrero, leader of the Spanish prelates at the Council, 1562–5.

that were put forward, so that the material was prepared and organized, and all that now had to be done was to finish the task. Once it was decided that residence was *de iure divino*, all obstacles would disappear by themselves; the bishops would recognize their duty, and it would become a matter of conscience. They would no longer be thought of as hirelings, but as shepherds. They would recognize that God had given them their flock, and that they would have to account for it to Him; that they could not pass the responsibility on to others; that dispensations would not help them; and then they would do their duty. He went on to establish that this was Catholic truth, with many references to the Old and New Testaments and to the Fathers. This opinion was approved by the majority of the congregation, and its defenders worked hard to produce authorities and arguments. Others opposed this view, saying that it was new, and unheard of either in ancient times or even in this century, before Cardinal Cajetan raised the question and supported this side; and even he abandoned it, because in old age he accepted a bishopric and never resided in it. In every age the Church has held that the pope can dispense. In every age nonresidents were punished or admonished for breaking the laws of the Church only, not the laws of God. In the first Council the matter was discussed, but the dispute became so dangerous that the legates, being prudent men, skillfully managed to end it. Their example should be followed. The books which were written about it afterwards gave great scandal and made it obvious that self-interest inspired the dispute. For the Scriptures and the Fathers contain only exhortations to perfection; the only foundation for the obligation to reside is in the canons, and these are laws of the Church.

Some held the opinion that neither the time nor the place was opportune for dealing with this question, and that no good would come from deciding it; but on the contrary, there was danger of many evils. This Council had met to stamp out heresies, not to create a schism among Catholics, which would happen if they condemned an opinion held, if not by a majority, at least by half of them. Some held that the originators of this view had not devised it for the sake of truth, but to encourage residence more; but their hope was not a very rational one, for men are no more careful not to transgress the laws of God than they are not to transgress the laws of the Church. Some believed that men are more careful to keep Lent than the Ten Commandments; that if Easter confession and Communion were commandments of God, no more people would go than do already; that to say Mass in vestments is a law of the Church, and no one disobeys it; that whoever disobeys the canons which carry penalties will break laws even more easily when he has no temporal punishments to fear, but only the justice of God; that no bishop will be influenced by this decision, but that it would give occasion to plots against the Apostolic See and the restriction of the authority of the Pope (as was already whispered about by some) and the weakening of the Curia, which was the honor of the clergy, whose status depended on it. If the status of the Curia were lowered, the Church would be less esteemed everywhere; therefore it was not just to deal with such a matter without informing His Holiness and the college of cardinals, who were chiefly affected by it.

The opinion of Paolo Giovio, Bishop of Nocera, should not be left out; he said in substance that the Council had met to treat a serious wound, the corruption of the Church, which everyone was persuaded was the cause of the absence of prelates from their Sees. Everyone said this, but no one had sufficiently reflected on it. But no wise doctor would try to remove a cause without first being sure that it is the cause, and that if he does this he will not cause other greater evils. If the nonresidence of prelates was the cause of corruption, then there would be less corruption to be seen in that Church in which in our age the prelates have resided. The popes for the last hundred years have remained in Rome and have done all they could to educate the people; but that city is no better than before. The most corrupt places are great cities which are capitals of kingdoms, whose prelates have not neglected to reside there, and poor cities who have not seen a bishop for a hundred years are the least corrupt. The old prelates who were here at the Council, who had been permanently resident in their Sees (of whom there were some), could not show that their See was better than the neighboring one which did not have a bishop. People who talked about flocks without shepherds should consider that parish priests have the cure of souls as well as bishops. They claim that there cannot be faithful Christians where there are no bishops; but there are mountain areas which have never seen bishops, and which cathedral cities could take as models. They should praise and imitate the zeal and diligence of the Fathers of the first Council, who had encouraged prelates to reside in their Sees by means of penalties, and who had begun to remove the impediments which hindered them; but they should not deceive themselves with the hope that to deal with nonresidences was to reform the Church. They should rather fear that just as residence is encouraged now, so posterity, seeing the inconveniences that arose from it, might come to encourage nonresidence. They should not attempt to bind so tightly that the bonds could not be loosed if this became necessary, as would happen with this *ius divinum*, which they were thinking of bringing in after one thousand four hundred years. Where a bishop was causing harm, like the Archbishop of Cologne, he would use this doctrine to defend his disobedience to the pope, if the pope summoned him to account for his actions, or if the pope wanted to exile him so that he did not spread the rot. He added that he saw the zeal of the prelates who favored the article, but also believed that some of them might make use of it to escape from obedience to the pope; and the more the pope was obeyed, the more the Church would be united. He would like to remind them that the same argument could be used by parish priests to escape from obedience to their bishops; when the article was expounded, they would say that the bishop cannot depose them, or restrict their authority by means of reservations. And like shepherds appointed directly by God, they would claim that the flock was more theirs than the bishop's, and this claim would be unanswerable. The Church had been preserved by means of its hierarchy; this measure would lead it into a democracy, and anarchy, which would destroy it.

## Chapter Four

. . . the legates and the deputies met to summarize the opinions of the Fathers. On the first article, concerning residence, they found themselves in disagreement. Simonetta[1] favored the opinion that it was *de iure positivo;* and so he said that it was the majority opinion, even of those who thought residence was *de iure divino,* and that this question should be omitted. Mantua,[2] without saying what he thought himself, said that the majority had asked for a declaration on the matter; of the other legates, Alt-Ems[3] followed Simonetta, and the other two (though with some caution) followed Mantua. The difference of opinion was expressed politely, but was quite bitter all the same. For this reason the legates held a general congregation on the twentieth, in which the question below was read from a written text.

Because many Fathers have said that it should be declared that residence is *de iure divino,* and others have said nothing, and some are of opinion that such a declaration should not be made; in order that those deputed to do so may draw up the decrees immediately, easily, and safely, will your Lordships declare with the one word *placet* whether or not you want there to be a declaration that residence is *de iure divino.* The decree will be made according to the majority opinion, as has always been done in this holy Council—it being understood that this could not be calculated from the speeches because of the variety of opinions. And would you

---

1 Cardinal Giacomo Simonetta, legate.
2 Ercole Gonzaga, Cardinal of Mantua, legate.
3 Mark Sittich von Hohenems, Cardinal of Alt-Ems.

please speak clearly and distinctly, and one by one, so that each man's vote may be noted down.

When this had been done, sixty-eight had said *Placet* without qualification; thirty-three had said *Non placet* without qualification; thirteen, *Placet consulto prius sanctissimo domino nostro* [Yes, provided that His Holiness is consulted first]; and eighteen, *Non placet, nisi prius consulto sanctissimo domino nostro* [No, unless His Holiness is consulted first]. The thirteen were different from the eighteen, because the thirteen really wanted the declaration, but were prepared not to want it if the Pope did not want it. The eighteen really did not want it, but were prepared to accept it if the Pope wanted it. A subtle difference, but each man thought he had done his master the better service. Cardinal Madruzzo did not want to answer the question, but referred to his speech in the congregation, which was in favor of *ius divinum*. The Bishop of Budua said that the ayes had it, and that he thought the declaration should be published. When the votes were counted, it was seen that more than half were in favor of the declaration, and that only a quarter were against it, and that others, even with a qualification, were with the first group. There were bitter words, and the rest of the congregation was spent in discussion of this subject, not without much confusion. When the Cardinal of Mantua saw this, he ordered silence, exhorted the Fathers to be humble, and dismissed them.

The legates consulted among themselves what to do; and they all agreed to give the Pope a detailed account of all that had happened and to await his reply. Meanwhile, they would carry on with the other articles. Mantua wanted to send his secretary, Camillo Oliva, posthaste with letters of credence, and Simonetta proposed putting everything in a letter. They decided to do both, and they wrote a long account of what had happened and gave it to the secretary, who left Trent the same evening. Although this was done with the greatest secrecy, the Spaniards discovered it. They complained bitterly that they saw an unbearable grievance begin;

that everything that was dealt with was done so not only with the advice of Rome, but the decision was taken there, too; that the Council, which had met in that same city twice before, had been unsuccessful and had been dissolved without anything coming of it, in fact, causing a scandal, because the Fathers decided nothing, and Rome everything; so that everyone quoted the blasphemous proverb, "The Council of Trent was guided by the Holy Ghost sent from Rome, from time to time, in the papal bags."

[*The news of the debate on residence arrives in Rome.*]

Many prelates had written from Trent to their friends in Rome, saying different things according to their different opinions. At the Curia there was great confusion and consternation, and they already seemed to see Rome empty of prelates and deprived of all privilege and precedence. They saw clearly that the cardinals living in Rome would not be allowed to hold bishoprics; that pluralism was sure to be prohibited; that no bishop or parish priest would be able to hold any office in Rome; that the pope would not be able to make any dispensation in any of these cases, which is the greater part of his power, and so the authority of the pope would be greatly diminished. They remembered what Livy had said, that the authority of a ruler is not easily brought from the top to the middle, but easily from the middle to the bottom. They discussed how the decree would increase the power of the bishops, who would deny the right to papal provisions and take to themselves the right to appoint to benefices. They noted that the bishops outside Italy, and even some Italians, had always been ill disposed to the Curia out of envy, and because they could not easily enter it; and that those who claimed to stay far away from Rome for conscience' sake should be watched, because they would be worse than the others, if they had a chance. These puritans had more ambition than the others, although it was hidden, and they wished to raise themselves by destroying others, as Paul IV had well shown in practice. And because the Spaniards were

217

united on this matter, and because it was known that Vargas[4] was encouraging them to go on with it, many whispered that the king[5] was behind it. To tax the clergy he needed to overcome two difficulties. He had first to gain the consent of the Pope and second, to overcome the resistance of the chapters and colleges. These were full of noblemen, exempt from the jurisdiction of bishops, and had in the main been appointed to their benefices by the Pope, and so had no scruples about opposing the king. Now the bishops were appointed to their Sees by the king, and they were completely dependent on him. If he were to increase their power, freeing them from subjection to the Pope and making the chapters and colleges subject to them, he would be able to acquire with ease absolute power over the clergy. . . .

The Pope spoke to the Venetian and Florentine ambassadors to tell their governments to recommend the Pope's point of view to their ambassadors at Trent, and to tell them to persuade their prelates not to take part in negotiations contrary to the Pope's interests, and not to be so warm in support of residence. He then called all the bishops who were still to be found at the Curia, pointing out the need for their presence at Trent and the service that this would do him, loaded them with promises, gave financial aid to the poor ones, and sent them off to the Council. He did this to increase the numbers for the time when the subject of residence would be raised, all the more because forty Frenchmen were to arrive, and he expected nothing good from them. In order not to have the French against him, whose ambassadors would soon arrive in Trent, he decided to make a gift to the king of a hundred thousand scudi, and to lend him as much again, in the name of merchants, if the king gave enough security both for the principal and for the interest, under the following conditions, without deceit. He was to revoke the edicts [of toleration] and make war for the sake of religion. With the money he was to raise Swiss and German troops, who would be

4 Francisco Vargas, Spanish ambassador to Rome.
5 Philip II.

not be allowed to anyone; and if it could be allowed for good reasons, on what conditions. . . .

The actions of the Council had not been followed so eagerly in the past as they were now, when all the princes wanted it; ambassadors from all parts were sent to it, and a great number of prelates were present at it— four times as many as there were before. More important still, it had been sitting for six months, and those months had been spent in daily and constant discussions; and many couriers and prelates had been sent from Rome to Trent and from Trent to Rome. But when the decisions taken at this session were printed, everyone remembered the Latin proverb about the mountains giving birth.

[*A reform of procedure, July, 1562.*]

When the congregation was over, the legates and the other Pope's men came together to discuss what they had heard, and how every day the prelates were more eager to say new, seditious, disrespectful things, which ought not to be called liberty but license; while the theologians were too long-winded and took up too much time, arguing among themselves about nothing and often discussing irrelevancies. If they continued in this way, the Council would never end. Besides this, there was danger that the disorder would increase and produce some dangerous effects. Giovan Battista Castello, the speaker, who had exercised the same office in the previous part of the Council under Pope Julius, recalled how Cardinal Crescenzio used to interrupt the prelates without any regard for them as soon as they began to wander from the point, and he would cut them off short, and make the prolix ones shorten what they had to say, and sometimes silence them altogether. If this were done once or twice now, the deliberations of the Council would be shortened, and the occasions for irrelevant contributions would be removed. The Cardinal of Varmia[1] was not pleased by this reminiscence; he said that if this

---

[8] Stanislaus Hosius, Bishop of Varmia (or Ermeland), East Prussia.

was how Crescenzio behaved, then it was no wonder that His Divine Majesty had not allowed the Council to make much progress. Nothing was more necessary to a Christian council than liberty. If one read about the councils of better times, one would see that they began with discord and contention, even when the emperor was present (who was most powerful in those times), but in the end, the Holy Ghost changed it into marvellous concord; and this was the miracle which calmed the world. At the Councils of Nicæa and Ephesus, the disputes were very great, so it was no marvel that at the present Council there were some differences of opinion expressed in polite fashion. Whoever tried to avoid these differences by human and violent means would make the world think that the Council was not free, and so it would lose its reputation. It would be good to leave it to God, who wanted to regulate councils Himself and restrain the impetuosities of those who had assembled in His name. The Cardinal of Mantua agreed with Varmia and criticized Crescenzio's procedure, but added that it would not be contrary to the liberty of the Council to reduce abuses by making decrees about the manner and time of speaking, giving each man his turn. Varmia approved of this, too, and it was decided to do this in the next sessions. . . .

## Chapter Eight

[*In the congregation held on the twentieth day of July, 1562 . . .*]

The Cardinal of Mantua admonished the prelates to give their opinions in congregation quietly, without shouting, and briefly, and he told them of the rules which had been made for the congregations of divines in order to do away with controversy, confusion, and prolixity. These were read and approved by the congregation. . . . The rules can be summarized in seven points.

I. That on each subject that was proposed, only four of the theologians sent by the Pope would speak: two secular priests and two regulars; the legates would decide which ones.

II. That the ambassadors of the princes would choose three of the secular theologians sent by the princes.

III. That each of the legates would choose a secular theologian from his own household.

IV. That of all the other secular theologians, from the households of the prelates, only four would be chosen to speak on each topic, beginning with the senior Doctor.

V. That of the regulars, each general would choose three of his own order.

VI. That none of the theologians should speak for more than half an hour. If anyone went on for longer, he would be interrupted by the master of ceremonies. If anyone spoke for a shorter time, he would be praised all the more.

VII. That any theologian who did not have a chance to speak on a certain subject could hand the deputies, in writing, his opinion on the matters proposed.

With these rules they calculated that thirty-four theologians would speak, and that they could be heard in ten congregations at most.


## Chapter Nine

*[September, 1562: the question of the chalice is raised again.]*


On this subject there were three opinions. One was extreme and negative, to the effect that it should in no way be granted. The second was affirmative, to the effect that it should be granted in Council, with the conditions and safeguards that seemed good to the Council. This opinion was supported by fifty of the wisest Fathers. Among them, some wanted legates to be sent to the areas which were asking for the chalice to find out whether it would be expedient to make the concession, and under what conditions. The third or middle opinion was that the matter should be left to the Pope. But this party was subdivided. Some wanted to leave it to him absolutely, without saying whether he should grant it or deny it; and others, to do so, together with a declaration that he should grant it. Some wanted to restrict him to particular countries; others, to leave him free. All the Spaniards absolutely refused it because Ambassador Vargas had written from Rome that this would be best for religion and the service of the king, and because of the danger to the Low Countries and to Milan. For when they saw their neighbors enjoy the right of the chalice, they would demand it themselves; and whether it was granted or denied, the door would be opened wide to heresy. The Venetian prelates, influenced by their ambassadors, held the same opinion for the same reason.

I shall mention only the leading figures and the remarkable things that they said. Cardinal Madruzzo, who spoke first, said that the chalice should be granted without any exception; the three patriarchs, that it should be refused absolutely; and the five archbishops, who followed, that it should be left to the Pope. The Archbishop of Granada, who had promised the imperialists his support in order to have theirs on the matter of residence (for which he was pressing most strongly), said that he did not support it or reject it, but it could not be concluded in that session, and it was necessary to postpone it to another. . . . Giovan Battista Castagna, Bishop of Rossano, who was absolutely against the concession went on to talk about those who asked for it and those who favored the request, saying that they were not good Catholics; if they were, they would not ask for something unfit which gave scandal to others. He said openly that the aim of the request was to introduce heresy; and he spoke in such a way that everyone realized that he was referring to Maximilian, King of Bohemia.

The Archbishop of Braga (or Bragança)[1] said that he was informed that in Germany there were four sorts of men: true Catholics, obstinate and open heretics, concealed heretics, and those weak in faith. The first did not demand, but opposed the concession. The second did not

---

[1] Bartolomeu dos Mártires, Archbishop of Braga—not Bragança.

care. The third wanted it in order for their heresy to remain concealed, because they could dissemble in everything else, but this one thing discovered them; so it should not be granted to them in order not to encourage their errors. But the weak in faith were only such because of their low opinion of the authority of the Church, and especially the authority of the Pope. They did not ask for the chalice out of devotion, which is only seen in persons of holy life, whereas they were sunk in the vanities and pleasures of the world. They even went to confession and Communion once a year unwillingly. They did not show such a fervor of devotion that they should ask to receive Communion under both forms. He concluded that they should imitate the diligence of the Fathers of Basel, who chose four or six prelates out of the body of the Council, as its legates, who, accompanied by theologians who were good at preaching, visited the provinces named by His Imperial Majesty, and wherever they found penitent men who wanted the chalice out of devotion or because they were accustomed to it, and who otherwise wanted to return to the Church, received them and granted them the chalice. . . .

Antonio Corrionero, Bishop of Almeria, said that he was confirmed in his opposition by the arguments used by the other side. If God gives many helps to the impenitent, such as preaching, miracles, and good inspirations, He gives the sacraments only to the penitent; if one wished to act out of charity, the first care should be to keep the Catholics, rather than to regain the heretics. They ought to imitate the Council of Constance, which prohibited Communion with the chalice, taught by Jan Hus, in order to keep good men in the Church. This is what ought to be done now with regard to the Lutherans. This concession would open the door to an infinite number of evils. They would demand clerical marriage and the abolition of images, of fasting and of other holy things, always making out that their demands were the only means to reunite them with the Church. Every little alteration of the laws would have serious consequences, and especially alterations in favor of the heretics. He would not advise the Pope to do it, though if it were to be done, it would be not as bad if he did it. The people would be less scandalized in that case than if it was the Council which made the concession, because although the Council had great authority with the people, supreme authority was with the Pope. If it were to be granted, it ought not to be committed to the bishops, even if they were known to be good men, for some time, because, moved by private interests, they might become wicked and of perverse faith. . . .

After everyone had expressed his opinion, the legates, who wanted to give satisfaction to the emperor, did not see how they could do so in the Council, because the party that was opposed to conceding the chalice was in the majority. So they decided to have the matter referred to the Pope, hoping that they could persuade some of the anti-chalice party to support this as a compromise. They asked Giacomo Lomellino, Bishop of Mazzara, and the Bishop of Ventimiglia to do this skillfully and cautiously. The legates themselves spoke to the three patriarchs and persuaded them, and by this means they gained all the prelates within the Venetian Empire, which was a considerable number. Having gained a number that they thought sufficient, they imagined that the difficulties were overcome. All they had to do was to write a letter to the Pope in the normal manner, informing him of all the opinions.

## Chapter Ten

[*September, 1562: the ambassadors met to force the Council to reform the Church.*]

All the ambassadors met in the house of the imperialists, saying that they wanted to discuss something which affected all princes. The Venetian and Florentine ambassadors were invited but excused themselves, saying that they could not take part without an express commission from their masters. In this meeting, the Bishop of Pecs[1] made a long speech, saying that till then nothing useful had been dealt with in the Council. They had disputed uselessly about dogmas, helping no one— neither heretics, who are obstinately resolved not to change their opinion, nor Catholics, who share their opinion already. Concerning reform, nothing was proposed except minor and unimportant matters concerning notaries, quæstors, and other such matters. It could be clearly seen that the legates planned to order the next session, too, in the same manner, and to go on spending time on disputation, or making rules about order or about matrimony, or some other unimportant matter, in order to avoid, in the usual way, substantial questions of reform. With these and other arguments well expressed at length, he persuaded the ambassadors to unite and go to the legates, and to ask them in the next session to stop speaking about the sacraments and making doctrines and canons, because now was the time for a thorough reformation, for removing abuses and correcting evil customs, and ensuring that the Council would be fruitful. The secretary of Spain[2] did not want to agree because his king wanted the continuation of the Council decreed at the end of the session, and he feared that he would prejudice this by a change of procedure. So far, they had treated dogma and reform together; and this change might lead to the argument that a new procedure implied a new council. The Portuguese ambassador made a long and inconclusive speech, saying that he wanted reform, but in a more peaceable manner; and he left. The Swiss ambassador, seeing what those two had done, and considering that the Venetians had not come at all, feared to make a mistake, and said it would be better to think about it again before making a decision. All the others were resolved to go.

Lansac[3] spoke for them all, by general consent, say-

---

[1] Imperial ambassador to the Council.

[2] Ercole Pagnano, secretary to the Marquis of Pescara, Philip II's ambassador to Trent, who was absent at this time.

[3] Louis, seigneur de Lansac, French ambassador to Rome.

ing that they had been sent by their princes to help and favor the Council, and to ensure that it kept to the point, not considering doctrinal disputes (since no one had doubts about doctrine, because they were all Catholics, and it is superfluous in the absence of those they were attacking), but a good, holy, and complete reformation of manners. However, notwithstanding their protests, they saw that it had been decided to determine the principal points of doctrinal controversy, and to scarcely touch on reform at all. So they asked that the next session deal only with reform, and that articles be proposed more important and more necessary than those which had so far been discussed. The legates replied in their usual way. It was the Pope's wish and their own to do God service and the Church good, and to satisfy and please all the princes; but it was not convenient to break the procedure that had always been followed in the Council, which was to deal with doctrine and reform together. What had been done so far was only a beginning. They intended to do better; they would most readily receive the articles that the ambassadors might propose; they were surprised that the French had not sent the Canons of Poissy[4] to the Pope, who would have approved them. To this Lansac replied that since the Pope had confided all matters concerning religion to the Council, the French prelates, when they arrived, would propose these and many other things. The legates replied that they would be most welcome and most gladly heard; but it would not be appropriate to postpone the session that had been planned for this reason, because nothing would be dealt with which would be to the prejudice of their proposals. They added that great numbers of Fathers were resolved that the session be held, and it would be dangerous to displease them. And if they, to their great inconvenience, were awaiting at Trent those who at their ease postponed the visit they had promised, it was not fair to make matters worse by forcing them to be idle while they waited.

---

4 Nine articles on the reform of the Church, agreed upon at the Assembly of Poissy, 1561.

[*Pius IV's reaction to news about the twenty-second session, September, 1562.*]

When the Pope received news of the session and what had happened in it, he was very happy, because he was freed from a great vexation. He had feared that in the dispute over the chalice his own authority would be called in question. Now that the way was opened to end the disputes by referring controversial matters to him, he began to hope that the same would be done in the matter of residence and in any other controversy that came up, so that the Council would soon be over. However, he saw two things that might hinder his plan. The first was the arrival of the Cardinal of Lorraine[5] and the French prelates; this worried him a great deal, especially because of the grand designs of the cardinal which were quite contrary to the interests of the papacy —designs which were so much part of the cardinal that he was unable to hide them. The only remedy he could see was to make sure that the Italians outnumbered the Northerners to such an extent that in the voting, the Frenchmen would not be important. To this effect he continually urged all bishops to go to Trent, whether they were only titular bishops or whether they had retired, providing them with their expenses and loading them with promises. He also thought about sending a number of abbots, as had been done in some other councils; but after having taken advice, he judged it better not to show such partiality and provoke the others to do the same. The other hindrance which he feared was the idea which all the princes had of keeping the Council open without doing anything: the emperor, in order to please the Germans and make them favorable toward electing his son king of the Romans; the king of France, to do what he wanted with the same people and with his Huguenots. He thought much about the precedent set by the meeting of the ambassadors; they seemed to him a council of laymen in the midst of that of the bishops. He considered that the meetings of prelates

---

[5] Charles de Guise, Archbishop of Reims.

would be dangerous if the presence and presidency of the legates did not keep them in their place. The ambassadors, meeting together, might discuss matters extremely prejudicial to his interests. There was danger that they might go further and invite some prelate to join them, so that there might be churchmen among them, and that they might introduce license under the name of liberty. In this perplexity he was encouraged to hope for the best by seeing that the majority of the ambassadors had opposed the suggestions put forward, and that only the ambassadors of the emperor and the king of France had been united—and the French king, having no prelates, could do little. Nevertheless, it was necessary to hasten the end of the Council and to encourage misunderstandings among the ambassadors. And so he wrote immediately that they should hasten the congregations and put the agenda in order. Considering that to thank someone obliges him to persevere, he ordered that the Portuguese and Swiss ambassadors and the secretary of the Marquis of Pescara should receive praise and affectionate thanks from him because they had refused to agree, like the others, to that impertinent proposal. He had the Venetian and Florentine ambassadors thanked for the good intention they had shown in refusing to attend the meeting, but asked them not to refuse if they were invited in future, because he was sure that their presence would help the Apostolic See and hinder the evil designs of others. The Pope made no mistake in his opinion. They all replied that they had acted in this way because they knew that in these times the service of God required that the authority of the Pope be defended, and they had persevered in this decision. They testified that they felt all the more obliged by the courteous thanks of His Holiness to do that which they had done because it was their duty.

# BOOK SEVEN

## Chapter One

[*King Charles IX wrote to his ambassador at Trent to have the Protestants invited and reforms made.*]

When the French ambassadors left the session, they received a dispatch from their king, ordering them to ask for the postponement of that session. Although it was too late for this, they appeared before the legates and explained the new instructions given them by the king, to ask that the Council should apply itself to reform and await the coming of the French prelates. They added that once the subjects of Holy Orders and matrimony had been dealt with by the theologians and prelates, there would be no matter of doctrine left, and the arrival of the French would be pointless. They asked the legates to postpone these matters till the end of October, and meanwhile to concern themselves with reforms, or to discuss doctrine and reforms on alternate days, rather than (as in the past) to postpone all the reforms to the days immediately before the session, so that there was hardly time to see the articles, let alone discuss them.

The reply was that the proposals deserved and would receive careful consideration, so that they might be satisfied so far as was possible. They asked for a copy of the instructions sent by the king in order to discuss the matter better. The ambassadors gave them a document which may be summarized as follows. The king had seen the decrees of July 16, concerning Communion *sub utraque* [under both kinds], and the two articles on the same subject which had not yet been discussed, and the articles which had been proposed in congregation concerning the sacrifice of the Mass, and he praised all that had been done. All the same, he was unable to refrain from repeating the universal comment that matters of morals and discipline had been left out or passed over

231

lightly, while decisions about controversial dogmas, on which all the Fathers agreed, were hurriedly made. He thought that this comment was unjust, but nevertheless asked that his ambassadors' proposals should be seen as necessary to remedy the ills of Christendom and the disasters which had fallen upon his kingdom. He had learned by experience that neither heavy nor moderate punishments brought back those who had left the Church, and so he had thought it good to have recourse to a general council, and had asked the pope for this. He was sorry that he had not been able to send his prelates sooner, because of the troubles in France; but he saw clearly that to achieve peace and unity in the Church, it was inappropriate to be stubborn and rigid in carrying on the approach already begun by the legates and bishops. What he wanted was that in beginning the Council they should do nothing to alienate their adversaries, that they should invite them to come, and when they came, receive them in a friendly manner, hoping that by this means they would allow themselves to be instructed and return to the bosom of the Church. And because all those who were met at Trent were of the same religion, and neither wanted nor were able to doubt any part of it, it seemed to His Majesty that this controversy about religion was not only superfluous but offensive to Catholics, and it was a reason for their adversaries to move still further away from the Church. Whoever thought that they would accept the decrees of a council in which they had not taken part did not know them very well; anyone who thought that this would do any more than produce more books was deceiving himself. The king, therefore, thought it better to leave these disputes about religion until all the reforms they were waiting for had been made. This was what everyone should aim at in order that the Council (which was numerous, and would be still more numerous when the French arrived) might bear fruit. The king next demanded that because of the absence of his bishops, the next session should be delayed till the end of October; or that they should defer the publication of the decrees; or that they should await new instructions from the Pope, to whom he had written; and that meanwhile, they should busy themselves with reform. His Majesty understood that the ancient freedom of councils, in which kings and princes and ambassadors had always been allowed to declare the needs of their kingdoms, was somewhat changed, and so he asked that this power be maintained, and whatever had been done to the contrary revoked.

The same day, the imperial ambassadors appeared before the legates, asking that the articles sent by the emperor (which they had already presented to the legates) should be put forward in the Council. They asked most earnestly that the discussions of dogmas be postponed till the French arrived, and since reforms were not only of general use to the whole Church, but of particular value to each kingdom, they asked that two of each nation should be deputed to remind them of what deserved to be put forward and discussed in the Council. The legates made the same reply to them as they had done to the French ambassadors—that the Council could not without serious consequences alter the established order of treating dogmas and reform together, and if they tried to do this, other princes would oppose it. However, as a favor, they would so arrange matters that the theologians and prelates would examine the subject of Holy Orders, and immediately afterwards, they would deal with some reform proposals, observing all the time the customary procedure that everyone, whatever his status, could make any suggestions to the legates which he considered necessary, useful, or convenient. This was a more free procedure than deputing two spokesmen for each nation. After that, they would go on to discuss matrimony. The ambassadors were not satisfied with this at all, so the legates forwarded all their requests to the Pope.

The Frenchmen were dissatisfied and complained in front of everyone about the way in which the Pope had commanded other prelates to go to the Council, since it was clear that he did this in order to have a majority. The Pope's supporters themselves were not pleased that this was done so openly, and at the time that there was news of the coming of the French. They would have

liked their numbers increased for greater security, but
this should have been done so skillfully that no one
could say that it had been done for this reason. However,
the Pope did not work openly in this way out of tactless-
ness; it was a deliberate move to let the Cardinal of
Lorraine know that his plans would not succeed, so that
he would decide not to come, or so that the French
would take some opportunity to have the Council dissolved. It was not only the Pope who had this idea, but
the whole Curia, which feared to incur some harm
from the plans of the Cardinal; even if the plans did
not succeed (and it was not so easy to hope this), his
coming would hinder, disturb, and prolong the Council
all the same. It is certain that the Cardinal of Ferrara
tried to persuade Lorraine (who was a relation of his)
not to come, saying that it would have no effect and so
lessen his reputation, for he would arrive after all the
decisions had been taken.

[*A meeting of the anti-papal party, September, 1562.*]

When the congregation was finished and the prelates
departed, Pecs remained with his Hungarians and some
Poles and some Spaniards, to whom he made a speech.
He said that there was no danger that the emperor
would be involved in war because of the truce between
him and the Turks, so Ferdinand wanted nothing more
than the reform of the Church, which would be put into
effect as soon as some of the prelates at the Council
helped him. He exhorted and begged them, out of reverence for God and out of the love that every Christian
ought to have for the Church, not to abandon such an
honorable, just, and useful cause. Each of them ought to
put in writing what he thought should be done for the
service of God, without thinking about any human considerations, and to aim at reforming the whole body of the
Church, not just a part of it. Granada made a supporting
speech, showing the need for reform and the opportunity.
He thanked Pecs for his admonition, and he said that
they would talk among themselves about this. The Spaniards met together for this purpose, and they talked

about the need for reform, and the hope of success as a result of the attitude of the emperor (from which their king, who was most pious by nature, would not dissent), and because the French prelates, who were expected in a short time, would help the work of reform with love and diligence. They went on to detail various abuses, showing that the Curia was at the origin of all of them and not only corrupt in itself, but the cause of the corruption of the whole Church. Granada recounted how the papacy had usurped the authority of bishops by means of reservations, and how if this authority was not restored, the abuses would never disappear. It was necessary to lay the foundations before raising the noble structure of reform. An opportunity was provided by the discussion of Holy Orders; if it was decided that bishops received their authority from Christ, it would follow that it could not be diminished, and the bishops would receive again that which Christ had given them, which the ambition and avarice of others and their own negligence had caused to be usurped. Braga added that it was all the more necessary because the authority of bishops had been reduced to nothing, and an order superior to them was created (unknown in past times), that is the order of cardinals, who in early times were counted in among the other priests and deacons, and who only after the tenth century raised themselves above their proper rank. Even then they did not dare compete with bishops, but were considered inferior to them until 1200. But after this they not only came to equal bishops, but exalted themselves higher, so that at the present they treated bishops like their household servants. The Church would never be reformed until bishops and cardinals returned each to his proper place.

These proposals were applauded, and the speeches were considered first-rate. And so they resolved to choose six of their number to write down all that was necessary for the reform in general and the institution of bishops in particular (the point at which they decided to begin). The men chosen were Granada; Gaspar Cervantes [de Goeta], Archbishop of Messina; the Bishop of Segovia; and Martin de Cordoba [y Mendoza], Bishop of Tortosa.

The last-named was the cause that things went no further, because he had a secret understanding with the papal party. So he excused himself from accepting the charge, alleging first of all his own inadequacy and the fact that the time did not seem to him to be quite ripe, adding afterwards that Pecs' motives were not pious ones, but that all he wanted was to use the reforms to force the Pope to grant the use of the chalice (which others opposed). Seeing that they were disposed to listen to him, he went on and persuaded them not to act at once but to wait. However, they did not delay long, because the next day Granada, Braga, Messina, and Segovia asked the legates for an audience and urged the discussion of the article already proposed in that same Council by Cardinal Crescenzio (and approved, but not published), to the effect that "bishops are instituted by Christ and are superior to priests *de iure divino.*" The legates conferred together and replied that since the Lutherans claimed that bishops and priests were the same, it was just to declare that bishops were superior; but there was no need to say on what grounds, or who it was that instituted bishops, because these matters were not controversial. Granada replied, on the contrary, they were, and if they let the theologians dispute, they would realize the necessity of deciding this point. But the legates would not agree at all. After both sides had lost their tempers, the Spaniards left without having obtained anything, but they resolved to persuade some of the theologians to raise the matter, and to mention it at the time of declaring opinions in congregation. When the papal party heard about this, they spread the story among the theologians that they were forbidden by the legates to speak about this question.

## Chapter Two

Although the congregations of theologians took up almost the whole time, the prelates, talking among themselves, showed more interest in reform (some supporting it, others opposing) than in the subjects treated by the theologians. The frequent and public discussions of reform which could be heard all over Trent, and which the imperial and the French ambassadors encouraged, led the legates to consider it necessary not to appear to be opposed to it, especially because they had promised the ambassadors to propose it after the discussion about Holy Orders. Besides, they had heard that a speech by Ambassador Lansac to a meeting of many ambassadors and prelates had been received with great applause. He concluded that if the reform proposed and requested by the emperor was so hated and feared, at least they should find out a way, without making new ordinances, to have the decisions of the ancient councils implemented, by removing the hindrances which encouraged abuses. The legates had the proposals of the imperialists collected, together with all the requests about reform which had so far been made, and the replies which they had given, together with a summary of the decisions taken at the French assembly [the Canons of Poissy], and of the requests of the Spanish prelates. They sent all these to the Pope with the message that it did not seem to them possible to simply go on talking about this; it was necessary to show the world that their heart was in the matter by taking some action and coming to some decision, which would to some extent satisfy the ambassadors of the princes, especially in those matters where their national interests were involved. They could do this in such a way as not to endanger the power of the Pope and the prerogatives of the Church of Rome.

When the Pope had seen the instructions of the king of France, nothing was more unpleasant to him than the prolongation of the Council. His idea had been that in the next session of November 12, they would settle all the business that was left, and if anything was left over, at the worst the Council would be finished, suspended, or dissolved at the end of the year. The French ambassador residing at the Curia urged him to postpone the discussion of dogmas until the coming of the French prelates, and in the meantime to deal with reform. To this the Pope replied that as far as waiting for the prelates was concerned, he had been informed that the Cardinal of

Lorraine had decided to wait until Bourges was captured and then accompany the king to Orléans, which showed that his departure from France would be a late one and might never happen at all. It was not fair to keep so many prelates waiting in Trent because of such distant plans. The requests to prolong the Council were aimed at making him and the prelates spend money, and they were not made because the French wanted to come to the Council. If they forced him to spend money in this way, he would not be able to go on giving help to the king. He made a great deal of the fact that they had been waiting for the French at Trent for eighteen months, while they produced various frivolous excuses. He also complained about the way in which he was treated; if the Council showed him any respect (which happened rarely enough), the ambassadors there lamented that the Council was not free. Yet they were the ones who asked him to prolong the Council, which was the most unfair thing and the one most hated by the prelates. He concluded that when it was certain or plausible that they would come, he would have preparations made for their coming. He added that he had arranged to be informed by a fast courier as soon as the Cardinal set off, and then he would have preparations made; but it was not fair to make the Fathers wait with nothing to do. As for reform, it was more necessary to have him present for that than for matters of dogma which did not affect him, since he was a good Catholic, and it was certain that he would not be able to disagree with the others. But it would be appropriate to listen to his views on reform, which concerned him, since he was a second pope, with many benefices and three hundred thousand scudi's worth of income from Church property, whereas the Pope himself was content with a single benefice. All the same, he had reformed himself and every part of his court, at the price of injuring and losing many officials. And he would have gone further, had he not seen clearly that by diminishing his income he was working for his enemies, weakening his forces and the sinews of his state, and exposing himself, together with all the Catholics who were under his protection, to the injuries of his enemies. So far as the areas outside his temporal jurisdiction were concerned, the destruction of discipline came from themselves and from the kings and princes, whose undue and importunate demands forced them into extraordinary expedients and expenses. He was in an unfortunate position, because if he refused the inappropriate requests that were made to him, everyone complained about him and thought themselves offended and injured; if he granted them, he was blamed for all the evil consequences. People like the king's ambassadors in Trent spoke about reform in general terms without it being possible to understand what they were getting at. Let them make specific requests, said the Pope, and declare what it was that they wanted reformed in the kingdom, and in four days he would satisfy them. The prelates at Poissy had made many reforms; he would confirm their decisions if he was asked; but for people to confine themselves to generalities and to criticize everything that was done without making any positive proposals showed a lack of good will.

[*In October, 1562 the legates wrote to the Pope for advice what to do; the congregation of cardinals discussed how to reply.*].

The congregation thought that the proposal to end the Council was of greater moment [than the institution of bishops, etc.] not because it did not seem to them obviously necessary to bring it to an end, but because they did not see how. For since there were so many subjects to discuss, and since they could not persuade the prelates to speak briefly and to discuss them without entering into controversy (things necessary to a speedy ending), it was impossible to think in terms of closing the Council except in the distant future. To suspend it without the consent of the princes seemed a dangerous and scandalous matter, especially since the legates had a few days before reported that the ambassadors Ferrier[1] and Pecs had said that when the Council was sus-

---

[1] Arnaud du Ferrier (1508–85), French ambassador to the Council, later ambassador to Venice 1563–7 and 1570–82.

pended, they would not leave Trent and would not let the prelates leave either until their princes had instructed them so to do. It would take a long time for this to happen, for there was no doubt that each of them would want to know what the others thought before replying himself. And so, they were unable to decide to do anything but urge the legates to hurry business on. The coming of Lorraine gave them more to think about, for they had heard from various places that besides the question of the election of the Pope, he was coming with the idea of proposing many innovations concerning the collation of bishops, plurality of benefices, and no less important, Communion with the chalice, the marriage of priests, and Mass in the vernacular. On the assumption that he would not leave France until he had had a reply from the Abbé de Manne, who was sent by the king and himself [to Rome], they advised recalling the Cardinal of Ferrara and offering Lorraine the post of papal legate in France (which it might be hoped would stop him, because he so much wanted to lord it over the clergy there that in former times he had been unable to resist engaging in intrigue to become Patriarch of France); but when he arrived, more prelates and some cardinals should be sent to Trent to counterbalance him. The Cardinals de la Bourdaisière and Navagero were nominated; but then the decision was postponed because they wondered whether this would offend Lorraine and provoke him to do worse, and because they were not sure that these men were equal to his opposition, and also because they wanted to have the opinion of those who were at Trent first, so that they would not take offense. They also reflected that this would increase expenses, which was something not to be done unless the consequences were extremely useful. And so, it was resolved to write to the legates that they should under no circumstances permit the slightest discussion of the election to the papacy, and that if it was impossible to avoid it, rather than give permission, they should return to Rome so as not to harm Italy and the college of cardinals.

## Chapter Three

*[Speech by Diego Lainez, the General of the Jesuits, concerning the institution of bishops, October, 1562.]*

Lainez spoke for more than two hours, most opportunely, most vehemently, and in a most magistral manner. His speech was divided into two parts. He spent the first part in proving that all authority had been given to the Pope, and that no one else in the Church had the slightest authority unless through him; the second part discussed all the arguments that had been adduced in the previous congregations to prove the contrary. The substance of his argument was that there was an enormous difference between the Church of Christ and lay communities. The latter first came into existence and afterwards developed their constitutions, so they were free, and all authority came from them, and they delegated it to the magistrates without depriving themselves of it. But the Church neither created itself nor its constitution; it was Christ, the first ruler, who ordained its laws and then founded (or as Holy Scripture says, built) the Church. As a result, the Church was born a slave without any kind of liberty, power, or authority, but was completely subjected. To prove his point he quoted places in Scripture where the body of the Church is compared to ground that has been sown, to the draft of a net, and to a building; he added the place where it is said that Christ entered the world to unite His faithful, to collect His sheep, and to instruct them by His teaching and by His example. Then he added, "The first and chief foundation on which Christ built the Church was Peter and his successors, according to the words which He said to him: 'Thou art Peter, and upon this rock I will build my Church'; by 'this rock,' some of the Fathers understood Christ Himself, and others, faith in Him, or the confession of faith, but the most Catholic interpretation was that which understood it as Peter himself, who in Hebrew or Syriac is called Cephas, that is, 'rock'." He went on to say that while Christ was alive as a man, He governed the Church alone and with absolute power; and when He was about to leave this world, He left the same constitution, making St. Peter His vicar, and Peter's successors, to govern the Church as He had, giving them all His power and authority, and subjecting the Church to them in the same way that it had been subject to Him. This Lainez proved from St. Peter, because the keys of the kingdom of heaven were given to him alone, and consequently the power of letting in and keeping out, which is authority; and to him alone was said "Feed (that is, rule) my lambs," an animal which does not do anything on its own initiative. These offices, that is, to be keeper of the keys and to be shepherd, being perpetual, should be given to a perpetual person, that is, not just to the first holder but to the whole succession. And so, the pope of Rome, from St. Peter to the end of the world, is a true and absolute monarch, with complete and absolute power and authority; and the Church is subject to him as it was to Christ. . . . There was no speech in this Council which was more praised or criticized according to the different opinions of the hearers. The papal party said it was the most learned, hardhitting and well-argued speech that they had heard; some thought it was a speech of flattery, others thought that it was heretical; and many let it be known that they were offended by the harsh judgments he had made, and that they intended in the congregations to come to take every opportunity to refute him and to convict him of ignorance and rashness.

## Chapter Four

[*Plans to end, suspend, or transfer the Council, October, 1562.*]

The Curia in Rome and the papal party in Trent were as much troubled by the Spaniards and their adherents at the Council as by the expectation of the arrival of Lorraine and the French. In fact, they were rather less worried about the French when there was reason to hope that something had happened to stop them, as when the news went about that they were to pass All Saints' Day with the Duke of Savoy. At the court of France, before he left, and during the journey, in various places, the Cardinal (whether out of vanity or as part of a plan) let it be known to many that he intended to raise many issues which involved the lessening of the authority of the Pope, and which were contrary to the interests of the Curia. When the news of what he had said arrived by various routes in Rome and Trent, they left the impression in both places that in general the intention of the French was to keep the Council going for a long time and, as opportunity offered, to reveal and put into practice various plans. There were already conjectures that he had an understanding with the emperor and with other princes and rulers of Germany, and although they were sure that the king of Spain did not have a complete arrangement with these others, all the same, there were good reasons for believing that he, too, wanted to make the Council go on for a long time, or at least that he would not let it be wound up. As a counterweight they thought of stressing the abuses current in France, and of making sure that the ambassadors came to hear that there was a plan to remedy them, because all the princes who were clamoring for the reform of the Church would not want to have their own abuses remedied. And so, when the serious work of reform began which would be prejudicial to their interests, they would cease (and make their prelates cease) doing things prejudicial to the interests of the papacy. After some packets of letters had passed between Rome and Trent, this idea was thought a good one, and the abuses that were found in France most of all, and to some extent in other kingdoms, were collected. This was the beginning of the reform of the princes, which will give us much to write about later on.

Besides this, in Rome, it was considered a good idea for the legates to dampen the ardor of the prelates, using their authority and position more than they had done in the past. In Trent, the legates thought it a good idea to keep their supporters among the prelates united, edified, and satisfied, so that even if the other side increased in numbers, they, too, would increase and would prevail. They also thought it good to set about ending the Council, or suspending it, or transferring it without regard to anyone. They wrote (and had many of their supporters write) to their friends and patrons in Rome to say that the best solution would be to arrange matters so that some prince asked for the suspension, taking the first opportunity that presented itself. They asked Rome for various briefs translating the Council, suspending it, and so on in order to be able to use whichever they needed. They also advised the Pope to go to Bologna; so that, besides receiving information more frequently and more quickly, and being able to take the necessary action in a moment, he would have a pretext to transfer the Council to that city at the slightest opportunity, or to suspend it; warning him that just as they had not said anything about this to Cardinal Madruzzo, he should not let his uncle, the Cardinal of Trent, hear anything about it. It was certain that the Cardinal of Trent, for various reasons of his own, would do all he could to stop the Council from leaving Trent. . . .

## Chapter Five

[*The arrival of the French, in November, 1562.*]

The Cardinal of Lorraine arrived in Trent, being met a mile away by Cardinal Madruzzo with many prelates, and met again at the city gate by all the legates, who accompanied him to his lodgings. He rode between the Cardinals of Mantua and Seripando—an honor they thought it necessary to do him because Del Monte and Santacroce had done the same when they were legates in Bologna (when the Council was being held there), and he was going to Rome for his red hat. That evening he visited the Cardinal of Mantua, and the next day the legates gave him an audience, together with [French] ambassadors Lansac and Ferrier. He presented the letters written by the king to the Council, and he made a long speech on the same subject. He said he was at the service of the Apostolic See, promising to tell the Pope and the legates about all his plans, and saying that he did not want to ask for anything unless this was all right with His Holiness. He said he did not want to pry into unprofitable questions, and he added that the two controversies about the residence of bishops and the source of their authority, about which everyone was talking, had weakened the authority of the Council and had damaged its good reputation with the outside world. For his own part, he was inclined towards the *iure divino* point of view, but even if he were certain, he would not see the point of laying this down formally. The aim of the Council ought to be to bring back to the Church those who had left it. He had been at a colloquy with the Protestants, and he had not found the points of difference so great that it was impossible to reach a solution, once abuses were reformed. No time was more opportune for bringing them back than the present, for they had never been so closely joined to the emperor. Many of them, the Duke of Wurttemberg, for example, were interested in taking part in the Council. It was necessary, however, to satisfy them by making a beginning of reform, and the service of God required that their Eminences busy themselves with this. He explained that the king wanted suitable reforms to satisfy the needs of his people. At present he was fighting the Huguenots; if abuses were not reformed, he would have to fight the Catholics, too, for he would have lost their obedience. These were the reasons for His Majesty's sending him to the Council. He complained that of all the money which the Pope had promised to lend the king, he had only been able to touch twenty-five thousand scudi, which was paid out by the Cardinal of Ferrara, because of the conditions that had been imposed: abolishing the ordinances concerning religion made by all the Parlements of the kingdom—a task of such difficulty that there was no hope of touching a penny. In conclusion, he said he had brought the ambassadors new instructions; and so, once he had spoken in the king's name to the general congregation of the Council, he would do nothing but declare his opinion freely in his capacity of archbishop. He wanted to keep out of secular affairs, leaving them to the ambassadors.

The legates replied as each saw fit without consulting among themselves first. They praised his devotion to the Apostolic See and offered on their side to keep him informed of all that was going on. They explained how patient they had been in tolerating the liberty—or rather license—of speech of the prelates, so that they would not have a chance to say that the Council was not a free one. The breaches of propriety arose not from the proposals they had put to the assembly, but from the excessive freedom taken by the prelates, who had wandered off into discussions of other questions. Now that His Eminence had joined them, they were sure that with his help they could put down such license and reconcile any disagreements, and in future they would proceed with such decorum that the world would be as edified as it had previously been shocked. As for the Protestants, their insincerity was well known. When they showed themselves ready for concord, then it was time to suspect them of creating opportunities for more discord. It was certain that they had asked for a council because they thought it would be denied them. At the same time that they were clamoring for it, they were putting obstacles in its way. At the present moment, those Protestants who had met at Frankfort were doing all they could to stop the Council going further, and they were making efforts to persuade the emperor to put some obstacle in its path. They hated the word "council" as much as the word "pope." In the past, they had used it simply to disguise and excuse their apostasy. There was no point in hoping for their conversion, but only in keeping those who were still good Catholics. They praised the king's piety and good intentions, and they explained the Pope's desire to reform the Church, and how he had reformed the Curia without regard for the fact that he reduced his own income. He had kept on writing to the Council urging reform, and the legates themselves were very much on the side of reform, but they were hindered by the contentions of the prelates, which took up almost all the time. If there was danger of losing the obedience of the French Catholics, this was a matter to discuss with His Holiness. As for the loan, they said that the Pope was so well disposed toward the king and the kingdom that the king must be sure that the conditions the Pope had imposed on the loan were the result of absolute necessity. After the exchange of various compliments, it was finally decided that he would go to the general congregation on the following Monday to tell the Fathers why he had come and to read the king's letters to them.

The legates were worried by the Cardinal's words, about wanting to keep out of secular affairs and to leave them to the ambassadors, because they were not consistent with what Lansac and Ferrier had said a few days before, when rejoicing at the Cardinal's arrival because it would free them from all responsibility, since (so they said) His Eminence would take all the decisions. The legates concluded that they must keep a lookout for these dissimulations, especially because Cardinal Simonetta had received reliable news from Milan that the French abbots who were lodged at St. Ambrose had said they would unite with the Spaniards, Germans, and others, and that they were going to deal with matters that would not please the Curia. Besides, whenever the Frenchmen talked together, they were heard to say that the time that should be spent in talking of reform should not be wasted on abstract questions; that the first thing to do was to abolish pluralism, and the Cardinal wished to be the first to give up his other benefices; that dispensations should be given for nothing; that annates, preventions, and minor collations should be abolished, and there should be only one provision for each benefice. They claimed that the Pope had a wonderful opportunity to win eternal glory for himself by doing all this: satisfying and uniting Christendom by reforming abuses; and that in return, they would pay His Holiness half a tithe. They said that they were resolved not to leave before they had attempted all these things, even if they had to remain there for a long time. If they saw that they could not have their way, they would not make a clamor but return to France and carry out the reforms in their own house. The legates were also fairly certain that the Cardinal had an understanding with the emperor and, still more important, with the king of Bohemia, both of whom were openly inclined to do something to annoy the German princes. The princes clearly hated the Council and wanted it to go no further, but wanted it somehow to be dissolved in a way that would be to their advantage and to the discredit of the Council and the Apostolic See. The legates also had their suspicions about the king of Spain because the Count of Luna's[1] secretary was told that it had been decided to send Martin Gastelone (formerly secretary to Emperor Charles V) to bring the Count his instructions from Spain by word of mouth, because it was not desirable to write them down. They compared this with reliable news from France, that before he left, the Cardinal of Lorraine had shown the king of Spain the petitions which he meant to put forward at the Council; and being sure that he had been urged in Germany to exert pressure for reform, they feared that the arrival of the Cardinal would produce some great change. They were not pleased at all by what he had said, during the audience, about Germans coming to the Council, especially considering the discussion which he had had already with the Duke of Wurttemberg. And in brief, they could not but suppose that a man of such authority and prudence would not lack a secure foundation for his plans, and so they thought that they should let the Pope know about all this immediately. The legates had observed that when special messengers arrived in Trent or departed from it, the prelates had occasion to talk about it, to investigate the reason, to whisper and make a clamor, and to lay plans of their own, which might, now that the Cardinal had arrived, produce dangerous results. Consequently they sent their messages secretly and wrote that

---

[1] The Count of Luna was Philip II's ambassador to the Council.

in Rome, the couriers should be told to leave their guide and all their baggage at the last post before Trent so as to enter the city unhurriedly with nothing but the dispatch. . . .

## Chapter Six

At this time, a new matter of dispute was being prepared because the Count of Luna gave the legates to understand that he was to come to Trent as the ambassador of the king of Spain and not as the ambassador of the emperor, but before coming he wanted to know what precedence would be given him. The legates summoned the French ambassadors and explained the situation to them, saying that they were greatly worried about the problems of precedence; and they asked them to find some sort of compromise. The French replied that they had not been sent to make compromises, but to take the place that was theirs—the one which was always granted to their king. They did not intend to do anything to the prejudice of the king of Spain, but to do him all the honor and service which was appropriate to the relationship and friendship between him and their king; and they had been charged, if their proper place were denied them, to declare that the acts of the Council were null and void, and they were to leave, together with all the French prelates. The Cardinal of Mantua proposed to give the Spanish ambassador a seat apart from the rest, opposite the legates, or below the ecclesiastical ambassadors, or below all the secular ambassadors. But the French would not accept any compromise, insisting that he take his place after them, and nowhere else.

In the congregation of December 1, Melchor Vosmediano, Bishop of Cadiz, speaking about that part of the last canon in which it was declared that the bishops appointed by the pope are true and legitimate, said that he was not pleased with the way in which it was expressed because there were also bishops who were neither appointed by the pope nor even confirmed by him, and who were true and legitimate bishops all the same. As examples, he mentioned four suffragans appointed and ordained by the Archbishop of Salzburg, whose appointments were not confirmed by the Pope. Cardinal Simonetta did not let him go any further, saying that everything that the Archbishop of Salzburg and the other primates did was with the authority of the pope. Brother Tommaso Casello, Bishop of Cava, and the Patriarch of Venice got up together, saying that he should be expelled as a schismatic. Egidio Falcetta, Bishop of Caurle, shouted, "Away with the schismatic!" And there was a commotion among the prelates—whispering and stamping of feet—some attacked the Bishop of Cadiz and others defended him, to the great displeasure of those prelates who were not Italian. If the Cardinal of Lorraine was displeased, he did not show it. The legates restored order with difficulty and had the next speakers follow. When the congregation was over, the Cardinal Lorraine said in the presence of many prelates of the papal party that this was a great insolence, that the Bishop of Cadiz had said nothing wrong, and that if he had been a Frenchman he would have appealed to a freer council; and that if it was not possible for everyone to speak freely, they would not be able to stop the French from leaving and from holding a national council in France. It was known that the bishop had said nothing wrong, and the canon was altered from "the bishops appointed by the pope" to "the bishops who had taken office by authority of the pope."

The following day, since it was time to fix the day for the session, the Cardinal of Mantua proposed that it should be adjourned until the seventeenth; and if the reform decrees which they had been discussing could not be put in order by that time, they should be postponed till the following session. The Cardinal of Lorraine agreed about the date, but on condition that they did not leave out anything relevant or put anything off to the next session, in which it was necessary to begin the universal reform. The Archbishop of Prague, the Bishop of Pecs, and the Polish ambassador agreed with this. There was much contention. Some wanted to do what the Bishop of Nîmes suggested and postpone the ques-

ions to another time. Others wanted to decide them on
he spot. It was decided to fix the session for the afore-
aid day, with two congregations a day so that they
vould deal with all the business. If not all the decisions
vere taken, they would publish the decrees which had
)een agreed upon, and put off the undecided matters to
another time. In the following session, they would dis-
:uss reform before entering into doctrinal matters. The
Cardinal of Mantua also criticized the noise which had
)een made the day before, and he ended by saying that
f they had not previously spoken with the respect and
everence appropriate to their own status and to the
presence of the legates, who represented His Holiness,
and of the cardinals and ambassadors, who represented
he princes, these dignitaries would have walked out so
as not to tolerate such disorders. The Cardinal of Lorraine praised this rebuke, adding that it was not a good
:hing for the legates to be forced to walk out of the congregation, and that it was only right that the disturbers
of the peace should be punished. The Bishop of Cava
was not prepared to apologize for what he said, and still
ess to accept the rebuke in silence, although it was
phrased in general terms. He said that the disturbances
would stop when their causes were removed, and that if
the words of the Bishop of Cadiz had offended him personally, he would have borne with it out of Christian
charity; but if charity requires us to put up with insults
to ourselves, it demands that we bitterly resent insults
to Christ, whose Divine Majesty is offended whenever the
authority of His vicar is questioned. He thought that he
had said the right thing. He went on to say the same
thing in different words, and everyone thought that his
tone was petulant.

Giacomo Gilberto de Nogueras, Bishop of Alife, declared his opinion that there was no better foundation
for theories about the institution of bishops than the
words of St. Paul to the Ephesians, if they were carefully
considered and properly understood. It was very true
that Christ ruled the Church with absolute power while
He was alive, as others in congregation had judiciously
remarked. But it was a great falsehood to add to it (as

had been done) that He had abandoned this form of government after He had ascended into heaven. He exercised it more than ever; and this is what He said to His apostles when He left them, "I shall be with you till the end of the world"; and the work of the Holy Ghost is added to this. Even at the present time, it is not only the interior influence of grace which comes from Christ as head, but also an exterior help (although invisible to us) which gives the faithful opportunities for salvation and repels the temptations of the world. Besides all this, He has also appointed certain members of the Church as apostles, pastors, and so on, in order to defend the faithful from errors and lead them toward unity of belief and knowledge of God. To these men He has given what is necessary for exercising this sacred duty, and that is the power "of jurisdiction," as it is called. This is not given to all equally, but more to some than to others, and it comes directly from Christ. Nothing is more contrary to St. Paul than to say that it is given to one man who deputes it as he pleases. It is true that it is not equal for everyone, but varies according to how God has distributed it. He has ordained that St. Peter and his successors should have the supreme authority in order to keep the Church united, as St. Cyprian says. This authority is not total or absolute; it does not turn will into law, as the proverb has it. As St. Paul says, it is authority to help the Church, not to harm it, so it is not great enough to abolish the laws and canons which are the foundation of the government of the Church. Here he began to mention the canons quoted by Gratian, in which the ancient popes admitted that they were subject to the decrees of the Fathers and to the constitutions of their predecessors.

However, the Cardinal of Varmia did not let him go on, and he interrupted to say that he was supposed to be talking about the superiority of bishops, and that what he was saying was irrelevant. To this he replied that if one dealt with the authority of bishops, it followed that one had to discuss that of the pope. And the Archbishop of Granada got up and said that others had spoken about this unnecessarily, not to say perniciously, and so Alife could discuss it, too (he referred to what Lainez had said). The Bishop of Cava, mentioned above, got up and said that others had spoken about this, but not in the same way. The prelates began to whisper. Simonetta made a sign to Cava to stop, and by telling Alife to speak if occasion arose, he quieted the murmurings. Alife went on mentioning the canons which he had begun to cite, when Varmia interrupted him again, not speaking to him, but delivering a set speech to the Fathers about this matter. He said that the heretics claimed to prove that bishops appointed by the pope were not true and legitimate bishops, and that this opinion ought to be condemned. But there was no difference between Catholics and heretics about whether or not true bishops are instituted *de iure divino* [take their authority directly from God], and so the question was not for the Council to decide because it had only met to condemn heresies. He reminded the Fathers that they should not say anything that might give rise to scandal and urged them to leave these topics alone. The Bishop of Alife wanted to reply to the Cardinal, but Simonetta, with the help of some other prelates—and with some difficulty—calmed him down. After him Antonio Maria Salviati, the Bishop of San Papulo, spoke. He said that they had all assembled together for the service of God, and that they all had good intentions, though some travelled one way and others another; and as he went on he said various things which served to harmonize men's opinions, and still more to reconcile the men themselves. So the congregation had a quiet ending, and the Cardinal and the Bishop exchanged kind and respectful words.

On December 4, the Cardinal of Lorraine stated his opinion on the same subject, and he declared at length that God had given jurisdiction directly to the Church. He quoted the passages from St. Augustine (that the keys were given to Peter: not to an individual, but to one body; that Peter, when Christ promised him the keys, represented the whole Church; that if he had not been the Church's representative, Christ would not have given him the keys), and he showed his excellent memory by reciting them word-perfect. He went on to say that the bishops received their share of the Church's jurisdiction directly from God. He explained what this share consisted of, and mentioned, among other things, the power to excommunicate. He spent a long time expounding the passage in St. Matthew where Christ laid down the method of correction, brotherly and judicial, to be used by the Church, and its power to expel the disobedient. Then he began to attack this opinion, too, taking various arguments from the words of Christ to St. Peter and from St. Leo the pope's interpretation of them. He gave many examples of bishops who had recognized the entire jurisdiction of the Apostolic See. He spoke with such eloquence and in such a way that no one could have a clear picture of what he actually thought. He went on to say that councils had their authority directly from God, quoting in his support Christ's words: "Wherever there shall be two or three met together in my name, I shall be in the midst of them." He mentioned the council of the apostles which ascribed their decision to the Holy Ghost, and the fact that councils described themselves as assembled in the Holy Ghost, and the fact that the Council of Constance openly said that it had its authority directly from Christ. Then he added that when he spoke of councils, he included their head, and that nothing was of greater service to Church unity than to confirm the authority of the pope. He himself would never have consented to anything which might diminish it, and all the French prelates and clergy were of the same opinion. Moving on to the institution of bishops, and speaking with the same ambiguity, at length he concluded that it was a question which could not be answered. He therefore exhorted the congregation to pass it over, and he offered a draft of the canon which omitted the words *iure divino* and put "instituted by Christ" in its place.

The French prelates, who spoke after Lorraine that same day and on the following days, spoke neither with the same ambiguity nor with the same respect for the pope's authority. They openly supported the idea that the authority of bishops was *de iure divino*, repeating and amplifying the arguments of the Cardinal. While they spoke, he leaned his head on his hand, as if he were displeased with what they were saying; but all the same he was considered to be acting from ambition, as if he had organized matters so that his opinion would be commented on. Although the French were openly defending the position taken up by the Spaniards, the Spaniards were not happy with this, whether because the Cardinal had spoken in an ambiguous manner, or because he and the other French prelates had declared that it was not necessary to decide the *de iure divino* question at the Council, but that it should rather be passed over. They were most displeased with the formula proposed by the Cardinal where the phrase was omitted, even though it was for their sakes rather than for any other reason that the words "instituted by Christ" were included.

The French and the Spaniards had the same aim, to deal with the ambition and avarice of the Curia, which exercised an arbitrary and useless power, and which drew a great quantity of money from Christian states by means of dispensations and collations to benefices. However, the Spaniards thought that if they brought this into the open they would cause scandal, and that they would not achieve their aims because the Spanish people were devoted to the authority of the pope, and because the king and his council hated innovations. They thought that the pope would easily be able to create such difficulties with the princes that they would never be able to declare what they believed. It was more fitting to follow national custom and to operate more indirectly; to declare that the authority of bishops and their duty to reside came from Christ and were *de iure divino*; to raise the reputation of bishops with the people; to resist the attacks that the Curia might make upon them, and so in time reform the Church and recover the power usurped by the Romans without harming the service of God or the peace of the kingdom.

The nature of the French, on the other hand, is to proceed openly and impetuously, and so they despised these subtleties. They said that Rome would find ways of making them come to nothing, and that for success they needed so much time that one could not rest one's hopes on such methods. The thing to do was to openly and directly attack the abuses that were all too clear and manifest. It was no more difficult to attain their main aim than to attain the pretended one, which would be worthless if they did attain it. In another respect, their opinions were no less different from those of the Spanish. They all agreed that it was necessary for the execution of the decrees of the Council to be impossible to evade. All the same, the French and the Spaniards differed as to the means whereby the Pope could be prevented from ignoring or altering the decrees of the Council under the pretexts of dispensations, *non obstantibus,* and other Roman clauses. The French wanted a definition of the superiority of the Council over the Pope, or for it to be laid down that the Pope could not alter or dispense from the decrees of the Council. This would have been a complete remedy. The Spaniards thought that this was too difficult to bring about, and that it should not be attempted because the Pope would always be supported by the princes, were he to complain that there was an attempt to diminish his power; and he would be supported by the majority of the Italian prelates for patriotic and personal reasons. It seemed sufficient to them for the Council to pass decrees, intending afterwards to obtain from their king a *pragmatica* on the subject, which would prevent papal dispensations on these matters from coming into Spain.

The legates sent a courier post-haste to Rome with a copy of the proposal of the Cardinal of Lorraine, and the opinions of certain canonists about it, to show that the pope's authority was being eroded. They asked for instructions. When the Cardinal heard about this, he was upset. He complained that when he had given them a copy before he made the proposal in congregation, they had seemed to be pleased with it; but that afterwards, they had acted as if they did not trust him. He said that it seemed odd to him that they should be suspicious of what he and his prelates did. He complained that the Italians had insulted his country, claiming to have heard with his own ears some prelates quoting the scurrilous proverb which was now current all over Trent, "after the Spanish scab, we have caught the French pox." The other Frenchmen and the Spaniards, too, took every opportunity to complain about the same thing. As usually happens, this increased people's interest, and the two nations became more and more suspicious of one another, which was extremely dangerous. Neither the legates nor the more prudent prelates, who attempted to resist the wave of suspicion, were strong enough to stop it.

The Frenchmen were irritated, and they resolved to test how much liberty they had. They agreed that the Cardinal of Lorraine should not take part in the congregation of the seventh, but the prelates, whose turn it was to speak, would express themselves freely; and if they were rebuked, the ambassadors would protest. To let both sides know that this would happen, Lansac, in the presence of many of the papal party, said to Antoine le Cirica, Bishop of Avranches (one of the prelates), that he must say freely and fearlessly that the protection of the king was sufficient to support them. News of this was brought to the legates, and this was the reason that the prelates were heard with great patience, although they said that the institution and jurisdiction of bishops was *de iure divino,* like that of the pope, and that the only difference between them was one of rank, and that the authority of the pope is limited by the canons. They explained and commended the practice of the French *parlements.* Whenever any papal bull was presented to them which contained something contrary to the canons received in France, they declared that it was illegal and forbade it to be implemented. This liberty was the reason why the papal party was more careful about what it said, although the beauty of the proverb encouraged some of the lighter-minded prelates to take some part.

The pretext for the Cardinal of Lorraine's remaining at home was the news of the death of the king of Navarre,[1] which arrived the same day. The king had been wounded by a harquebus at Rouen, in September, and the wound did not heal, but at length proved mortal. On

---

[1] Antoine de Bourbon.

his deathbed, thanks to Vicenzo Lauro, a doctor, he took Communion in the Catholic manner. Then he wavered toward the doctrine of the Protestants, and finally, on November 10, he died. This accident had a great effect on the affairs of the Council, because when Lorraine heard the news, he changed his plans completely. The king had played a most important part in giving the Cardinal his instructions before he left, and so now, the Cardinal was not sure whether the queen and the others were completely behind him. Besides this, he saw a manifest crisis in French affairs, and he wished to be in France to support his party. The Prince of Condé was an open rebel, with little confidence in the queen and those around her; the Cardinal of Bourbon was a man of little ability; the Cardinal of Montpensier was not much trusted; the constable was old and had many powerful rivals. So the Cardinal was confident that they could all be set aside: his brother would dominate military affairs, and he himself would dominate political ones. He was occupied with these schemes and did not think much about the Council of Trent, although he was still present there. The other Frenchmen said openly that they should thank God for the king's death, because he had begun to falter and to make an alliance with his brother and the other Huguenots.

The next day, which was December 8, was entirely taken up with ceremonies on account of the election of Maximilian as king of the Romans. For this reason, the Archbishop of Prague celebrated the Mass of the Holy Ghost, and all the Council attended. The Bishop of Tininia preached a sermon in praise of Maximilian, and the Archbishop of Prague invited the cardinals and ambassadors to supper.

The Diet met in Frankfort as before. The Prince of Condé sent not only to ask for help from the Protestant princes, but to negotiate an alliance between the Huguenots and the adherents of the Augsburg Confession. They should join together particularly to demand a new, free council, which would undo everything that had been done in Trent, and he gave them hope that the French Catholics would come, too, because this is what had been promised to the French ambassador, who was afterwards created cardinal and called de la Bourdaisière. However, the German Protestants did not like the idea of a council, as long as it was possible to have peace in Germany without one. And so, a book was printed in Frankfort which was full of excuses and arguments as to why they had taken no part at Trent and did not want to do so; it declared that everything that had been and would be done there was useless.

The king was first of all anointed and crowned king of Bohemia in Prague, in the presence of the emperor, his father, and of the archbishop, who had gone from Trent to Bohemia to perform the ceremony so that the king would have a vote in the imperial Diet. When they went to Frankfort, they had to wait for the canons of Cologne to elect their archbishop, because the See was vacant. As a result, the princes had a great deal of time to discuss various matters, since they remained in Frankfort the whole time while waiting for the coronation in Bohemia and the election in Cologne to bring the electors up to their full number of seven. These matters were much thought about in Rome, where it was feared that the Diet might send a deputation to Trent to make a protest; that some new form of coronation ceremony might be used (since the old one had been abolished), which might show an inclination to break with ancient rites; or that the new king might make some promise prejudicial to the power of the Pope. However, the emperor and the king were extremely skillful in preventing the Diet from discussing religious affairs before the election. This was on November 24, and the coronation was on the last day [of the month]. On this last occasion the electors and other Protestant princes remained at Mass till the Gospel had been recited, and then walked out. Another novelty was that the papal nuncio was given precedence over the electors, and they over the other ambassadors. After the coronation, the king began to try to persuade some of the Protestants to adhere to the Council of Trent. In order not to be taken by surprise, they assembled together and presented their reply to the emperor—a reply which had been promised twenty months before to the imperial

ambassador at the convent of Naumburg, but put off till
now. In this reply they explained why they had demanded
a free council in many previous imperial Diets, and why
they were demanding one again now. They added the
conditions which they considered necessary. If these
were observed, they were prepared to take part in a future general council. There were ten conditions.

I. That it should be held in Germany.

II. That it should not be held on the initiative of the
pope.

III. That he should not preside over it, but be a part
of the council, and subject to its decisions.

IV. That the bishops and other prelates should be
freed from their oath to the pope so that they could declare their opinions freely and without hindrance.

V. That Holy Scripture should be judge at the council,
and every human authority excluded.

VI. That the theologians from the states adhering to
the Confession of Augsburg, who were sent to the council, should have not only the right to be consulted, but
the right to vote; and that their safe-conducts should
cover not only their personal safety, but their practice of
their religion.

VII. That the decisions made in the council should not
be made by majority vote, as in worldly affairs, but that
the most correct opinions should be preferred—those derived from the word of God.

VIII. That the acts of the Council of Trent should be
declared null and void, since that Council was one-sided,
attended by only one of the two parties, and not organized in the manner that had been promised.

IX. That if religious unity did not result, the arrangements made at Passau would remain in force, together
with the religious peace made in Augsburg in 1555,
which would remain valid, and everyone would have to
observe it.

X. That they should be given suitable and adequate
guarantees of the observance of all the preceding articles.

When the emperor had received the articles, he promised to work for unity and for the holding of a council

which they could not reasonably refuse to attend, provided that for their part they would lay aside their hatred and other emotions contrary to peace among Christians. He also offered to go to Trent for this purpose, and he resolved to go to Innsbruck as soon as the Diet was over. This was only four short days' journey from the Council, so he would be able to do whatever was necessary in a short time.

## Chapter Seven

At this time, the controversy about residence changed its nature. Those who hated the idea no longer tried to show by means of reasons and authorities, as they had done up to now, that it was only a law made by man, but they began to frighten the other side by saying that to call it a law of God was to weaken the authority of the pope; because it followed from this that he could not increase or diminish the number of Sees, divide them or join them together, change or transfer them, leave them vacant or appoint administrators for them or give them *in commendam*. They said that he would not be able to limit, still less to take away, the power of absolution; and that this decision would with one stroke condemn all the dispensations popes had ever made in the past, and it would take away their power to grant them in the future. The other side saw very well that these consequences necessarily followed, but did not see anything wrong with them. On the contrary, this was precisely the belief and practice of the primitive church, and this question had in fact been raised just for the purpose of taking away these inappropriate powers from the pope. But now they, too, gave up offering reasons and authorities in proof of residence being *de iure divino*. They concentrated on showing that when this declaration had resulted in bishops' residing again, this would increase the papal power and the standing of the clergy, and especially that of the pope, who had lost his authority in so many parts of Christendom because the bishops, by being absent from their dioceses and by governing through inefficient substitutes, had allowed new doctrines hostile to the pope's authority to spread and to take root. If all bishops resided, the authority of the pope would be preached everywhere; where it was still recognized it would be strengthened, and where it had been shaken it would be restored. Neither side was able to conduct the discussion in these terms without letting the real opposite aims be perceived all too well through their attempts to hide them. They were all wearing masks, and yet they all knew one another.

[*Outbreak of the religious wars in France, 1562; their effect on the Pope and the Council.*]

That summer there were no less than fourteen armies raised at one time in different parts of the kingdom. Sons fought against fathers, brothers against brothers, and even women took up arms on both sides in order to preserve their religion. There was hardly any part of the provinces of Dauphiné, Languedoc, and Gascony which was not fought over several times. In some places, the Catholics won; in others, the Reformed. There was so great a variety of happenings that it would be a long business to describe them, and anyway it would be irrelevant. We only want to mention what happened outside Trent if it has some connection with the affairs of the Council, as have the following events. Where the Huguenots were victorious, they threw down images, destroyed altars and sacked churches, using the gold and silver ornaments for minting money to pay the troops. The Catholics, where they were victorious, burned French Bibles, rebaptized the children, and made couples married according to Reformed rites perform the ceremony again. Most unhappy was the fate of Catholic priests and Reformed pastors—they were tortured cruelly when they fell into the hands of the other side. Under the pretext of doing justice, there were many executions, especially on the Catholic side. In July, the Parlement of Paris issued an *arrêt* which made it legal to kill all the Huguenots, and it was ordered to be read every Sunday in every parish. Then another *arrêt* was issued which declared that all who had taken up arms in Orléans were rebels and public enemies; that they and their descendants were infamous; and that their goods were confiscated. Condé was excepted from this, on the pretext that he was forced to be with them. Although there was much negotiation between the two sides, and the queen mother and the Prince of Condé even had a personal interview, the ambition of the great nobles prevented any compromise, so that it proved impossible to calm down the disturbances.

After the death of the King of Navarre, who might perhaps have prevented the outbreak of open war, the queen demanded help from all the princes in order to try to recover obedience by force of arms. As a result of the disturbances in France, the inhabitants of the Netherlands learned to be more and more disobedient and obstinate, and the authority of the king [Philip II] grew less and less every day. The governors could do nothing about it, and the king did not want to take the advice of Cardinal Granvelle, the chief minister, who counselled him to go and live in the Netherlands to oppose his royal presence to the ill disposition of the people and the contempt of the nobles. That prudent king realized that it was still more dangerous for him to be despised when he was there, and he feared that he would not win the Netherlands, but rather make it even more disobedient, and lose Spain in the bargain. King Philip thought that if the French rebels submitted to their king, then he could take action against his own, so he offered the queen extensive military help, sufficient to make the whole kingdom submit. The queen refused troops and asked for money, knowing well that if she accepted troops she would be forced to rule France not according to her own interests, but according to those of Spain. A compromise was reached, and she accepted six thousand men. With these men and her own forces, under the command of the constable and the Duke of Guise, a battle [the battle of Dreux] was fought on December 17, in which three thousand Huguenots and five thousand Catholics were killed. The Commanders on both sides were taken prisoner, Condé and the constable.

Neither of the armies was routed, thanks to the valor of the two who were second-in-command, Guise on the Catholic side and Coligny on the Huguenot side. The queen immediately appointed Guise commander-in-chief. Coligny maintained his army under arms, kept the territories he had won, and extended them still further.

All the Fathers assembled at Trent gave thanks to God for this victory (as it was described, although it did not really deserve the name), walking in procession, and celebrating High Mass. At Mass, François de Beaucaire, Bishop of Metz, made a speech in which he told the whole story of the disturbances in France from the death of François II. He described the success of the last war, and he gave the whole credit for it to the Duke of Guise. He went on to say that the cause of these disturbances was Martin Luther. Although he was a small spark, he had kindled a great fire, which had swept first over Germany, and then over the other parts of Christendom—apart from Italy and Spain. He asked the Fathers to help Christendom because only they could put out that fire. He said that it was the twenty-sixth year since Paul III had begun to treat this illness (he was referring to the Council). It was postponed, and then disguised. Then it was held, but various factions clashed with one another until it was transferred to Bologna, where there were various delays, and even more bitter conflicts. Then it was recalled to Trent, and it was dissolved because of the wars. Now they had reached the last stage. There was no more possibility of dissimulation. This Council would either reunite or ruin the whole world. And so, the Fathers should pay no attention to private interests; they should not carry out private plans or say what others told them to say, when religion itself was in question. If they had their eyes on any other matter, then it would be all up with religion. All this was said with frankness tempered with adulation, flattering first the Fathers, then the Pope, the emperor, the king of the Romans, and the king of Poland. He went on to praise the French queen mother and the king of Portugal, and finally exhorted everyone to reform Church discipline.

When the Cardinal of Lorraine heard that the prince [of Condé] was a prisoner, he was very happy, particularly for his brother's sake. He wanted to return to France even more quickly now so that he could use his position in court and council to help his brother and have him advanced to a rank still higher, now that Navarre and the constable, to whom he had had to give place, had disappeared.

At this time, the Pope was full of suspicion because the emperor had announced that he was going to Innsbruck, believing that he would not do this without grand designs and confidence in his success. He thought the emperor had a secret understanding with France and Spain. As he did not know what it was, he could not tell whether it was intended against him or not. So he began to think of going to Bologna himself, and of sending eight or ten cardinals to Trent; of drawing closer to the Italian princes; and of supporting the prelates who were well disposed toward him in the Council, while he looked for some opportunity to dissolve or suspend it. And to prevent the reform of the Curia from being discussed at Trent at this time, he took action about this, too. He reformed the *rota,* publishing a brief dated December 27, which laid down that no judge could come to a decision (even if the case was a clear one) without the matter having been laid before the whole college, unless the parties themselves agreed; that judgments pronounced *ut in schedula* [as listed] should be produced within fifteen days; that cases affecting the judges and their relatives, including those of the second degree of relationship and of their household, should not be judged in the *rota;* that the parties involved should not be forced to accept an advocate; that they should not come to decisions against what had been published unless two-thirds of them agreed; that they must retry any case where there was any suspicion of collusion. In the same bull, he imposed a limit on fees. With other bulls, which were published on the following January first, he reformed the *segnatura,* the Roman tribunals, and the office of the fiscal advocate, laying down the charges that it should have. But these reforms were far from putting an end to the customary extortions; on the contrary, from breaking the new rules, men learned to violate the old ones, which had been observed to some extent.

At the Curia, it was thought that the French Catholics had gained a complete victory, and that the Protestants had been wiped out. The courtiers rejoiced, believing that now the French had obtained by force of arms what they had been expecting from the Council. And since there was no more need to have regard for Germany, which had protested against the Council, the pressures for having a council would be removed, and it could be suspended or postponed, so freeing them from their anxieties which had grown every week as they heard the news of innovations at Trent. But the Pope did not invest much hope in the news. For he was reliably informed that the Catholic forces had not increased, and those of the Huguenots had not diminished; and that the battle would provide an opportunity for both sides to negotiate about peace, which could only be to his disadvantage and would give rise to still more innovations at Trent. And so he was even more afraid and troubled than before.

## Chapter Eight

[*January, 1563: the French ambassadors presented thirty-four articles of reform to the legates. The reader should compare these suggestions with those implied by Sarpi's book* On Benefices.]

I. Priests should not be ordained unless they were adult and their good life could be vouched for by popular witness; their sins of the flesh should be punished according to the canons.

II. Holy Orders should not be conferred all at the same time, but a man should prove himself worthy of minor orders before his ordination as a priest.

III. No one should be ordained a priest without being given a benefice or cure of souls at the same time; following the ruling of the Council of Chalcedon, which did not recognize the title of presbyter without the office.

IV. Deacons and other officers in minor orders should have their functions restored so that they did not appear to be mere titles used in ceremonies and nothing else.

V. Priests and other ecclesiastics should follow their calling and not meddle in affairs other than God's ministry.

VI. No one should be made a bishop unless he was of reasonable age, pure in life, and learned in theology, so that he could both teach his flock and set it an example.

VII. No one should be made a rector unless he was of proven good life and one who could teach his people, celebrate the sacrifice of the Mass fittingly, administer the sacraments, and explain their effects to those who received them.

VIII. No one should be made an abbot or a prior unless he had taught theology in a famous university and had his master's degree or its equivalent.

IX. The bishop should preach himself or have others preach, in sufficient number according to the size of the diocese, every Sunday and feast day, in Lent, in Advent, and on fast days, and whenever convenient.

X. The rector should do the same, when there were people to listen.

XI. Abbots and priors should read the Holy Scriptures and set up guest houses so that their ancient functions of education and hospitality would be restored to monasteries.

XII. Bishops, rectors, abbots, and other ecclesiastics incapable of performing their duties should be given coadjutors or should give up their benefices.

XIII. Concerning the catechism and brief instruction in Christian doctrine, the proposal of the emperor to the Council should be put into force.

XIV. A man should be given only one benefice, and the differences between different sorts of people and between compatible and incompatible benefices (a new distinction, unknown to the ancient decretals, and the cause of great disturbances in the Catholic Church) should be abolished; and monastic benefices should be given to monks, and secular ones to the secular clergy.

XV. Whoever at present should possess two or more benefices should retain only one, which he was to choose quickly, or else he would suffer the penalties laid down in the ancient laws.

XVI. To remove all tincture of avarice from the priesthood, there should be no asking for any return for the administration of holy things on any pretext whatsoever, but it should be established that the rectors with two or more assistants should have enough to live on and provide hospitality. The bishop should arrange this buy uniting benefices or assigning tithes, or if this was impossible, the prince should do it by means of gifts and money collected from the parish.

XVII. In Masses in the parish, the Gospels should be expounded clearly, according to the capacity of the people. The prayers that the parish priest and the people recite together should be in the vernacular. After Mass in Latin, there should be public prayers in the vernacular, and if possible at the same time or at another time, hymns or psalms which had been approved by the bishop should be sung.

XVIII. The ancient decree about Communion in both forms (made by Popes Leo and Gelasius) should be confirmed.

XIX. Before the administration of any sacrament there should be an explanation of it in the vernacular, so that the ignorant would understand its use and efficacy.

XX. According to the ancient canons, benefices should not be conferred by deputies but by the bishops themselves, and within six months; or else the duty of presentation would fall on the bishop's superior, and so on up to the pope.

XXI. Expectatives, regresses, resignations in confidence, and commendams should be abolished and banished from the Church, as contrary to the decretals.

XXII. Resignations of benefices in favor of someone else should be completely wiped out from the Curia, since appointing or recommending a successor was something prohibited by the canons.

XXIII. Simple priories, from which the cure of souls had been taken away (contrary to the foundation statutes) and assigned to a perpetual curate with a tiny portion of the tithes or other income, should be restored to their original state as soon as a vacancy occurred.

XXIV. Benefices which do not carry the duty of preaching, administering the sacraments, and so on, should have some spiritual duty imposed on them by the bishop, with the advice of the chapter. Or as an alternative, they should be united with neighboring parishes, for there should be no benefices without duties attached.

XXV. Pensions should not be imposed on benefices, and taxes on them should be abolished, so that ecclesiastical incomes would be spent maintaining the priests, giving to the poor, and in other pious works.

XXVI. Bishops should be given complete ecclesiastical jurisdiction over the whole of the diocese once more; and all exemptions should be abolished except for the heads of religious orders and the monasteries subject to them, and for those who hold general chapters who are legitimately exempt. But it should be provided that they should not be exempt from correction.

XXVII. The bishop should not exercise his jurisdiction or deal with important diocesan matters without the advice of the chapter. The canons should be in residence all the time, and they should be satisfactory in life and learning, and at least twenty-five years of age, because before that age they do not legally have full possession of goods, and so should not be given to bishops as counsellors.

XXVIII. The rules concerning consanguinity, affinity, and spiritual relationship should either be observed or altered, but dispensations from them should not be allowed, unless in the case of kings and princes for the public good.

XXIX. Considering that many disturbances had occurred over images, the Council should provide for the instruction of the people concerning them; and if any abuses or superstitions had been introduced into the cult of images, they should be removed. The same should be done in the case of indulgences, pilgrimages, relics of saints, and religious sodalities and fraternities.

XXX. The ancient public penances for serious and public sins should be revived and put into practice in the Catholic Church; and to appease God's wrath, the practice of fasting and other penitential exercises and the practice of public prayers should be restored.

XXXI. Men should not be excommunicated for every kind of offense, but only for the most serious ones, and those in which the sinner carries on in the same way after having been warned.

XXXII. In order to do away with or shorten lawsuits over benefices, which have infected the whole of the clergy, the new distinction between petitionary and possessionary should be abolished; and also nominations by universities. Bishops should be commanded to give benefices not to people who ask for them, but to people who try to avoid them but who deserve them. Deserving cases are people who, after a university degree, have spent some time preaching, with the permission of the bishop and to the satisfaction of the people.

XXXIII. In the cases where lawsuits over benefices still took place, a steward should be put in charge, and the litigants should choose arbitrators. If they did not, then the bishop should choose for them; and these should settle the case within six months without possibility of appeal.

XXXIV. Episcopal councils should be held at least once a year; provincial councils, every three years; and general councils, when there was no impediment, every ten years.

[*January, 1563: the Bishops of Ventimiglia and Viterbo arrive in Rome, the latter with the thirty-four articles.*]

The Pope heard the articles of reform read the first time with extreme impatience, and he interrupted to comment that their aim was to abolish the datary, the rota, the segnatura, and in the end, to abolish all his apostolic authority. Afterwards, he was mollified to some extent by the bishop's explanations. The bishop gave His Holiness the hope that he could, by granting some demands, moderate others and sidetrack the rest. The bishop explained Lorraine's instructions to him, to the effect that princes asked for many concessions in order to obtain the ones they really wanted, which were not the ones which threatened the power of the pope, but which were things like Communion in both forms, the use of the vernacular, and clerical marriage. If His Holiness would be willing to satisfy them in these respects, he would find this an easy way to be honored by the Council and to attain the ends he desired. The bishop told him that the French bishops themselves did not care for many of the articles, and they were prepared to put obstacles in their way. Having heard this, the Pope ordered the articles to be discussed in congregation, at which the Bishops of Viterbo and Ventimiglia were present, in order to explain in detail what had been happening. At the congregation, it was decided that theologians and canon lawyers should be consulted about these proposals, and each of them should give his written opinion. To cause a diversion on the French side, the Pope told the Cardinal of Ferrara to let the king have forty thousand scudi without any more conditions, and to tell him that most of the proposals of his ambassadors in Trent were useful for the reform of the Church. He wanted to see the proposals not only decreed, but implemented as well. But he did not approve of all of them, since some of them would lessen the authority of the king, who would lose his right to grant abbeys, which was a great help to him in rewarding his faithful servants. In former times, kings had found that they had bishops who were too powerful and at the king's expense, and they had asked the popes to limit this power; and here were his ambassadors proposing that the bishops should be given back their excessive liberty, although his predecessors had very wisely had it limited. As for the authority of the pope, it was impossible to take away what Christ had given him; Christ had made St. Peter and his successors shepherds of the whole Church and the administrators of all ecclesiastical goods. To take away the right to grant pensions was to take away the power to give alms, which was one of the pope's most important duties throughout the world. By favor of the pope, bishops were given the power to appoint to certain benefices, but it was not just to extend this power so far as to prejudice the power of the pope himself. Just as tithes were owed to the Church *de iure divino,* so the tenth of these tithes was owed to the pope, but for convenience it had been commuted into annates. If this was inconvenient for the kingdom of France, the Pope would not refuse a compromise, provided that this did not involve the Apostolic See's giving up its rights. But as he had made clear many times, this could only be discussed by the Pope personally, and the Council had nothing to do with it. Finally he told the Cardinal that he should suggest to the king that he consider all these things and give new instructions to his ambassadors.

The Pope also sent to Trent the opinions concerning the articles delivered by various cardinals, prelates, theologians, and canon lawyers in Rome, with instructions that this subject should be postponed as long as possible. The article concerning residence and the abuses relating to the sacrament of Holy Orders would give the Council enough to discuss for a long time; when it became necessary to put forward these articles, they should begin with those that were most harmless, ones relating to manners and to doctrine, and put off the discussion of the articles which concerned ceremonies and benefices. If they were forced into discussing these, too, they should suggest objections to the prelates on the Pope's side, and they should enter the discussion, giving him time to decide what to do next. That is what he wrote to the legates.

[*At the council.*]

There was a dispute between the Frenchmen and the Italians. The Italians said that the Council of Florence was a general council, and that the Council of Constance was partly official and partly condemned, and that the Council of Basel was schismatic. The Frenchmen, on the contrary, argued that the Councils of Constance and Basel were general councils, but that the Council of Florence was not, and that only a few Italians and four Greeks had taken part in it. Nor did they allow that the pope had all the authority of Christ, even with the restrictions and limitations proper to a mortal man, but they contented themselves with saying that he had authority equal to that of St. Peter. The members of the papal party were extremely suspicious of this move, seeing that the other side wanted to make the life and actions of St. Peter the model for the pope. This would be, as they said, to reduce the Apostolic See to nothing. They claimed that the pope had an unlimited power to act in any situation according to the demands of that situation, even if it was contrary to what his predecessors had done, even St. Peter himself.

The disputes would have gone much further, but the legates, in order to call a halt so that they could send the Pope news of what the Frenchmen and Spaniards were saying and receive his instructions as to what they should do, and in order to raise a subject which would divide their opponents, turned to the matter of residence. Lorraine and Madruzzo had composed a statement on this subject and presented it to the legates a few days before, and the legates had given it their approval without thinking more about it. However, afterwards they asked the advice of the canon lawyers, who did not approve of the passage which said that bishops were commanded by God to look after their flocks personally. So the legates thought that the Pope would make the same criticism and changed the words and made the proposal in congregation in this revised form. These alterations deeply offended Lorraine and Madruzzo, who believed that they had been slighted. Lorraine said that in future he would not make any proposals or negotiate with other prelates, but that he would confine himself modestly to giving his own opinion, although he could have been of service to the legates if he had been given a chance. Madruzzo could not refrain from saying that there was a secret council within the Council, which claimed more authority than the Council itself. The legates, seeing that everything they did turned out for the worse, gave up holding congregations. But this was not good enough, either, because the prelates held private congregations of their own, while the legates held continual consultations. The Archbishop of Otranto and others who aspired to be made cardinals and who were sure of achieving their aim if the Council broke up, agreed to make objections to everything so as to cause a disturbance. They went about energetically, even at night, making arrangements and having papers signed. Although the legates wanted this done, most of them disapproved of the manner in which it was done as a bad example which might cause grave scandal. On the other side, too, there were some who wanted the Council dissolved; but each side was waiting for an opportunity to make the other responsible for it. And so, each side became more and more suspicious of the other.

## Chapter Ten

On March 9, [1563] the news arrived in Trent that the Duke of Guise, the brother of the Cardinal of Lorraine, on his return from the siege of Orléans, had been shot by Jean Poltrot [de Méré], a private gentleman who was a Huguenot. Six days later he died from the wound, to the sorrow of the whole court. After he was shot, he exhorted the queen to make peace and said openly that whoever was opposed to peace was an enemy of the kingdom. The assassin was asked whether he had accomplices, and he named Admiral Coligny and Theodore de Bèze; although afterwards, he denied Bèze's part, but continued to assert Coligny's complicity. Afterwards, he wavered, so that no one knew what to believe. When the Cardinal heard the news, he increased his bodyguard. After he had recovered from the sorrow of losing a brother who had been close to him and before doing anything else, he wrote a letter to console their mother, Antoinette de Bourbon—a letter which was full of exquisite conceits, to be compared (or as his followers said, to be preferred) to those of Seneca. At the end of it, he said that he had decided to go back to his church at Reims and to spend the rest of his life preaching the word of God, instructing his people and bringing up his brother's sons in Christian piety; and that he would not give this up unless the kingdom had need of him for public affairs. The letter had hardly been dispatched from Trent when the city was full of copies, which the members of the Cardinal's household importuned everyone to take. So difficult is it to still one's self-love, even on an occasion of great sorrow! After this the Cardinal, considering his affairs, changed all his plans as a result of this event. This in turn caused a change in the affairs of the Council. He had been the instrument—and an extremely efficient one—through whom the emperor and the queen of France[1] had operated up till then, and so they were forced to put off some of their plans and to proceed more slowly. However, human affairs are like the sea: when the wind has dropped, the waves remain turbulent for some hours after. In a similar way, the great mass of the affairs of the Council could not easily stop, but went on from its own momentum. But it is certain that the duke's death was an important factor in the quiet period which came some months later.

## Chapter Twelve

[*News arrives in Trent of the Pacification of Amboise.*]

May began with fresh discussions of the peace made in France, since letters arrived from the king for Lorraine and the French ambassadors, telling them about it and instructing them to inform all the Fathers present at the Council, either in general or in detail, according to what they thought best. The letters were dated April

---

[1] Catherine de'Medici was not "the queen" of France, but the queen mother.

15, and were chiefly concerned in showing that the peace was not aimed at favoring the introduction or establishment of a new religion in that kingdom, but that on the contrary, it was aimed at taking the easiest way to unite the whole people in the same holy Catholic religion and to end civil war, conflicts, and disasters. But he added that what would help this aim most of all would be a holy and serious reformation, such as had always been hoped for from a free and general council. So he had decided to send President Biragues to Trent to ask for this. He also wanted his ambassadors already present at Trent to take every opportunity to let the Fathers know how strongly he felt the ruin and the troubles which differences in opinion over religion had given rise to in his kingdom; with the apparent ruin, and still greater danger of the state. Rather than run that risk again, he had decided that if the general council did not do its duty and do what was expected toward a holy and necessary reform, he would hold a national council. He had done his duty to God and man by making frequent approaches to the Fathers and to the Pope to obtain a remedy for the common evil from the general council. In order to obtain what he wanted the more easily, he had sent Seigneur d'Oissel to the king of Spain and Seigneur d'Allègre to the Pope, and had ordered Biragues, after he had carried out his instructions at the Council, to go on to the emperor to see if these princes would help him attain this excellent aim.

It is certain that the Pope was greatly displeased by the news of the peace because it was to the prejudice of his authority, and also because it had been concluded without his taking part, although he had contributed so much money to the war. The king of Spain was still more displeased, since it seemed to him that he had lost both his effort and his money. His troops had taken part in the victorious war, and he had been put to great expense, so it seemed unfair to him that peace should be made without consulting him and to the prejudice of the religion which he had taken up arms to maintain and defend. He had a particular interest in the matter because peace in France weakened his position in the Low Countries, since it was obvious that if the French Huguenots prospered, the people of Flanders would be encouraged to continue with their rebellion. . . .

The French realized that as long as the Italians remained in the majority, they would not be able to obtain anything useful from the Council. They began to give up hope of the Council as long as it remained in Trent. They cut off supplies of money to the theologians sent by the king, allowing them to go or stay, whichever they pleased. One by one, almost all of them went. At the end, there remained the two Benedictines, who were paid for by their monasteries, and Ugonio, who was maintained by the papal party, having his board and lodging in the monastery, and fifty scudi every three months. . . .

[*April–May, 1563: Cardinal Morone's mission to the emperor at Innsbruck.*]

It was said that the German princes were sure that they could obtain nothing good from the Council, and that the best thing to do was to bury it with honor; and that they promised Cardinal Morone to connive at this and to take no offense if the Council was brought to a close. Whoever considers how the Council ended, without these princes having any of their demands satisfied, will be inclined to believe in the truth of this rumor. However, when he notices that after this mission the imperialists did not cease making demands, he will consider that it is unfounded. But it is possible to take a path which avoids both absurdities, and to believe that at that time these princes gave up hoping and decided that they would not oppose the ending of the Council; yet they did not consider it honorable to beat a retreat, but rather to reduce their demands gradually, so as not to let everyone know of their lack of judgment in being hopeful in the first place, and in disbelieving in the observation of St. Gregory Nazianzen. He said that he had always seen disputes become sharper and sharper in meetings of bishops. I am not sure which is the truth in this case;

it is one of those things which I have not found out. But it is certain that this was the time of the beginning of the catastrophe in the affairs of the Council, which never seemed as if it would have a quiet ending.

# BOOK EIGHT

## Chapter One

After this time [May, 1563], the Cardinal of Lorraine began to be less violent. In France, it had become clear from the experience of past events that it was impossible to obtain from Trent anything that would be of service to the kingdom. It was also clear that things were moving easily toward peace, so that one might hope that the king's subjects would return to their obedience without any more thought having to be taken concerning religious matters. It is also possible that the French had heard from the emperor about his meeting with Morone; and the Pope had been trying to persuade the queen through his nuncio. Anyway, the French decided not to press the affairs of the Council so enthusiastically, but rather to try to win over the Pope. If anything useful were to come out of Trent they would welcome it, but otherwise, they would simply devote themselves to making sure that nothing harmful came out of it. So the queen wrote to Rome, offering the Pope her aid in bringing the Council quickly to an end, in holding back Lorraine and the French prelates from attacking the authority of the pope, and in making the Huguenots leave Avignon and the neighboring country. At the same time, she wrote to the Cardinal of Lorraine, telling him that things were going well in France so far as peace was concerned, and that the only thing lacking to perfect them was his presence in France. He could do much more good there than in Trent, where he had learned from experience that he could do nothing of use. So he should make arrangements to return as quickly as possible, to try to satisfy the Pope in every way and make him his friend, and to think no more of the affairs of the Council than he was forced to by his own conscience and honor. She added that he would have the same authority in the kingdom as before; and so he should hasten his return.

## Chapter Two

*[June, 1563: Lainez defends the pope's authority.]*

Lainez, the General of the Jesuits, when he came to declare his opinion, replied to all the things which the others had said the Curia did not agree with; and he spoke as warmly as if the subject had been his own salvation. He said a great deal about dispensations. He said it was wrong to claim that there was no power of dispensation other than the power of interpreting the law, because it would mean that a good theologian had more authority than a great prelate; and to say that the pope, by means of dispensations, could not loose what God had bound, was to teach men to put their own conscience before the authority of the Church. But this "conscience" could make mistakes, and often did, and so to leave every Christian to rely on his conscience was to plunge him into an abyss of dangers. It could not be denied that Christ had the authority to dispense from any law; it could not be denied that the pope was the vicar of Christ. And since a deputy and his principal were judges in the same court, it could not be denied that the pope had the same authority as Christ. This was the privilege of the Church of Rome; everyone should take heed that it was heresy to take away the privileges of that Church, which was the same as denying that it possessed the authority Christ had given it. He went on to speak of the reform of the Curia, which he said was superior to all individual churches, and even to many of them assembled together. If it was in the power of the court of Rome to reform each of the churches which had a bishop at the Council, and if none of them had the power to reform the Church of Rome, since "no disciple and no servant is above his master," it followed that the Council did not have the power to reform it either. Many people spoke of things as abuses which turned out to be necessary, or at least useful, when they were examined carefully. Some people claimed to want the Church to return to its state at the time of the apostles—the state of the primitive Church; but these people could not distinguish one age from another, or tell what was appropriate for each. It was clear that by Divine Providence and goodness, the Church had become rich; nothing could be more impertinent than to say that God had given these riches, but not the right to make use of them. Concerning annates, he said that it was *de iure divino* that people should pay tithes and firstfruits to the clergy, just as the Hebrews had done to the Levites; similarly, just as the Levites paid a tenth of this tenth to the high priest, the clergy had the same duty to the pope. The income from benefices were the tithes, and the annates were the tenths of these tithes.

## Chapter Three

[*June–July, 1563. Following more disputes over precedence (cf. pp. 249ff.), the French ambassador, du Ferrier, drew up a protest to the Pope which was not delivered but was printed; and it is important, as Sarpi says, because it shows the aims and ideas of the French.*]

The substance of what he said is as follows. The Council had met as a result of the efforts of the brothers Francis and Charles, kings of France, so the ambassadors took it hard that they were forced either to depart or to agree to lessening the dignity of their king. The prerogative of the king of France was known to whoever had read the *ius pontificum* and the histories of the Church of Rome. Those who had read about the councils knew what place they had held there. The ambassadors of the "Catholic King" had in past general councils followed those of the "Most Christian King." Now a change had been made. This change was not the work of the Fathers, who, had they been free, would not have tried

to deprive any prince of his rights; nor was it the work
of the "Catholic King," who was a close friend and relation of their king. It was the work of the father of all
Christians, who had given his eldest son not bread, but
a stone, and not a fish, but a serpent, to harm with its
sting the French king and the French church together.
Pius IV was sowing seeds of discord between the two
friendly kings, changing forcibly and unjustly the traditional order of seating the ambassadors, lately followed at the Council of Constance and the Lateran Council, in order to show that he was superior to councils. But
he would not be able either to damage the friendship of
the two kings, or to go against the view of the Councils
of Constance and Basel that a council is superior to the
pope. St. Peter had learned to avoid making judgments
about worldly affairs, whereas his successor (but not
follower) claimed to have power to give kings honors
and take them away. The law of God, international law,
and civil law all took account of the eldest son, whether
his father was alive or dead, but Pius refused to place
the eldest king before the others who were born long
after him. Even God was unwilling to diminish the dignity of Solomon out of consideration for David; and Pius
IV, without respect for the merits of Pepin, Charles,
Louis, and other kings of France, claimed to take the
prerogative from their successors by his decree. Against
divine and human laws and without any reason, he had
condemned the king, taken away the most ancient of his
rights, and pronounced judgment against a widow and
an orphan. The ancient popes had never done anything
without the approval of a general council while it was in
session; but Pius had—without consulting the Council
which represented the whole Church—deprived of their
rights the ambassadors of a king who was a minor, ambassadors sent not to him but to the Council. In order
that nothing could be done about this, he had tried hard
to prevent his decree becoming known, commanding the
legates to keep it secret on pain of excommunication.
The Fathers should consider whether these things were
done by Peter and other popes, and whether they, the
ambassadors, were not obliged to leave the Council,

where Pius had left no trace of its liberty and no room for laws; for nothing was proposed to the Fathers and nothing was published which had not first been sent from Rome. They solemnly protested against Pius IV, reverencing the Apostolic See and the Pope and the Holy Catholic Church, but simply refusing to obey him and to accept him as the vicar of Christ. As for the Fathers there assembled, they had always had great respect for them; but since everything that was done was done not in Trent but in Rome, and the decrees that were published were those of Pius IV rather than those of the Council of Trent, they would not accept them as decrees of the general council. Finally, he commanded the prelates and theologians in the king's name to depart, to return when God should have restored to general councils the form and liberty that they should have, and when the king should have been given his proper place.

## Chapter Four

[*July 15, 1563—the twenty-third session: eighteen articles on the reformation of the Church.*]

I. The first article, on the highly controversial question of residence, declared that according to God's command, everyone who was given the cure of souls ought to know his sheep, say Mass for them, give them the spiritual food of sermons and the sacraments, set a good example, look after the poor, and perform the other tasks of a good shepherd. These things could not be done by a man who did not look after his flock personally, and so the Council admonished everyone to look after his flock faithfully and sincerely. In order that no one should misinterpret the decisions taken in the time of Paul III on this subject, and believe that an absence of five months was permitted, it was declared that whoever held bishoprics, whatever his title, cardinals included, was obliged to reside in them; and that they could only absent themselves when this was demanded by Christian charity, urgent necessity, their obedience, or the interests of

Church or State. Such reasons for absence, unless they were well-known or urgent ones, should be approved by the pope or by the metropolitan; nevertheless, the provincial council should be informed and approve the leave of absence that had been given to ensure that no abuses occurred. In any case, the absent prelates should make provision so that their flock did not suffer in any way from their absence. And because a short absence was not worthy of the name, even without one of the reasons mentioned, it was declared that such an absence must not exceed the space of two months or three at the outside, whether continuous or sporadic, provided that there was a good reason for it and the flock did not suffer. This was left to the conscience of each prelate, with the admonition that they should not be absent during the Sundays of Advent and Lent, or during Christmas, Easter, Pentecost, or Corpus Christi. If anyone were to disobey this decree, besides incurring the penalties of Paul III's time against nonresidents, and besides falling into mortal sin, he could not with good conscience enjoy the fruits of his benefice for the time that he was absent. The same decrees applied to everyone who had the cure of souls; and when they absented themselves by permission of the bishop, they should put in their place a suitable vicar who was approved of by the bishop and given his due reward. This decree and that made under Paul III should be made public in provincial and diocesan councils.

The other articles were concerned with Holy Orders, and were as follows.

II. Whoever held a bishopric, whatever his title, cardinals included, should lose the revenues if he was not consecrated within three months. If he put it off another three months, he would lose the benefice altogether. If the consecration did not take place at the Curia it should be celebrated in the cathedral itself, or somewhere in the province, if this was convenient.

III. Bishops ought to celebrate ordinations themselves. When illness prevented them from doing so, they ought not to send their priests to be ordained by another bishop without examining them and approving them first.

IV. The first tonsure should only be given to men who had been confirmed and who had learned the principles of the faith, and could read and write, and who were choosing the clerical life to serve God, not to escape the secular courts.

V. No one could enter minor orders without the parish priest and the schoolmaster bearing witness to his character; the bishop must have his name published in church and have inquiries made concerning his birth, his age, and his way of life.

VI. No one was to be able to hold a benefice until his fourteenth year, and no one was to be exempt from the secular courts unless he held a benefice, or unless he wore the habit and had the tonsure and was appointed by the bishop to serve in some church, or unless he lived in a seminary or in a school or in a university, by permission of the bishop. As for married clergy, the constitution of Boniface VIII should be observed, on condition that they, too, should serve the Church in habit and tonsure, if they were so commanded by the bishop.

VII. When ordinations were held, the ordinands should all be called to the city on the Wednesday before, and the bishop should examine them carefully and make inquiries about them, with the help of whoever appeared there.

VIII. Ordinations should only be held at the times laid down in the laws, in the cathedral church, with the canons present; if it were to be held elsewhere in the diocese, it should be in the most suitable church, and in the presence of the clergy. Everyone should be ordained by his own bishop, and no one should be allowed to be ordained by another bishop unless he had a testimonial from his own.

IX. Bishops should not ordain one of their household if he was not one of their subjects, unless he had lived with the bishop three years, and unless he gave him a benefice immediately.

X. No abbot or prior was to be able to give the first tonsure or minor orders except to their subjects—members of an order; and neither these nor other religious colleges or chapters were to be able to give the secular clergy dimissory letters to confer minor orders.

XI. Minor orders should only be conferred on men who knew Latin, and with a period of time between conferring one order and the next. And since minor orders were a stepping-stone to the others, no one should be ordained unless there was hope that he might become worthy of the priesthood. After the last of these minor orders, a man should wait a year before becoming subdeacon, unless the bishop decided otherwise for the good of the Church.

XII. No one should be ordained subdeacon until he was twenty-two; nor deacon until he was twenty-three; nor priest until he was twenty-five; and members of religious orders should not be exempt from this rule.

XIII. Subdeacons and deacons should have experience in minor orders; they should hope to be able to live continently; should serve in the church to which they were assigned; and should consider it extremely fitting to receive Communion on Sundays and feast days, when they served at the altar. Subdeacons should not pass to a higher rank unless they had passed a year in their own; and they should not be given two ranks in one day by virtue of any privilege whatever.

XIV. Men should not be ordained priests unless they had been practicing deacons for at least a year, and had been found suitable for teaching the people and administering the sacraments. The bishop should ensure that they celebrate Mass at least on Sundays and on important feast days; and that they do their duty in a satisfactory manner if they had cure of souls. And if anyone were ordained to higher orders before lower ones, the bishop could grant him a dispensation if there was a good reason.

XV. Although priests are given the power to absolve from sins at their ordination, no one should be able to hear confessions unless he had a parish of his own or was approved by the bishop.

XVI. No one should be ordained without being assigned to some Church or place of devotion to exercise his priestly function; and if he left the place without informing the bishop, he should be forbidden to exercise this function. And no foreign cleric should be allowed to exercise his priestly function without letters from his bishop.

XVII. To restore the functions of the different orders from deacon down to *ostiarius* [doorkeeper] which had been in use at the time of the apostles, but had in many places fallen into disuse, so that heretics derided them as useless, these functions should only be exercised by those who had received the appropriate orders, and prelates should revive these functions. If it was impossible to find continent clerics for the exercise of the minor orders, they should take married ones, provided that they had only one wife, and provided that they were in other respects fit for that office.

XVIII. The last article concerned the foundation of seminaries. It was laid down that every episcopal church should have a certain number of children to be educated in a college near the church, or in another convenient church; that they should be at least twelve years old and of legitimate birth; they should be assigned to different classes by the bishop according to their numbers, their age, and their progress in ecclesiastical discipline; they should wear a habit and be tonsured; they should study grammar, singing, ecclesiastical computation,[1] the Bible, the homilies of the Fathers, the rites and ceremonies concerned with the sacraments, and above all, they should study what was concerned with hearing confessions. To pay for all this, where there was already money to educate boys, it should be applied to this seminary; and if there was need of more, the bishop and four of his clergy should tax all the benefices in the diocese and also apply simple benefices to this purpose. He should force everyone whose duty it was to teach, to teach in the seminary schools, either in person or with suitable substitutes; and in the future, teaching posts should only be given to doctors or masters in theology and canon

---

[1] Calculations concerned with the Church year—the date of Easter, for example.

law. And if in any province all the churches were so poor that seminaries could not be founded in each of them, then there should be one seminary or more for the whole province; and in the churches of great dioceses the bishop could, if he considered this desirable, found one or more extra seminaries, which would, however, be subordinate to the seminary of the city. . . .

There was no act of this Council which interested the world as much as the act of this session, when it was published, because everyone was curious to see what it was that had caused so many prelates to dispute in Trent for ten months, and what caused all the Christian courts to be busy. But, as the proverb has it, the mountains were in labor for the birth of a mouse.

The effect of what happened at this session was to destroy the good relations which had existed up to this time between the Cardinal of Lorraine and the Spaniards. The Spaniards complained that they had been deserted so far as the institution of bishops and residence were concerned—matters about which he had claimed innumerable times to be of the same opinion as they were. He had promised to work hard to have these opinions expressed in the decrees, without allowing anything to make him give up. They added that they did not trust him to keep his other promises, and they said that the Pope had won him over by promising to make him legate in France, along with other remarks that were hardly complimentary. He, for his part, said in his own defense that the offer of the legation was made to him to make his friends distrust him, and that he had replied that he was not interested until the Council had passed the reforms. However, they did not believe that he would continue to hold the same opinions, at least as far as the legation was concerned.

The legates were anxious to end the Council at the same time as they ended the session, and they proposed to hurry along the other business, which so far as matters of faith were concerned were indulgences, praying to saints, and purgatory. To this end they chose ten theologians: two generals from the orders of friars and two theologians for each prince, that is, for the Pope, France (few Frenchmen were now left), Spain, and Portugal. They charged them to consider how they could briefly refute the views of the Protestants on these matters; and when they had decided, their opinions would be put forward in a general congregation, and canons would be drafted at the same time as matrimony was being discussed to get through the business quickly, without listening to the arguments of the theologians, as had been done previously.

## Chapter Five

*[July–August, 1563: the legates present the articles of reformation to the ambassadors for comment before the Fathers discuss them.]*

The Count of Luna went around persuading the other ambassadors to demand that deputies should be elected to represent each nation who would consider what had to be reformed, because the legates' draft had been made to suit the interests of Rome, and so was not appropriate for other countries. The Cardinal of Lorraine and the French and the Portuguese ambassadors contradicted this, claiming that everyone would be able to express his opinion about the articles and propose others as they went along, so that there was no need to offend the Pope and the legates in this way, who could not bear to hear talk of "nations" at the Council. The imperialists also agreed with this opinion, and the count withdrew his suggestion, saying, however, that he had various comments to make about the articles which had been proposed.

The Cardinal of Lorraine advised the legates to make matters easier by taking out all the articles which would not pass without much dispute, adding that the fewer matters discussed, the better. The Cardinal of Varmia seemed astonished at this, and Lorraine, suspicious of him as he was, asked Varmia if he was amazed because he did not see in him the same warm desire for reform that he had formerly shown. He added that nevertheless he had the same aims and motives as before; but he had learned from experience that nothing perfect could be done in the Council, nor even anything fairly good, but that every attempt of that kind was bound to go wrong. Lorraine worked on Luna not to try to postpone reform altogether, saying that if there was anything which was not to the count's satisfaction, if he told Lorraine about it, Lorraine would work to get him what he wanted.

The imperial ambassadors gave their reply in writing before anyone else, on July 31. They said first of all that they wanted complete reform in the head and in the body, and that having read the articles, they had added some things and commented on others, and they asked for the articles to be revised in these respects and proposed for the Fathers to discuss. Since the emperor, with the ambassadors of many German princes, was holding a Diet in Vienna to discuss many matters pertaining to the Council, the legates must not be annoyed if (after hearing from His Majesty) they were to bring up still further considerations in the future. For the moment, they wanted to add eight articles to the ones they had proposed: that a serious and lasting reform of the conclave should be made in the Council; that the alienation of ecclesiastical goods without the free and definite consent of the chapter should be forbidden, especially in the case of the Church of Rome; that commendams should be abolished and also the appointment of coadjutors with the right of succession; that schools and universities should be reformed; that the provincial councils should amend the statutes of all chapters; that they should equally be given authority to reform missals, breviaries, calendars, and graduals—not only the Roman ones, but those of all the churches; that laymen should not be cited to Rome in the first instance; that cases should not be removed from the secular court to the ecclesiastical one on the pretext that justice had been denied, without first making sure that the charge was true; that there should be no conservators in secular matters. On the articles which the legates had shown them, they noted many things some of which were unimportant and best to omit. The important matters were as follows: cardinals should be selected from all regions so that the pope would be elected by all nations; the provisions concerning pensions, reservations, and regresses should be made retrospective; the right to kiss the Gospel at Mass should not be taken away from the emperor and the kings, whose duty it was to defend the Gospel; a declaration should be made concerning what worldly affairs were forbidden to the clergy, so as not to contradict what had already been decided in the decree on residence; in the article about not taxing the clergy, an exception should be made for the subsidy for war against the Turks and other infidels.

This reply contained matters difficult to digest; but it was not as unpleasant for the legates as the possibility that the Diet in Vienna would make some extraordinary demand for a change in the customary ceremonies, and for a relaxation of the laws of the Church.

## Chapter Six

[*August–September, 1563: attempts to hasten the end of the Council.*]

When the Pope saw the replies which the ambassadors had given to the articles proposed by the legates, he was confirmed in his opinion that it was necessary to put an end to the Council, or else some great scandal would occur. The inconveniences that he could foresee he did not take seriously, but he feared that there might be something worse which he had not foreseen. He saw the difficulty of putting an end to the Council without finishing the business for which it had been called, unless the princes were agreeable. He decided to use his influence with them to this effect. He wrote to his nuncios in Germany, France, and Spain; he spoke of these matters with all the ambassadors resident at his court, and also with the ambassadors of the Italian princes. What he said was that he would be more obliged to anyone who helped him to put an end to the Council than if he had helped him

with arms in some great need. He wrote to the legates
that his chief aim was to finish with the Council. To
this end they should make every concession that was
necessary, though they should concede as few harmful
things as possible. He left everything to their prudence
and their strength, provided that they put an end to the
Council as quickly as possible.

The legates, after having considered (together with
some prelates) the proposals of the ambassadors about
reform, and having at their request omitted six of the
articles, leaving thirty-two, gave the articles to the prelates to discuss on the twenty-first of August. The Cardinal of Lorraine held particular congregations of the
Frenchmen to examine the articles, which the legates
approved, not only because they were certain that he
was travelling in the same direction as they, but because
they wanted agreement to be reached before the discussions in the general congregation. They charged the
Archbishops of Otranto and Taranto and the Bishop of
Parma each to collect their supporters in their own
house and question them to find out what would be to
the general satisfaction. They did this for a few days,
and then a great murmur arose among the Spaniards and
the Italians who had not been invited, and who mutinied
and opposed the others.

It also happened that the Archbishop of Otranto went
to the Spanish ambassador's house, and the ambassador
told him that he did not want to have to tell the king
things that would not please him. He added that those
special congregations were so much disliked by the better prelates that he would have to tell His Majesty all
about them. The Archbishop said in excuse that it was
well meant, to smooth the way and provide against difficulties before the general congregation met. At this point
the Bishop of Ischia arrived to speak to the Count of
Luna on behalf of Cardinal Morone. The Bishop made
it clear that he disliked private congregations, and that
he believed that their purpose was simply to raise difficulties and to omit some of the articles in order to finish
the session more quickly. All the same, the legates, who
aimed at pleasing the prelates rather than the ambassa-

dor, were glad to receive the comments made in these congregations, and they altered the decrees accordingly, striking out some things and inserting others.

When they were about to make public the articles in this amended form, a courier from the emperor arrived with instructions for the Archbishop of Prague, who immediately asked the legates not to propose the reform of the secular princes,[1] until he had heard from His Imperial Majesty. The Count of Luna supported this request. The legates were extremely worried because France, and now the emperor and Spain as well, seemed dissatisfied; and on the other hand, it was the common wish of the Fathers that all the reforms should be put through together. The legates met in the house of Navagero, who was ill, and, seeing that it was necessary to satisfy the ambassadors, they discussed whether to postpone all the reform proposals or just the article concerning the princes. Lorraine was of the opinion that they should only postpone that one article and propose all the rest. This would have been acceptable had they not been afraid of making the prelates suspect that they were going to omit the lay reform altogether, which would lead to both private and public reclamations. It was therefore resolved to satisfy the ambassadors by postponing the reform of the princes; but in order that the prelates should not take this the wrong way, they would postpone at least half of the other articles, including the most important, but would make the rest public in their amended form so that the session could be held and opinions given. The difficulty they foresaw concerning the decree on clandestine marriages made them hesitate all the same. On the sixth of September, twenty-one articles of reform were published, with instructions to begin the congregations the next day. Cardinal Simonetta and his adherents used all their skill in drawing up these articles so as to make compromises and to proceed in such a manner that little harm would be done to the Curia, and at the same time to satisfy the world, which was clamoring for reform, and the ambassadors,

[3] See p. 289-90; 299ff.

293

too. They aimed, above all, at pleasing the bishops, since to finish with the Council it was necessary that the bishops should agree to it with good will.

The aim of the bishops was a single one: more freedom. They believed that they would obtain this freedom when three provisions were made. First, parish priests must be dependent upon the bishops; this would happen when the bishops were given the collation to benefices with cure of souls. This, besides other difficulties, would interfere with reservations and chancery rules, and so make a great breach in the secret places of the Curia, for it was clear that this was to open the door for taking away collations altogether, which was to destroy the power and the very life of the Curia. So they hit upon a compromise, which was to keep reservations but give bishops the power to give cures to whomever they wished, under the pretext of examining them. To this end the eighteenth article was drafted with exquisite artifice, as everyone can see, which with specious show gave bishops the right to confer benefices on whomever they wished without taking away any of the profits of the Curia. The second provision concerned exemptions, a matter on which the bishops had received many concessions in the past; nevertheless, for full measure the eleventh article was added on this subject. There remained the exemptions of the religious orders; and the bishops hoped to be able to abolish them, or at least to limit them so that the religious would be largely subject to the bishops.

Since the beginning of the year, there had been a congregation discussing the reform of the religious orders, in which the generals had taken part, and in which the other religious at the Council had given advice. It had made great progress and decided on good decrees without any conflict, because, as it appeared outwardly, the religious themselves did not hate reform but, on the contrary, desired it. In reality, however, in the monasteries, they were quite sure that they would interpret and carry out reforms in the manner that would please them. So they considered it useful to have thorough-going reforms in writing, just as all their rules are honored more in writing than in observance. But when people began to speak of limiting exemptions and at least partly sub-ordinating the religious to bishops, all the generals and the theologians of the orders mutinied, and they joined forces with the ambassadors of the princes, showing them how useful the orders were to peoples, cities, and governments; offering to remedy abuses, if there were any sort of abuses among them; saying that they would accept every reform, and that when they returned to their houses, they would be still more strict than the reforms ordained; but arguing that to place monasteries under bishops was to harm them, because bishops did not understand monastic life and its severe discipline, and so they would upset everything. The bishops said that privileges always damage laws; that to revoke them was a good thing, so that matters returned to their natural state; that to abolish privileges was not to innovate but to restore things to their ancient state. On the other side, the religious replied that the exemption of regulars was so ancient that it could no longer be called a privilege, but rather common law; that when monasteries were subject to bishops, their own discipline and that of their canons was so strict that they were fit to oversee everyone; that if they wished to restore ancient practice, they should do so completely; that when the bishops returned to their ancient state, then monasteries could be placed under them as before; but that it was not right that they should demand to oversee monasteries before they were in a position to be a guide to the religious life. The religious orders were supported by the ambassadors, and by the legates, on account of the interests of the Curia, which would have lost a powerful instrument if the orders had ceased to be dependent on Rome alone. Some prelates also supported them, agreeing that their arguments were good ones. This controversy lasted for several days, and it died down gradually as every day the bishops who had raised this storm discovered greater difficulties.

The third provision concerned the hindrances which the bishops received from the secular magistrates who, in order to preserve the temporal power, would not allow the bishops to exercise the absolute power which they wished to exercise not only over the clergy, but over the people as well. To this effect the article on the reform of the princes was made, which has been mentioned already, and which will be discussed fully in its place.

[*The king of France writes to the ambassadors in Trent (August 28), concerning the reformation of princes. For the text of the articles, see pp. 299ff.*]

He said that he had received the articles which the legates had given the ambassadors, and had found things far distant from his hopes. The articles cut the claws of the kings and lengthened those of the clergy. He would not put up with this, and he commanded them to tell the Fathers this with force, prudence, and dexterity. They must explain that every prince was obliged to do all he could to favor the Council so long as matters marched as they should; but that to hide the wound that was the cause of the present evils, and to make another by acting against the interests of the kings, was something very different from what he had expected. He had noticed how lightly they had passed over the reform of the clergy, which had given scandal to those who had left the Church of Rome; and how they had given themselves the authority to take from kings their rights and prerogatives, to go against royal orders and immemorial customs, to excommunicate and anathematize kings and princes. All these were matters which tended to sow the seeds of disobedience and sedition, and to instigate the rebellion of subjects against their prince, since it was clear to everyone that the power of the Fathers and of the Council did not extend further than the reformation of the clergy, without touching on matters of state and secular authority and jurisdiction, which is completely distinct from the ecclesiastical; and that whenever Fathers and councils had taken it on themselves to discuss such matters, kings and princes had offered resistance. As a result, there had been many rebellions and wars which had greatly harmed Christendom. He exhorted them to attend to their own business; to do what was necessary for the needs of the present; and to give up attempts which had never come to any good, and which would have particularly evil consequences at this time. The king added that if the Fathers did not yield to these arguments, his ambassadors would oppose them firmly. Having come out in opposition, they would not wait for the judgment of the Fathers or submit themselves to it, but would leave the Council and go to Venice, letting the French prelates understand that they were to remain at the Council, doing what would serve God. And being certain that if any matter was raised contrary to the rights, prerogatives, and privileges of the king and the Gallican Church, they would not fail to stay away, as His Majesty wished them to do. He wrote also to the Cardinal of Lorraine, in the same way as he had asked the ambassadors to speak to the other prelates; that is, he told the Cardinal that he should not by his presence there approve anything that was done in Council against the king's rights, but should absent himself if he saw that the Fathers were going beyond their proper bounds. And he referred the Cardinal to the instructions which he sent to the ambassadors.

When the French ambassadors had received these letters and had informed the Cardinal of Lorraine about their contents, on his advice, they gave some of this information to the legates. They also spread a rumor about this information through the Council, so that the bishops would hear of it and stop demanding the reform of the princes. Then there would be no occasion for opposing them and making protests. However, the rumor had quite the contrary effect. The bishops had been quiet, expecting the reform of the princes to be proposed when the session was over, but hearing the news and seeing that there was an attempt to smother the reform, they began to discuss the possibility of proceeding no further with other business unless the article which concerned the princes was published and raised for discussion, together with the others. These private negotiations went so far that a hundred of them gave their word together to stand by their decision; they drew up a document which they all signed, and they went to see the legates, asking them to propose the articles concerning the reform of the princes and to give them to the Fathers. They made a kind of protest to the effect that they would not continue to discuss, nor would they come to any decision on, the other articles, unless these ones were decided, too. The legates spoke to them pleasantly, aiming and hoping to divert them. By means of prorogation, a temporary solution was reached till November 11.

## Chapter Seven

*[The Cardinal of Lorraine visits Rome, September, 1563.]*

A few days before the arrival of the Cardinal of Lorraine in Rome, the papal nuncio to France returned, sent by the queen to propose a conference between His Holiness, the emperor, the king of Spain, and the king his son, a gathering in which she would take part, too. The Pope thought this impossible to bring about. The suggestion did not displease him because it might be most useful in bringing the Council to an end; and so, he gave his word to send nuncios to the emperor and to the king of Spain to this effect. He sent the Bishop of Ventimiglia to Spain, recalling him from Trent, and sent the Bishop of Ischia to the emperor.

The Pope did great honor to the Cardinal of Lorraine by lodging him in the Vatican and, an unusual thing, by paying him an official visit in his rooms. One of the subjects they discussed was the conference: whether the Cardinal also thought that the plan was not feasible. They talked about the loan of a hundred thousand scudi, and it is not clear whether the Cardinal was working in favor of this or against it; but at this time, the Pope replied to a new request by the ambassador on this subject, that he would put it to the Council, and many thought this pretext was an idea of Lorraine's. However, their principal topic was ending the Council, a matter which the Pope recognized to be at once extremely important and extremely difficult. They were extremely open with one another. The Cardinal explained how he now thought that this was in his interest, and how after the death of his brother he saw clearly that there was no other means of maintaining his religion and his family in France, apart from allying himself with the Apostolic See. The Pope promised Lorraine to make his nominees cardinals, and he explained his intention to have the Cardinal succeed him as pope. In order to be taken all the more seriously, the Pope showed Lorraine how his greatness as cardinal was useful to the Pope's own plans in Italy. It is certain that the Pope had important aims in view, because the end of his talks with everyone was always, "We must end the Council and provide money, and then God's will will be done."

## [*The reform of the princes: September, 1563.*]

The legates published the remainder of the articles, the last of which was the reform of the princes, being forced to do so by the rebellion of the prelates. The section touching the princes has often been mentioned, and now we have come to the place where in order to understand what follows, it will be necessary to give details. It contained a prologue, thirteen articles, and a most pregnant epilogue. It may be summarized as follows. The Council has decided that besides its decrees concerning the clergy, it ought to reform the abuses of the laity, too. Concerning the immunities of the Church, the Council trusts that princes will be content to ensure that the clergy are obeyed as they should be. In addition, it admonishes them to make their magistrates and officials obey the pope and the decisions of the Council, in the same way that the princes themselves are bound to obey. To facilitate this obedience, the Council renews some of the laws of the Church and of the Empire in favor of the immunities of the Church—laws which everyone is bound to observe under pain of excommunication.

I. Clerics cannot be judged by secular courts, even if a man's claim to be a cleric is doubtful, and if he agrees to it himself, whether because he withdraws his claim or for some other reason, even that of the common good or the service of the king. They shall be proceeded against for murder only if the murder is genuine and well-known to be so; in the other cases permitted by the law, proceedings shall not be begun without the prior permission of the bishop.

II. In spiritual cases or in cases of matrimony, heresy, tithes, patronage, and benefices; in civil, criminal, and mixed cases which pertain in some way to Church courts, whether they affect men or goods (tithes, fourths, and so on) belonging to the Church, or patrimonial benefices, ecclesiastical fiefs, or the temporal jurisdiction of churches —in all these cases secular judges should not take part on either side. There should be no appeal to them, either because it is claimed that justice is being denied, or that there is some abuse, or because of a renunciation of claims. If anyone has recourse to a secular court in one of these cases, he is to be excommunicated and deprived of the rights which he was claiming. These rules are to apply even to cases which are pending.

III. Laymen are not to be able to appoint judges in ecclesiastical cases, even by the authority of the apostles or by immemorial custom. Clerics who accept such appointments, even on these grounds, are to be suspended from Holy Orders, deprived of their benefices and offices, and declared unable to hold them.

IV. The secular authority is not to be able to forbid an ecclesiastical judge to excommunicate without permission, or to withdraw or even to suspend an excommunication; nor is he to be able to forbid him to examine, cite, or condemn, or have his own spies or officials.

V. The emperor and all kings and princes do not have the power to make edicts or to issue orders which in any way concern clerics and ecclesiastical cases, nor can they interfere with clerics or with ecclesiastical causes, jurisdictions, and tribunals, not even with the Inquisition; but they are obliged to lend their "arm" to the ecclesiastical judges.

VI. The temporal jurisdiction of the clergy should not be disturbed, even in the case of *mero e misto imperio*.

Their men should not be summoned to appear in secular courts, even in secular cases.

VII. No prince or magistrate should give a written promise to anyone, or give him any hope of receiving a benefice in their territory, or promise to obtain it for him from a prelate or a chapter. If anyone obtains a benefice in this manner, he should be deprived of it and declared unable to hold it.

VIII. Princes and magistrates do not possess the power to lay their hands on the fruits of vacant benefices, under the pretext of wardship or patronage or protection, or in order to avoid disputes; they should not appoint administrators or vicars. Laymen who accept such offices should be excommunicated, and clerics should be suspended from Holy Orders and deprived of their benefices.

IX. The clergy should not be forced to pay taxes (gabelles, tithes, subsidies, and so on), even when they are called gifts or loans, either on their own goods or on the goods of the Church; an exception is made for those provinces where by ancient custom the clergy themselves took part in public assemblies in imposing taxes on both laity and clergy for the sake of war on the infidel, or for some other most urgent necessity.

X. Princes and magistrates do not possess the power to lay their hands on ecclesiastical goods, movable and immovable, on vassals, tithes, and other rights; nor on the goods of communities and individuals over which the Church has rights; nor to rent out pastures and grasslands which are Church property.

XI. Letters, judgments, and summonses from ecclesiastical judges, especially from the Curia, should be published and executed as soon as they are received. It should not be necessary either in this case or in the case of the taking possession of benefices to have to ask for permission (whether it was called *Exequatur, Placet,* or whatever), even on the grounds that this prevents deception and violence, except in fortresses and in benefices where princes have special temporal rights. If there is any suspicion of the authenticity of the letters, or fear of some great scandal or tumult, it is for the bishop, as the pope's delegate, to decide what needs to be done.

XII. Princes and magistrates do not possess the power to billet their officials, household, soldiers, horses, and dogs in the houses or in the monasteries of the clergy, nor to take anything from them to eat or for the journey.

XIII. If any kingdom, province, or other place shall claim to be exempt from any of these rules by virtue of privileges from the Apostolic See which are actually in force, the privileges must be shown to the Pope within a year from the end of the Council and confirmed by him according to the deserts of those kingdoms or provinces; and at the end of the year, privileges that have not been exhibited shall be invalid.

The epilogue was a warning to all princes to venerate the things of the Church as specially dear to God and not allow others to attack them; renewing[1] all the constitutions of the popes and the canons in favor of ecclesiastical immunities, and commanding, on pain of excommunication, that nothing should be commanded or executed, directly or indirectly, under any pretext, which might harm the clergy and their freedom and the property of the Church, whatever privileges and exemptions there might be to the contrary, even immemorial ones.

This is what had been first communicated to the ambassadors, and it was sent by them to their princes; and as a result of which the king of France gave that order to his ambassadors, which we have mentioned above [p. 296]. When the emperor had seen it, he wrote to Cardinal Morone that neither as emperor nor as archduke could he ever agree for the Council to discuss the reform of princes' jurisdiction, nor the abolition of their right to receive aids and contributions from the clergy. He considered that all the evils of the past had been caused by the attempts of the clergy to oppress the princes and their peoples; he warned them not to anger him further and cause still more unfortunate things to happen.

---

[1] Reading *renovando* for *innovando*.

## Chapter Eight

*[The Cardinal of Lorraine returns to Trent.]*

It is worthy of note that in congregation he made a long digression in praise of the good will of the Pope: his desire to see the Church reformed and the bishops restored to their ancient dignity, and the Council finished to the benefit of all Christendom. The Archbishop of Granada, when it was his turn to speak, also sang the praises of the Pope, and he credited him with even more good will than the Cardinal had; but he added that the Pope either believed himself unable to issue the orders he wanted, or that he lacked the authority to make his subordinates carry them out.

Here I have to make a great change in style. So far, I have always written in a style appropriate to the description of a variety of opinions, with plans cutting across plans and some men delaying what others had resolved, so that I had to halt the narrative to explain the conflicting opinions of different men. But from now on there was one aim only, and everything worked harmoniously toward it; events seemed to fly rather than to run toward the goal. For this I have a single explanation, which I give now in order not to have to repeat it: and that is, the general agreement to give the Council a speedy end.

## Chapter Nine

*[The twenty-fourth session, November 11, 1563. The reform decrees.]*

I. [Qualifications should be laid down for bishops and cardinals.]

II. Provincial councils should be summoned by the metropolitan or by the senior suffragan, within a year at most of the end of this Council; and at least every two years afterwards. . . .

III. Bishops have the duty of inspecting their dioceses (in person or by means of visitors) every year, if they can; or at least every two years in the case of the bigger dioceses. . . .

IV. Bishops have the duty of preaching in person (or, if they have a legitimate impediment, by proxy). Parish priests have the same duty of preaching in the parish church, and if there is some impediment, the sermons are to be given by someone appointed by the bishop, at the expense of the man whose duty it is and who usually gives them. Sermons are to be given every Sunday and solemn feast day, and every day during Advent and Lent, or three times a week. The bishop should tell everyone to go to his own parish to hear the sermon. No one should contradict the bishop in his sermons. The bishop should be responsible for the teaching of Christian doctrine in all parishes.

V. Serious accusations of crime against bishops should be judged by the pope; and if it is necessary to entrust the cases to someone outside the Curia, they should be entrusted to the metropolitan only, or to bishops appointed by the pope. Even then, they should only have authority to collect information, leaving the pope to judge. Minor cases should be judged by the provincial council, or its deputies.

VI. Bishops should be able to give dispensations to their subjects in "the court of conscience" for all irregularities and for all suspensions for secret offenses, except deliberate murder. They should be able to grant absolution in person or by deputy in all cases which had been reserved to the Apostolic See. They should even be able to grant absolution from grave heresy—but not by deputy.

VII. The bishop should make sure that before the administration of the sacraments, their nature and purpose should be explained to the people in the vernacular, in the manner of a catechism (which the Council would compose), which the bishop would cause to be translated faithfully into the vulgar tongue, and which the parish priests would read to the people.

VIII. Public sinners should be given public penance, though the bishops should be able to commute it to private penance. In every cathedral church a "penitentiary" should be appointed, forty years old and with a degree in theology or canon law. . . .

XIV. The Council detests and forbids all customs of paying for rights and possessions (except where the money is put to some pious use), declaring those who take the money to be guilty of simony. . . .

XXI. In the words of the decree *Proponentibus legatis* of the first session under the present Pope Pius IV, it was not the intention of the Council to change in any way the customary manner of proceeding in general councils, nor to add or subtract anything from what until now had been the canons of the Church and the form of general councils. . . .

The fourteenth article was praised by everyone, since it seemed to have abolished annates and the payment of the bulls which came from Rome for collation to benefices. But in the course of time, it was seen that they continued in force, and that there was no thought of abolishing or of moderating them. All that were abolished were the little abuses of the other churches, so that it remained true that people take motes out of eyes, but not beams. . . .

Concerning the last [twenty-first] article, which had been awaited for so many months, and which had raised the crucial issue of the liberty of the Council, seeing that it declared that the intention of the Council had not been to change its procedure, nor to add to or to take away anything from old laws or new, wise men said that as far as this Council was concerned, this was a declaration contrary to the fact, and published when it was no longer of any use, like medicine given to a dead man.

## Chapter Ten

*[The discussion at Trent about ending the Coun-
cil.]*

In Trent, when the session was over and matters had
been concerted between the legates and Lorraine, and
after the heads of the papal party had also been informed (Otranto, Taranto, and Parma) and the imperial
ambassadors, too, Lorraine began to let people know
about the plan to conclude the Council with one session
more. He said that he could not be in Trent for Christmas; that he and all the French bishops would have to
leave before then; that he wanted very much to see the
end of the Council; and that he would be sorry to leave
that honorable gathering, but he could do nothing else,
as he had had his orders. The imperial ambassadors let
all the Council know that the emperor wanted it over,
and that the king of the Romans wrote that it should
finish by St. Andrew's day,[1] or, at the latest, by the beginning of the following month. It was true that the king
wanted the Council over, not to please the Pope, but for
reasons of his own, because he had to call a Diet, and
did not want his father to have ambassadors at the
Council; and he said that the sooner the Council ended,
the better for the affairs of religion in Germany.

Most of the Fathers heard the news with great pleasure. On the fifteenth of November, Cardinal Morone held
a congregation in his own house. The two legates were
invited and the two cardinals and twenty-five bishops,
chosen from the most important nations. He pointed out
that the Council had been called to satisfy the needs of
Germany and France, but now the emperor and the king
of the Romans and the Cardinal of Lorraine and all the
princes wanted it ended. He proposed that they should
give their opinions about when and how to end it. The
Cardinal of Lorraine said that it was necessary to end

[1] November 30.

it so as not to keep Christendom in suspense any longer, and to make it clear to Catholics what they were supposed to believe. Also, it was necessary to repeal the Interim of Augsburg, which was to remain in force till the end of the Council, and so could not be ended in any other way; but its continuance was harmful to the Church. It was also necessary to end the Council to ensure that a national council was not held in France. As to the way in which the Council should be ended, he said that this could be done with a session which dealt with the rest of the reforms and hurried on to the catechism and the Index (which were already in progress), and which left everything else to the pope, without disputing about the articles on indulgences and images; and that they should not anathematize individual heretics, but only heretics in general. All agreed to this manner of ending the Council, except the Archbishop of Granada, who said that he would accept the judgment of the Spanish ambassador.

## Chapter Eleven

Late at night, on the first of December, a courier from Rome arrived in Trent with the news that the Pope had fallen into a dangerous sickness. He brought letters from Cardinal Borromeo to the legates and to the Cardinal of Lorraine to hurry up the ending of the Council as much as possible, without respect for anyone, to avoid the awkward situation which might occur: electing a pope while the Council was sitting. There were a few words in the Pope's own hand, which gave them full powers to do this, and he told Lorraine that he remembered his promise. And it is certain (to mention this point here, although it is out of place) that the Pope was resolved, if he did not recover quickly, to create eight cardinals and to make sure that the election of his successor went smoothly. The legates and Lorraine decided to bring forward the session and to finish the Council (with or without the propositions) within two days, because they could not have news of the Pope's death before then. They told the ambassadors about the news and their decision, and they discussed the matter with the most important prelates.

[*Twenty-fifth session: December 3, 1563—the reading of the decrees.*]

Concerning purgatory, the decree said that the Catholic Church (on the authority of the Bible, tradition, and the Council itself) has taught that purgatory exists, and that the souls there can be helped by the prayers of the faithful and by the sacrifice of the Mass. Bishops were ordered to see that sound doctrine on this subject was taught and preached, without raising subtle questions in the presence of simple people, or allowing the spread of uncertain and implausible ideas; forbidding excessive curiosity, superstition, and profiteering; and laying down that the prayers that the living were accustomed to offer up for the dead should be piously carried out, and also what was laid down in wills and in other ways.

Concerning the saints, the Council commanded bishops and others with the duty of teaching to instruct the people about the intercession and invocation of saints, the honoring of relics, and the legitimate cult of images according to the ancient doctrine of the Church, the general opinion of the Fathers, and the decrees of councils. They were to teach that saints pray for men, and that it is of benefit to call on them and rely on their prayers and help. Then in one sentence the decree condemned eight statements on this subject: that the saints of heaven ought not to be invoked; that they do not pray for men; that it is idolatry to ask them to pray for us, even individually; that it is contrary to the word of God, that it is contrary to the honor of Christ, that it is madness to beg them for things aloud or silently; that the bodies of saints (through whom God gives many benefits) should not be venerated; that their relics and tombs should not be honored; and that it is useless to ask for help by mentioning their names.

As for images: those of Christ, the Virgin, and the

saints ought to be kept in churches and honored. This is not because there is any divinity or virtue in the images, but because this is to honor what the images represent. Thus by means of images, Christ and the saints are worshipped. This was laid down by councils, especially the second Council of Nicæa. By means of narrative pictures, the mysteries of religion are taught to the people, and they are reminded of the articles of their faith. Not only the benefits of Christ, but also the miracles and examples of the saints are placed before their eyes, so that they may thank God and imitate the examples. Anyone who taught or believed the contrary was to be anathematized. Desiring to reform abuses and the occasion of pernicious errors, they ordered that, in the cases of representations of God in pictures of biblical subjects, it should be explained to the people that this was not done because He could be seen with the outward eye. All superstitions should be abolished which concerned the invocation of saints, the veneration of relics, and the cult of images. There should be no profiteering, no extravagance, and the images should not be painted in a sensual manner; on the feasts of saints and when there is an exhibition of relics, there should be no banquets. No new images should be placed in churches or elsewhere without the approval of the bishop, nor should people believe in new miracles or collect new relics. If there was some doubtful case or abuse difficult to stamp out, or grave difficulty, the bishop should consult the provincial council; and no new decrees should be made without consulting the pope. . . .

All the Fathers were commanded to sign the decrees, on pain of excommunication. The next day, Sunday, was spent in doing this. To do this in due order, something like a congregation was held: those who signed were four legates, two cardinals, three patriarchs, twenty-five archbishops, two hundred and sixty-eight bishops, seven abbots, thirty-nine proxies, and seven generals of religious orders.

## Chapter Twelve

[*Joy in Rome; the recovery of the Pope and the end of the Council.*]

In Rome, when the Pope fell ill, everyone feared that he would die, and there was much confusion at the Curia because, since a pope had never died while a council was in progress, everyone was terrified of what might happen. They had the example of the Council of Constance, which added other prelates to the cardinals for the papal election, and they feared that something similar or worse might occur. Although the Spanish ambassador declared that the ambassador in Trent and the Spanish prelates had been charged to make sure that the pope was elected by the cardinals, all the same (given their small number), they were not completely confident of this. There was great joy when it was understood that the Pope had recovered; he seemed to have escaped from great danger. The joy increased inordinately when it was heard that the Council was over. The Pope ordered a solemn procession to thank God for so great a benefit. In consistory, he showed how pleased he was about this; he said that he wanted to confirm its decrees, and even add other reforms. He wanted to send three legates to Germany, France, and Spain to exhort them to execute the decrees, to make concessions where this was honorable, and to give their opinion on matters of positive law. . . .

On the twelfth of March, the Pope created nineteen cardinals, mainly to reward those who had worked well at the Council, especially in the service of the Apostolic See. He was resolved not to include any of those who held that the residence or institution of bishops was *de iure divino,* although some of these were men who, according to custom, would have deserved such promotion; and he did not try to hide his decision from anyone or on any occasion.

# Glossary

ANNATES. That portion of the revenues of a vacant benefice which was paid to the pope.

BASEL (Bâle), Council of. Held 1431-49 to continue the Council of Constance. It declared the superiority of councils to the pope.

CANON. 1) A member of a chapter; 2) a law of the Church.

CATECHISM. A summary of Christian doctrine, usually in question-and-answer form. A catechism was composed as a result of a decree of the Council.

CHAPTER. The community of the clergy in a cathedral or large church.

COADJUTOR. Helper. Used especially of assistants to bishops, appointed by the pope and given the right of succession.

COLLATION. The granting of a benefice.

COMMENDAM. A benefice is held *in commendam* (provisionally) in distinction to one held *in titulum* (fully, legally). The term is used especially in the case of abbeys, which were sometimes held in this way by men who were not monks, and who drew the revenues but did not exercise authority over the discipline of the monks in the abbey.

COMMUNION UNDER BOTH FORMS. This means taking both bread and wine at the altar, instead of bread alone. The right of the laity to receive Communion in both kinds was asserted by Jan Hus and by the Czech "Utraquists." Ferdinand I raised this issue at the Council.

CONGREGATION. *Congregation* means "meeting." The term was used of two kinds of meeting at the Council. 1) A general congregation was a meeting of all members of the Council, including those without the right to vote. 2) A particular congregation was a kind of committee—

a meeting of some members in order to discuss a specific issue.

CONSTANCE (Konstanz), Council of. Held between 1414 and 1418. It ended the Great Schism and condemned Jan Hus.

CURIA. *Curia* is medieval Latin for *court* (legal or royal). It is now used to refer to the papal court, the pope's household and officials. I have adopted this term to translate Sarpi's *corte romana*, "the court of Rome."

DECRETALS. Collections of canons and of decisions in canon law cases. Such collections include Gratian's *Decretum* (1151).

ELECTION. Sarpi often uses the term *eleggere*, which I have sometimes translated as "choose" (its normal meaning) and sometimes by "elect."

EXPECTATIVES. An old English word for *litteræ expectativæ*, papal letters giving the recipient a claim to a certain benefice as soon as it became vacant.

LEGATES. Papal ambassadors and governors.

MERUM ET MISTUM IMPERIUM. In sixteenth-century legal writings, these terms referred to absolute and limited power respectively. In ancient Rome, they referred to criminal and civil jurisdiction.

METROPOLITAN. A chief bishop or archbishop. Where Sarpi uses this term, I have tended to translate it as "archbishop."

ORDINARY. A diocesan bishop, so-called because he exercises power by common right (*iure ordinario*). I have tended to translate Sarpi's term *ordinario* by "bishop."

PREBEND. A share in the revenues of a chapter, enjoyed by a prebendary or canon.

PREDESTINATION. The doctrine that God from all eternity destines some men to salvation and others to damnation.

PROVISIONS, PAPAL. Letters from the pope to a bishop, instructing him to provide the cleric named in the document with a specific vacant benefice.

RESERVATION. The pope's reservation of the right to appoint to certain diocesan benefices.

RESIDENCE. The residence problem was that of encouraging or forcing bishops to reside in their sees and priests in their parishes, instead of living at the courts of princes, as many bishops did.

SERVITES. An order of mendicant friars founded in the thirteenth century.

SESSION. A formal meeting of the Council, beginning with High Mass and a sermon, and proceeding to voting and the making of decrees. There were twenty-five sessions in all. Sarpi describes the first session in detail as a model for the rest.

VOTE. Sarpi's word *voto* sometimes means "opinion" and sometimes "vote." Voting took place at the Council by writing *placet* (yes) or *non placet* (no) on a ballot paper.

—H. R. Trevor-Roper, general editor of *The Great Histories Series,* is the distinguished Regius Professor of Modern History at Oxford University. He is probably best known to American readers for his book *The Last Days of Hitler,* which is a classic in the field of modern German history and was the result of official investigations carried out by him at the behest of British Intelligence in an attempt to unshroud the mystery surrounding the dictator's fate. The book has already been translated into twenty foreign languages. Professor Trevor-Roper is a specialist in sixteenth- and seventeenth-century history and has published other notable works, including *Archbishop Laud* and *Men and Events.* He has contributed numerous articles on political and historical subjects to the journals and is familiar to American readers of *The New York Times Magazine* and *Horizon.*

—Peter Burke has edited an anthology on the problems and perspectives of the Renaissance, has contributed essays on the cultural and intellectual history of the Renaissance to publications both in England and in America, and has lectured on these topics over the BBC. He is presently a lecturer in European history at the University of Sussex.

# Index

315

# INDEX

854

0962

# Date Due